America's Heroes

Untold Stories of Honor,
Courage and Sacrifice
Volume I

as told to
Scot King

Correlated by:
J.D. Tynan
and
J. Jackson Owensby

Argus Enterprises International, Inc.
New Jersey***North Carolina

America's Heroes: Untold Stories of Honor, Courage and Sacrifice, Volume I © 2011. All rights reserved by Remember The Wounded Ride, Inc.

No part of this book may be reproduced or transmitted in any form or by any means, graphic, electronic, or mechanical, including photocopying, recording, taping, or by any informational storage retrieval system without prior permission in writing from the publisher.

A-Argus Better Book Publishers, LLC

For information:
A-Argus Better Book Publishers, LLC
9001 Ridge Hill Street
Kernersville, North Carolina 27285
www.a-argusbooks.com

ISBN: 978-0-6155734-8-9
ISBN: 0-6155734-8-7

Book Cover designed by: William Reynolds and Dubya

Printed in the United States of America

Untold Stories of Honor, Courage and Sacrifice

Dedication

This series is dedicated foremost to those brave men and women who sacrificed themselves and all that they held dear in the service of their country in her time of need. It is my honor to thank those brave men and women who bared their souls so that their stories of honor, courage and sacrifice could uplift their fellow man in time of change and turmoil.

The series is specifically dedicated to the Benevolent and Protective Order of Elks of the United States of America, an American organization whose generosity to our nation's children, veterans and elderly is truly an inspiration. Without their dedication, many would suffer greatly. The overwhelming support and assistance from individual Lodge's across the country, without which the collection of these stories would not have been possible, is greatly appreciated.

I also wish to express my particular appreciation to Remember The Wounded Ride, Inc., a tax-deductible organization whose goal is to assist in relieving the burden carried by the families of wounded veterans and first responders and to those organizations that seek to aid those who have made the sacrifices demanded of them by their nation and to their families whose sacrifices were no less great.

Finally, I dedicate this to those American youths, male and female, who will answer the call and accept the sacrifices that the United States of America will undoubtedly make on them at some time in the future when danger to our way of life is most imminent. May the United States of America ever stand, and may her youth ever be prepared in her defense.

Scot King

Introduction

On battlefields of long ago and today, America's Veterans have made sacrifices for all of us. Through their service, their pride, and their patriotism, the men and women of our armed forces have made our nation what it is today. They defended our freedoms. They fought for justice. They preserved our ideals. And through it all, they forged our character. Our veterans are our real heroes. Indeed, our great nation was built by their actions.

Since 1917, the Benevolent and Protective Order of Elks has demonstrated its compassion for the veterans of our armed forces through numerous programs and activities. Since 1946, our Order has maintained the pledge, "So long as there are veterans, the Benevolent and Protective Order of Elks will never forget them."

Oregon State Elks Association member, US Marine Corps Veteran Corporal Scot King, began what he has termed his "Remember-The-Wounded Ride" on May 7th, 2011. Corporal King has been riding his bicycle thousands of miles throughout America for our veterans. He is visiting Elks at many of our 2,034 lodges as well as speaking at Elks' state association meetings, in order to raise awareness and support especially for those wounded in combat. In addition to Elks officers and members, he continues to meet with many government officials and veterans. His ride will continue until he has visited all of the forty-eight contiguous states.

In every state in our nation there are hospitals, nursing homes, and VA medical centers that house veterans who deserve our utmost respect and support. In addition, Elks throughout America are helping to provide needed services and financial assistance for the families of our servicemen and servicewomen through the Elks Army of Hope and in connection with USO programs. The renewed attention provided by Corporal King's "Remember-The-Wounded Ride" is aiding members of Elks lodges provide this assistance.

I proudly salute Corporal Scot King for this tremendous undertaking and wish him continued success in demonstrating that "Elks Care and Elks Share."

David R. Carr, National President
Benevolent and Protective Order of Elks, U.S.A.

November 30, 2011

Preamble

A chance meeting can change your life, can alter the world, can cause a paradigm shift of unbelievable magnitude. At least, it can for an individual, and it has: mine.

A couple of years ago, I was window-shopping in downtown Portland with my girlfriend, my son and her daughter. We were enjoying a beautiful summer day. I had some trash in my hand that I wanted to throw into a garbage dumpster. So I walked over to the dumpster which was close by and threw the stuff in. Even as I was putting the debris in the bin, there was a guy digging through the dumpster. I was thinking, *"Well, it's just another bum, or another vagrant digging through the garbage."*

At that particular time in my life, I wasn't a very nice person when it came to acknowledging those kinds of people who were not doing anything for society but who were just living from day-to-day by going through dumpsters. I really didn't think much about it until he looked up at me and said, "Hey. Semper Fi."

To any Marine, that expression which ordinarily is only used between Marines, means "Always Faithful." I turned and looked at him. That's when I noticed the tattoo on his arm, an eagle over an anchor with the letters U.S.M.C. There stood a Marine.

I swear—and it's hard for me to put this into words—at that instant, meeting that Marine, my life was changed forever. As I said earlier, I wasn't the nicest person in the world, but I felt compelled to help; this man, this Marine; a feeling I have never had before. So, I pulled out my wallet and I gave him money. I told him, "I've never done this before," and as I was giving him some money to make his day better, I told him, "It may not be much, but I hope it is enough so that at least today you won't have to dig through the garbage to find your next meal."

I didn't know his story. I don't know if he was booted out of the Marine Corps, or if he was on drugs or alcohol, or if he were simply homeless. Regardless, at that point it didn't matter to me because the only thing I knew was that I wanted to help. He was a Marine. I was a Marine. It really hit me hard when that realization came home. Too large a percentage of homeless are combat-affected Marines. I think it's bull-shit, our veterans shouldn't be homeless, our veterans shouldn't have to dig through a goddam garbage bin to get their next meal, let alone have to survive on this.

I didn't have any idea where this was going to lead me, but I must admit that I became very emotional, barely able to talk to this man after I gave him the money. Even now it hurts to talk about it, because after looking back, I know that the unkind remarks I had often made, the actions I took, and the other things I said rubbed off on my son, Kalib. He was starting to call them 'bums' and that shouldn't happen. My son was a young boy. It wasn't right for me to do that; I had taught him wrong. As I said, I didn't know where it was going to lead me, and I decided to go on with my day. But things began changing.

Days would go by and I would go to Subways or McDonalds restaurants and buy extra food. Then I would go look for homeless people and give the food to them. Sometimes, I would have blankets in my truck and I would stop and give a homeless person a blanket or a jacket to help them, the same people I used to deride. It could have been in pouring down rain or snow. I just wanted to help them.

After a week or so, my girl friend noticed a huge change in the way that I approached things when it came to the homeless or even people in general. Like I said before, I was selfish; seldom thinking of others, and that was terrible. I started to realize that life is too short.

Now, if there is anything I can do to help others, I try. Other people began to notice the change in me, including my sister, a person who would never say anything good about anybody unless she meant it. She was pleased with the way I did things for others.

My transition continued over the summer, however, two months later, to my shock, I lost my job. I thought, *"You know what? I could be one of these people who would have dig through garbage cans."* I was certain that it wouldn't happen because I would get back up on my feet and take whatever job I had to in order to survive. Actually, it was very humbling to lose my job. First time I had ever lost a job. I had been working since 1979, even working part-time while I was in highschool, and after finishing school was never out of work for more than a week or two. All of a sudden, I found myself at home rather than working, stuck with a house payment and other bills, without an income; boy, that was difficult.

I'll continue to tell the world that the meeting with that Marine changed my life. This happenstance might have been a blessing as it gave me the occasion to commit to a cause in which I believe. Otherwise I probably would have only continued to help others a little as best I could while working and earning a living.

This idle period gave me the time to figure out what I wanted to do and how to do it. So I started doing research on where and how I could help others. I felt certain that I wanted to do something involving the military. Being a Marine and loving our military and our first responders, I found some holes in our system.

One of those holes is that combat-affected veterans and their families are struggling mightily. Financial aid isn't easily available to help transition the entire family back into civilian life, once the loved one is wounded or traumatized by combat. These men and women are coming back with these terrible and horrific injuries, and they are continuing to suffer emotionally as well as financially.

An example could be that a wounded veteran comes into the Military Hospital in San Antonio, Texas. Rehab can and likely will be for an extended period of time. In order to facilitate and accelerate the recovery, it is most desirable for at least one member of the family to be there for the duration as the patient needs all the support he or she can get. It is documented that recovery is much more successful and much faster if there are family members on hand to help.

A lot of these men and women have families that are located at great distances. Therefore someone is leaving their job, their home and the rest of the family to be with their wounded loved one, and that could be for months or even years.

Then what happens? Well, now, they are struggling because they moved to an area they aren't familiar with, they have to find a job; they have to pay their rent, utilities and their food. The bills don't stop, they keep coming. Now they have to maintain two households. **And who's paying for that?** Many military families live on a shoestring budget to begin with, and now the expenses are doubled in order to be close to the loved one.

This is a huge gap in our system that needs to be addressed. People are losing their homes, their cars, their jobs; they are having trouble buying groceries. It's a tragedy when our young men and women in uniform who have been traumatized or wounded are unable to meet basic needs and made even more tragic when the families are forced to rely on food stamps to survive.

Over the next several weeks, I talked with a lot of my friends and asked them, "What can I do to increase awareness about the situation, and raise money that is so desperately needed to care for the men and women in uniform and the first responders?" That's when I came up with a great idea. *"I've always been athletic; maybe I'll back-pack across the United States. I could visit every state capital and talk to veterans along the way. If I can find enough sponsors, then maybe I can generate money to help these veterans and their families."*

At the time, I had the idea of having each veteran tell his or her story for a book and possibly a documentary. It was my hope to make Americans, especially the younger generation, aware of the sacrifices made by our veterans, male or female, in all branches of the military services and in all wars, to preserve their liberty and their individual rights. That awareness might cause people to get involved in helping our veterans and their families.

I had a talk with my best friend, John Keating by name, and I mentioned this to him and he said, "Scot, back-packing is going to take you a long, long time, and being away from your family for four or five years—for that's how long it will take you to back-pack to all the state capitals—probably wouldn't be a good idea. Why don't you ride a bicycle across America?"

I thought, *"Hey, I'm a recreational rider, I can ride a bike like anybody else."* So I said, "John, that's a fine idea."

Being a Marine, I decided to approach the situation just as the military would. First, define the mission. Second, do the planning. Third, initiate the operation.

THE MISSION

Raise the awareness of the American public to the plight of the combat-affected veteran and his/her family and raise funds to alleviate the situation and ease the burden on the family.

THE PLANNING

I started doing research and began putting packets together to find sponsors. It was a totally grass-roots effort; it was just me at the beginning. I found a few people to help me. My friend, Jeff Nelson, was there for me – big time. Together, we did some shows at the Veterans Memorial Coliseum to raise seed money to help make this mission possible. One thing led to another. Sam Seelbath, another friend of mine, said, "You know what, Scot? You should become a 501-c non-profit. That way, you can help even more families."

I thought that was a great idea. So, I began the paperwork and then my friend, Jerry Reed, from Operation Military Embrace—another great organization that I support—helped fine-tune everything, and in June of 2011, we were granted the 501-c-3 non-profit status by the I.R.S.

One thing that I didn't know—or I miscalculated—was the effect that such an undertaking would have on people in my life. The impact on my family life has been tremendous. It has been very difficult on my family and my friends as well. I felt like I was doing the right thing, but I made a lot of mistakes. I didn't have everything as ready at home as I should have. It caused a lot of tension and strife. I told myself that I would never make those mistakes again, as I plan on another ride to complete the second leg of the mission. I will have my family better prepared.

I regret the pain that I put my family through. Five weeks before I was to take off on the first leg from Salem, Oregon, my mom who is a huge supporter of mine had a massive stroke. It was a really tough situation for Mom and the rest of my family. We all had to pitch in to help Mom, even as we prepared for the ride. But that is what family is all about.

Additionally, my step-father became very ill with cancer and it was really rough on him as well, trying to care for my mom but he couldn't handle it, he was overwhelmed. My sister, Jennifer, to whom I owe everything, took care of Mom better than anybody ever could, and for that I will always be grateful and always owe her because I wasn't there to help. That was hard; she really wanted me at home to help, but she knew that I was committed to the ride, so she understood why I had to go.

When I started on this ride I was aware that I would need to stay on this mission through thick or thin. I have to this point and I will until I finish. Through rain, snow, hail and heat. Of course, I paid a heavy price, especially not being able to help out with Mom. And then my step-father passed away June 30th of this year. That was a blow as well, because my stepfather and I were very close. Not being there made my riding that much more difficult, because everything that I have known was changing. My family's home went up for sale and I couldn't help. That was quite difficult.

    I lost my home as well. After nineteen years. I tried everything I could to save it but it wasn't enough. Still, my girlfriend—one hell of a woman—put it all in prospective. It was just a box, only a shell. It wasn't really that important. I can get another one someday. There are a lot of people going through the same thing that I am. I'm not a rich man when it comes to money, but I can tell you where I am rich and that is rich in the fact that I know a lot of good people. I have met and will meet a lot of great people on this bicycle trek and I am certain we are going to help a tremendous amount of people.

    While doing my research, I realized that I needed to work with as many other people and organizations as I could. I was doing a lot of research on organizations throughout this country and wanted to work with an organization that fit in with what I was doing and had the same moral compass that I had, and the same beliefs that I had. I needed a group that would see things a lot like I see things: a belief in God, a belief in ourselves, a belief in country. I looked at many good, even great organizations such as the American Legion, the VFW et al, but for some reason I was looking for more. I recalled that my grandfather was an Elk for fifty-one years. I remembered as a kid going down to the Elk's Lodge every now and then with my grandfather, to hang out and help him. The Benevolent and Protective Order of the Elks was a great organization then, a very big organization. Three important things the Elks do big time: take care of our children, take care of our veterans and take care of our elderly. To me, those are three BIG reasons why anyone that is invited should become an Elk. And you must be invited to join by a member in good standing of the BPOE. I am honored that I was allowed to become an Elk. The Elks Order is number two in giving loans or grants for school kids that want to go to college; second only to the United States Government.

This great organization was to serve as my backbone, to be there for me when I would ride into a city or a state. If I would need a place to stay, or a hot meal, or a helping hand, I knew that I had only to ask an Elk. "Elks care, Elks share," was not only a motto but a way of life as I would learn on my trek.

I calculated that to visit the capital of each of the "lower 48" states was going to take me a minimum of two years and encompass roughly twenty thousand miles, so I decided to do the mission in two phases. The first phase would be the northernmost states and the second phase would be a southern route.

To begin the first segment of the mission, I would depart from Salem, Oregon on May 7, 2011 and my route would take me to Olympia, Washington; Boise, Idaho; Helena, Montana; Salt Lake City, Utah; Denver, Colorado; Cheyenne, Wyoming; Bismarck, North Dakota; Pierre, South Dakota; Lincoln, Nebraska; Topeka, Kansas; Jefferson City, Missouri; Des Moines, Iowa; St. Paul, Minnesota; Madison, Wisconsin; Springfield, Illinois; Indianapolis, Indiana;; Lansing, Michigan; Columbus, Ohio; Charleston, West Virginia; Harrisburg, Pennsylvania; Albany, New York; Montpelier, Vermont; Augusta, Maine; Concord, New Hampshire; Boston, Massachusetts; Providence Rhode Island; Hartford, Connecticut; Trenton, New Jersey; Dover, Delaware; Annapolis, Maryland; Richmond, Virginia and end the first leg in Washington, DC. on October 25, 2011. A daunting undertaking of course, but then, I'm a Marine. And Marines don't quit in the face of adversity. Also, at the very least, by the time I finish I will know the name of each of the state's capitals as well as the name of some of America's finest.

So, as I commenced this trek, I found myself looking forward to meeting many of America's greatest heroes from World War II, the Korean War (not just 'conflict'), the Vietnam War, Gulf War I, the Afghanistan War and the Iraq War. And I am both proud and eager to present them to you. In doing so, I want to explain that when you learn of their stories, your emotions will be touched. Deeply touched. But probably not as deeply as mine. As I listened to these heroes while they bared their souls to me—and on many occasions were almost unable to express the emotions and the feelings they were having—I was able to see the grief in their eyes. Grief and sorrow and joy and pride. And I could see the tears that they shed and the smiles that some memories would bring back. I was able somewhat to relive their traumas with them and to ease a little of the pain they were feeling. It isn't possible for me to relay to you in mere words the anguish, the grief, the sorrow and the joy that these brave men and women felt and now are trying to share with you. But if you will open your minds and your hearts, you will understand a little of the great sacrifices these Soldiers, Sailors, Marines, Coastguardsmen and Airmen—male and female—and their families have made for us. Now, America's heroes – our heroes.

Untold Stories of Honor, Courage and Sacrifice

ROLL CALL

One of the harder parts of this segment of the mission was to decide whose story should come first, as we have World War II veterans, Korean veterans, Vietnam veterans and Iraq veterans. Each was important, each was stirring and touching, each deserved to be headlined, but everyone could not be the first. When in doubt, do it the Marine way. So,

Veterans, Atten' Hut! Line up by your last name alphabetically. Veterans: By the Numbers: Sound Off.

- BECKER, GUNNER D. FORESTBURG, SOUTH DAKOTA. PFC, UNITED STATES ARMY, YOB 1986, DECEASED 01/13/2005
- BERST, VILIS L. LINCOLN, NEBRASKA. DENVER, COLORADO. SERGEANT, UNITED STATES ARMY, 803 TANK DESTROYERS, YOB 1920
- BRADLEY, GEORGE. DENVER, COLORADO. SERGEANT, UNITED STATES ARMY AND UNITED STATES MARINE CORP. YOB 1925
- ESTES, CLARENCE A. ST. LOUIS, MISSOURI. SERGEANT, UNITED STATES ARMY NATIONAL GUARD, YOB 1960
- FULKS, JAMES, COLONEL, BAD, MONTANA. UNITED STATES MARINE CORPS, RTD. YOB 1946
- GESSFORD, LYLE D., MAJOR, BOISE, IDAHO. UNITED STATES ARMY, RTD. YOB 1944
- HENDERSON, REED. SWAN LAKE, IDAHO. UNITED STATES ARMY, 28TH INFANTRY, YOB 1922

- Hohm, John A. Jefferson City, Missouri, Sergeant, United States Army, 11TH Airborne, YOB 1923
- Ingels, Gregory C. Iowa, Kansas United States Army, YOB 1949
- Jensen, Dennis D. Genoa, Utah. Lieutenant, United States Army Aviation, YOB 1949
- Lengkeek, Peter J. M. Chamberlain, South Dakota. Sergeant, United States Army, YOB 1973
- Lind, Dell, Bismarck, North Dakota. Seaman First Class. United States Navy, YOB 1947
- Martin, John B. Preston, Idaho. United States Army Air Corps, YOB 1921
- Moszer, Jerome P, Lieutenant Colonel, Bismarck, North Dakota. United States Army National Guard, YOB 1963
- Olzweski, Robert. Sanger, North Dakota. CW-4, United States Army, YOB-1948
- Reynolds, William E., Helena, Montana, Seaman 2ND Class, United States Navy Aviation Cadet and 2ND Lieutenant, United States Marines Reserve. YOB 1920
- Sable, Marty S., Yakima, Washington. Sergeant. United States Army, YOB 1956
- Scow, Orval H., Helena, Montana. Sergeant, United States Army, Airborne, YOB 1922
- Sparks, Richard D. Lovell, Wyoming United States Army, YOB 1945
- Wadsworth, Shawn. West Virginia. United States Army, YOB 1978
- Warrick, Devon W. Preston, Idaho. United States Army, Infantry, 7TH division, YOB 1919

Becker, Gunner Duane.
PFC United States Army
1986 - 2005

Throughout American history, many brave men and women have stood up in defense of their country and fought for the preservation of freedom and the American way of personal liberty and individual rights. Many of those brave people sacrificed greatly to be of service to their fellow citizens and many made the ultimate sacrifice. Among those who paid the highest price was Private First Class Gunner Duane Becker. While serving as a crew member on a tank under the command of Staff Sergeant James L. Parker, Gunner was handling a heavy machine gun in the interior of the tank when the gun was accidently discharged. A round from the gun struck Becker in his head.

The following is information from the records of the United States Army. At the age of nineteen, PFC Gunner D. Becker, of Forestburg, South Dakota in Mosul, Iraq, died of what the Army referred to as 'non-combat related injuries'. He was assigned to 2nd Battalion, 63rd Armor Regiment, 1st Infantry Division, Vilseck, Germany as a crew member on an Army tank. According to the scant Army records available for public review, Staff Sergeant Parker, the tank commander, was court-marshaled in the incident. Major Roughneen served as Parker's defense counsel. Evidence presented showed that Parker did not fire the weapon that killed Becker, according to Roughneen's account. An unidentified sergeant on the crew accidentally pulled the trigger as he and PFC Becker were handling the heavy machine gun without Parker's knowledge. The accidental discharge sent a .50-caliber round into Becker's head, killing him instantly. Parker was convicted of dereliction of duty for not instructing his crew — the sergeant and two privates first class — to clear their weapons as they entered Forward Operating Base Marez in Mosul.

The rest of Gunner's story is told by his mother.

*****

I don't deal with this sh— stuff well, as you know. It's every parent's worst nightmare: having to bury your kid. It's not natural, it's not. My son was Gunner Duane Decker He was just nineteen when he was killed and he was buried on his twentieth birthday. And then they say it's a non-combat related injury, but it's still a head gunshot. People know. So you deal with all the ... Before you even find out for sure that it was friendly fire, before you know what happened, the rumors are flying that it was suicide, so you have all that to deal with; and then you have to stop the lies. Gunner was just about ready to come home. They were three weeks from being done. They were three weeks out, three weeks; a month at most. They left Germany for a one-year deployment on February 14, 2004 and he died on January 13, 2005.

He was home for two weeks R & R over the Fourth of July and I really wasn't sure that I would be able to keep him alive long enough send him back to the Army, back to Iraq. He wasn't in South Dakota eighteen hours before he had already bought a Camero. And he put two sets of rear tires on that Camero. Two sets in just two weeks. He loved to drive and drive fast. He would call home from Iraq, and say, "Have you been out to the County Comfort, Mom?" I would say, "Why?" He would say, "I was just wondering if my skid marks were still out there on the corner."

They still had been out there for a month. Everywhere I went, anywhere in a twenty-five mile radius, from here to Mitchell and back, every road—might as well have drawn a circle with a radius of twenty-five miles of this house on every road, he had skid marks everywhere; two sets of tires worth. That's my boy. There were a lot of times I thought that God, if I could just get him back into his Army tank, he's gotta be safer in a tank than he was in that Camero.

He would get up in the morning and he would come upstairs and stand in front of the window and stretch and he'd look outside at that red car and he'd say, "Huh, maybe those 'Chevies' aren't as bad as I thought."

I said, "What did you mean by that?"

"Ah, I would have thought for sure that I was going to blow that sucker up last night, but it got me home again."

He built a sparkler bomb while he was home. It was so big it knocked – it rattled all the windows out of a cabin over at one of the lakes. He said, "The guy that owned the cabin came screaming out of there, was going to chew ass. Mom, he saw me and then he stopped dead in his tracks, and he said, 'I'll be damn. How long are you home for?' I told him, 'I've got about another week left.' 'Well, let me shake your hand. I've got to buy you a beer. Come on, let's go'. Gunner said to me, "Last year, he would have chewed my ass up one side and down the other for the same thing."

Gunner was home for the Fourth of July and said, "Mom, when in the hell did everybody turn so patriotic?"

"What do you mean?"

"Everywhere I go; red, white and blue this – red, white and blue that – flags here, American flags there. The music on the radio," he said. "It's like I went away and when I came back, everybody had turned into another discipline, but it's patriotic. When did that happen?"

I said, "It's always been that way, Gunner; it's just now your eyes are opened to it." He just didn't have that perception of the 4th of July before.

Gunner left for basic training in August of 2003. He was home for Christmas in 2003. He went to Germany in January, 2004. He was in Germany for about five weeks and deployed to Iraq in February 2004. He was home for R&R for two weeks over July 4, 2004 and died the 13th of January, 2005.

At his grave, his memorial has really impressed some people. The tank on the back, where it says "Forestburg_tanker." And the way written, it was capital

'F', small 'o', capital 'R' small 'e' … when I broke into his email account, that's what I found: Forestburg underscore tanker. And I knew I was going to use that somewhere, somehow. And when I broke into his email account, I was actually quite impressed with myself. Not only did I get into it, it was a hell of a lot cleaner than his bedroom or his car ever was or any vehicle that he ever drove. Way cleaner. There wasn't a whole hell of a lot of … I mean, unless somebody beat me to it, there wasn't a lot of stuff there. A little, but it was very, very clean.

Some of his buddies still drop by from time to time, three of his Army buddies have been by so far. What makes me feel good is when I find one of them on Facebook. And here I sit, cropping the pictures, cropping the pictures and here's this beautiful little boy and I'm cropping the pictures, and finally, I get one that says, "Benjamin Gunner Mallory. Because Ben Mallory was the kid in the bottom of the tank when Gunner was handing the gun down to him, when the gun went off. The trigger hit the bottom of the floor of the tank or something and that's all she wrote. Gunner had been bending over the gun and handing it down, and was hit in the head.

I guess the impact of the news put me into a state of shock.

It wasn't until the Army came and gave us the full three hundred fifty-eight page fu.... report with all the guys' names magic-markered out that explained what had happened. I talked on the phone to guys three tanks away that were sprayed with gray matter. You know what? Guys that didn't even know Gunner but were there when this shit went down, standing three tanks away have tracked me down and told me. Despite what anybody says, Gunner was a true soldier and died in the defense of his country.

The person in charge of this, Staff Sergeant Parker was court-martialed. He was found guilty of negligent homicide in the death of Gunner Becker. He was also found guilty of dereliction of duty and was given six months of jail time or whatever they call it. It is my understanding that from the time he was found guilty, he lost all his rank and went back to being a private while he was in jail. Apparently his family got some money to live on because I don't think that they came until he got out of jail and came home with them. But I could be wrong. He tried to talk to me twice since then on the phone, but I just couldn't. It cost him his career, but he is the one. He's got to live with it the rest of his life. So, he's a prisoner, too. I can't hate him because I have never been in a war zone. I can't hate him, I wasn't there, I don't know exactly what happened that day. But it was a big mistake. It was a big enough mistake that in a court-martial in front of his peers in what I would call a jury, he was found guilty beyond a shadow of doubt. So, I will believe for the rest of my life that it was a big "fuck-up." Shit happens. I wasn't there. I can't judge him but I can't forget.

America is a grateful nation. Six plus years. It was six years in January and stuff still comes in the mail. Cards, dvds, music; even needlepoint not too long ago. The lady who made this frond is no longer living. She lived down by Sioux Falls. There's a group of people who makes these fronds for fallen heroes. This lady was an immigrant from Switzerland or Sweden or someplace like that. She did it on a scroll frame. I went to her house and saw her do another one. She sat at that machine like it was her sewing machine. Her name was Christine Yeager. She married her husband when he was in the service and he brought her home to America. She was a cancer survivor at the time she was making these fronds for many of us in South Dakota. She didn't survive cancer the second time. She was fifty-four years old when she died. I have a picture of the two of us together when she came up here.

That was when Gunner died and I was working every Saturday night bartending because we ... It's a little town. Gunner and I made a pact when he went back from R&R that we were gonna ... I said, 'You're not drinking, I'm gonna not drink, or at least, not drink very much. And when you get back from Iraq, we're going to go out and get shit-faced, falling down, puking drunk. It's only going to take a six-pack of beer, but we can do it."

Anyway, I got done with the melon season in Aberdeen, came home and started working Saturday nights just for something to do and to give the guy that owed the bar a chance to get away and do something else. And he still, pretty much, always takes Saturday nights off and let somebody else come in and work.

I needed a ... it was a Christmas tree, but it had to be flat and it was tree-shaped, and mounted ... and it was like ... a wall tree for Christmas. I did it in red, white and blue blown-glass stars. Some of them were striped with stars like the flag, some were just regular red, white and blue. At the top of the Christmas tree was a bundle with little, tiny red roses with yellow ribbons that lights up. We left it up. We left it up because we were all going to have a Christmas party when ... It was going to be a party when Gunner got home. In March. I mean, I did Christmas decorations here, things that would be able to hold from Christmas to March. Snowmen, because snowmen go all winter, that kind of thing. That was when I really first started the snowman deal.

Anyway, after Gunner died, I went to the bar and tried to go to work one night. I made it, but it was an ugly night, for me. I took the Christmas tree apart because it was like; really cold, a lot of snow, not many people, very boring and I needed something to do, so I dismantled that Christmas tree. I threw ninety percent of it away, but I brought this patch frond home and I put it someplace where it would be safe, where it wouldn't get lost and where it took me until the blizzard of 2011 to find it. I had put it in the bottom of a big buffet drawer with a whole bunch of other stuff that I had looked through fifty-two times, but just didn't quite ... I really wasn't sure that I was ever going to find it again. But it's here. Because I was going to rework some pictures, I found the patch. Not only that, but I also found something downstairs that I had looked for some twenty years while I was talking to my mother-in-law.

I have learned to live with it. I don't really have a choice. It hurts, it hurts like hell; but life goes on.

So must I.

Berst, Vilis L.
Sergeant, United States Army
1920 -

Another great American hero sprang from the town of Lincoln, Nebraska ninety-one years ago in 1920. Like many of the patriotic Americans, Vilis L Berst was called to serve his country during a time of great peril. Germany had conquered Europe and Japan had attacked the United States at Pearl Harbor, destroying much of her naval forces. The year was 1942 and his country called. Although it was likely that should he have pursued it, he could have received a war-time exemption as he was engaged in what was called a 'critical skill' – in this case, farming – Vilis felt that it was his duty to do his part to defend his country in its time of strife and need.

Vilis went beyond what many would say is his duty and served in World War II during many battles, including the infamous Battle of the Bulge. His story is an inspiration to all patriotic Americans.

*****

Sergeant Vilis L Berst reporting for duty, Sir. I am a mid-westerner, hailing from Lincoln, Nebraska. A native 'Cornhusker', I was born in 1920 and I'm happy to say that I am still somewhat spry at the ripe young age of ninety-one. I grew up on a farm, having spent my youth helping my family and especially my father do the farming. The farm itself was a standard farm; raising crops, hogs, chickens, and children.

At the time the Germans started what we call World War II, I was just reaching twenty years old. Most of the news we got was from radios and just talking to neighbors, but we kept pretty much up to date on what was happening. Hearing about Pearl Harbor and the Japanese joining the Germans in the war, I felt that it was only a matter of time before the Draft Board would certainly take away the war-time exemption for farm workers; especially one that was only twenty or so years old and in excellent physical condition. It turns out that I was right.

I had gone to California to visit my sister and had been at her home for only two or three days when the Draft Board called me to come home to be drafted into the military service. I was enrolled in the United States Army in 1942.

The outfit where they put me was the 803rd Tank Destroyer Battalion. Tank Destroyer Battalions are normally attached to infantry units and we were no different. The units that we were attached to during the war included the 82nd Airborne Division; the 3rd Armored Division; the 2nd, 5th, 8th, 29th, and 30th Infantry Division as well as the 1st Belgian Brigade. We were used mostly for reconnaissance.

I served in the Army from 1942 to 1945. Our unit underwent basic training at Camp Hood, Texas. We were there to be trained in the desert and sand for desert warfare. We spent six to eight months near Camp Hood, engaged in pretty severe training. We had to crawl under barbed wire while live ammunition fired just above us. We also had to cross rivers and hills while in full gear, in addition to all of the desert warfare we practiced. We left the training grounds outside Camp Hood and went to live in the barracks at Camp Hood. We were there for only a short while and then we went Fort Lewis, Washington. We engaged in winter training up there. I even went up to Mt. Everest and did some winter training there as well. Afterwards, I left there and went to New York.

All of a sudden, I was in World War II.

It was just one of those things that had to be done, I suppose. There were a lot of my friends around there from my home town that were being drafted and I guess that was the reason I didn't resist the draft. Of course, I wasn't really looking forward to going to war, didn't really want to shoot anybody, but knew that I had to do my part.

Of course, even if you are busy, you miss things from home. I missed my parents most of all. I was only twenty-two at the time I was drafted. I wasn't married, so didn't have a wife or any children to worry about. I did have one sister and she was older than me. I only got married after I came back out of service.

While I did miss my family and the farm, I never had any urging to come home like a lot of the guys. I was never homesick even in basic training, and overseas it didn't seem to bother me too much.

We deployed to England on June 24, 1943. We spent close to a year in a little town by the name of Barnstaple, England, and we did a lot of training there in addition to cosmolining our vehicles and weapons to protect them from the elements. Later, we went to Plymouth, England, to the docks there to practice going across the English Channel. So, I don't think I got too anxious about coming home. Actually, didn't have the free time. Anyway, there were a lot of my friends over there.

I was a radio operator for a lieutenant. I rode in an armored car that was called an M-10, an armored car – a six-wheeler. It was operated by a driver; the lieutenant was riding in front passenger seat, and there was myself – the radio operator – and then there was a fourth person, a gunner. The outfit that I was in had quite a big radio in it, it was a big set for the lieutenant. There were a .37 mm cannon and a .50 caliber machine gun mounted on the turret. The vehicle would shield off small ammunitions, like machine guns and small arms.

I was in the Battle of the Bulge. We landed on Normandy Beach on day D plus seven (June 13, 1944-Ed). We helped capture the town of St. Lô. During the Battle, our unit was engaged in fighting in the Hurtgen Forest.

Like many other soldiers I saw evidence of the Holocaust. There were a great number of mass burial sites as well as quite a few buildings that had been used as gas chambers. The concentration camps areas were vile.

I was also at Hitler's Eagle Nest, his mountain top retreat at Berchtesgaden. When we got there it was all bombed and shelled out, but I stood in what had been a big picture window that looked out over the mountains. He had quite a sight up there.

There was one time when we were going through the Hurtgen Forest that we were pinned down by enemy machine gun fire. The Germans had blown a huge crater in the road which took up most of the roadway. There was no way to go around the large hole because the trees in the forest were so dense you couldn't get through them. So we had to wait for the bulldozer to come up and fill the hole so that we could continue our advance. It was so dark in the forest, even during the daytime that lights were needed. I had a lot of close calls, but was either blessed or lucky.

We were almost trapped at one time during the Battle of the Bulge, there was only one road for us to exit and we barely escaped. The Germans came close to pinning us down.

During the Battle of the Bulge, we were moving up, driving with just our little peep lights. There were just two of us, the driver and me in the M-10. The Lieutenant was outside the vehicle and the gunner was also outside, trying to direct traffic in the darkness. We came up to this road block, which was two tree logs, one laying on one side of the road and one a few feet further on laying on the other side of the road, each protruding almost halfway across the road bed. The only way to get through there was to do an 'S' turn between the two logs. The driver must have been getting tired as it was pretty late at night because as he made the turn, the rear wheel hit one of the logs and must have knocked it aside. That set thirteen mines off under our M-10. It blew the fenders off of the M-10, blew the tires off and it blew most of our gear that had strapped to the turret off as well. We never did find some of that stuff. The only one that got seriously hurt was the driver. He was in his seat with the hatch fastened down. He was blown up out of his seat, hitting his head on the cover overhead. I was in the back with the radio and it was just a ball of fire when the bombs went off. I didn't suffer any punctures, but I couldn't hear for a couple of weeks after that, and still have difficulty to this day. The Army said they were going to give both of us Purple Heart medals, but that was about the same time that we were getting ready to come home. Well, it ended up that this driver, who was from South Dakota, received two Purple Hearts instead of one. And I have yet to receive the one I was due. I believe he actually got two medals by mistake, as he was only wounded once. We had communicated back and forth over the years as he was trying to get the situation straightened out, but he passed away three or four years ago. I still communicate with his wife, and in fact, she sent me one of the Purple Hearts. That was good of her, but to this date, I am not legally entitled to the medal. She actually sent it to my daughter.

The news reached us that the war was over, but a few minutes later one of our men were shot by the enemy in an ambush. This was in Czechoslovakia. Several of our guys went out in a jeep and drove down the road. They ran into an ambush manned by German troops who were ignorant of the "Cease Fire" order, and were pinned down by gunfire. One of the guys, a Czech-American soldier, stood up in the jeep to see what was going on, and they shot him right in the head. His name was Charles Havlat. He was killed just nine minutes prior to the effective time of the surrender terms on May 7, 1945. He died after the war was declared over, and was the last known American soldier to die in the European Theater of Operations. He was from a little town near here, Dorchester, Nebraska. I still carry a picture of him in my wallet.

There was another guy from that town, also, but he has passed away, about a year ago. In fact, most of the guys that I served with are all gone now. I had been in touch with one of the sergeants, Walter George, but I haven't been able to talk to him recently. He was from Independence, Missouri, which isn't too far. I talk to his wife once in a while, but I haven't been able to speak with Walter. We send letters back and forth to keep up with the news, but most of the rest are all gone.

Altogether, I was proud to have served. I was awarded five bronze stars. I don't remember ... one was the Battle of Normandy, but I don't remember exactly what happened for them all. I'm supposed to be receiving a Purple Heart, but I don't know if it will ever go through.

I have tried three different times with gentlemen from the V.A., the Veterans Administration. Three different men have tried at different times, but they all tell me that my records were destroyed in a fire in St. Louis and they just can't find anything on it. But I think that if they would go the surviving widow in South Dakota and find out how her husband got his, that there might be some connections. It's not so much that I want it, but if I deserve it and if I earned it, I should have it. It's been a long time; sixty years or better.

I'm not sure that their lack of success has had any effect on me, at least I hope not. It's going to be hard for anybody to make it happen, because there's nobody left, now that my friend in South Dakota is gone. Unless there is somebody else up there could verify the events, I probably will never receive the Purple Heart. I'm certain there was a mistake made with him getting both Purple Hearts. In fact we were together all the way through from 1942 through 1945, even through basic training.

I have been rated as ten percent disabled because of the effect the explosion had on my hearing. My hearing is still bad and I have hearing aids for both ears that I got through the V.A. Actually, I get my medicine through the V.A. as well. It helps. I don't take all that much, but it's appreciated.

I had the great privilege to go on an honor flight not long ago. The flight went out of Omaha, but because I was from Lincoln, we went to Omaha the night before and stayed at the local Holiday Inn. We assembled at the old railroad depot and had a big banquet for us. Then they chauffeured us from the motel down Interstate 80. They even had a motorcycle brigade. They stopped all the traffic on the Interstate in our honor. The next morning, we got up at five o'clock in the morning. Then they put us on a plane and flew us from Omaha to Washington DC. There were more than fifty people on the plane and they had two busses waiting for us. They started touring us around and we went to the Vietnam Memorial Veterans Memorial first, which was quite impressive; but then they all were. But I think the Korean Memorial was probably the outstanding one. I think it may have been because it looked so real. It really impressed me. We got to see the changing of the guard and that was really nice. As was the Iwo Jima Memorial. We made a trip around that Memorial in the bus and the driver told us to keep our eyes on the flag as he drove around the memorial and it will seem that those guys are pushing the flag up, and sure enough, it really did. Afterwards, we went to the National Cemetery and that was quite impressive. Seems like every time we stopped, they had something for us to eat. They must have catered stuff out to these busses, because every time we returned to the busses, there was food waiting. I really enjoyed that trip; it was quite an honor for me.

One memorial we missed that I would have liked to see is the Holocaust Memorial. That would mean something special to me. We came up on a lot of those places where Germans had buried people in mass graves, shallow graves that were filled with dead bodies. We also found quite a few boxcars where the Germans had packed people in the boxcars and killed ... them. I also walked through one of those gas chambers that they had used. It was just a block building with one opening at each end. I guess they just walked them and gassed them. It's too hard to even think about, much less talk about it.

Even so, I would do it all over again if I were asked.

I am still a pretty active volunteer at the V.A. and just a month or so ago I got my 35-year pin from the V.A. I've been an active chairman with the Lincoln Elks Lodge for twenty-two years on the Veterans Hospital Committee. I have been an Elk ... I'm a fifty year member as an Elk. I'm quite proud of that. I really enjoy that organization and its community services. We no longer have a Veteran's Hospital, it's an out-patient facility now, but we used to have patients there and some thirty-five years ago we used to sponsor games and events as well as picnics for the veterans who were in the hospital and their families. Now that there aren't any, I volunteer – Sam Carter and I work together on that program. We call on nursing homes and retirement homes. There are two facilities, twenty veterans in one and more than twenty-four in the other. I carry a list of birthdays and carry a little pack of goodies; toothpaste, socks, lotion, shampoo and stuff like that. I give it to them along with a birthday card and we go to the bank and get a two-dollar bill and put it in the envelope along with the card. In the Sunday paper is a supplement, a celebration magazine that sometimes has a veteran in there. If it has his or her address, I make up a birthday card along with the two-dollar bill and send it to the veteran. The Elks has a program, Leather for Veterans, that provides leather gloves for wheelchair patients and I try to see that anybody in a wheelchair gets a pair of gloves. These veterans are very grateful. And they make us feel very much needed, and that's a great feeling.

I've been married for sixty-five years and my wife is still with us. I have two children, one boy and one girl. My son is the head of the X-ray at Bryan Hospital here in Lincoln and my daughter is a nurse at Radiology clinic here in Lincoln. She has three boys, all of whom were Eagle Scouts. One is in the military, overseas right now. Another is going to the University of Nebraska. The third is in Minnesota ... he is buried.

My son has a boy and a girl. They are both married, and we have two great-great-grandchildren. That is my life. I'm glad it turned out the way it did. It has turned out grand, thanks to many great people

I have been truly blessed.

Bradley, George
Sergeant, U.S. Army
Sergeant, U.S. Marine Corps
1925 –

With the average lifespan increasing and the number of veterans who have served in the military, it isn't too unusual to meet a former serviceman or woman. It is also increasingly common to meet someone who served in a war, as wars continue unabated. Less common is it to meet someone who has served in two wars, although as the result of the short span between Desert War I and Desert War II, meeting such veterans occurs more often than in the past. It is seldom that you meet anyone that served in different wars in different decades and it is extremely rare indeed to meet a veteran that has served in three wars that has spanned four decades. Or who has served in more than one branch of the military. Such an individual is George Bradley of Denver Colorado, a veteran of both the United States Army and the United States Marine Corps. And he has served in not one, not two, but three wars: World War II in the 1940's, the Korean War in the 1950's and in the Vietnam War in the 1960's and 1970's. Not just three wars, but in four different decades. Not just three wars but five tours of duty in combat zones. At the age of eighty-six, Bradley has seen action that few if any living people have ever seen or will ever see. With less surviving World War II veterans every year, individuals like George Bradley have characteristics that every young person in the world should emulate. Enjoy the story of one of America's most unique heroes, George Bradley.

*****

Sgt George Bradley, Denver, Colorado, present and accounted for. I really don't have much of a story to tell, and frankly, would prefer to forget most of what I do remember.

It just came up, the war I mean. The War to End All Wars, World War II. Germany started the war by invading Europe, but that didn't mean much to us at the time. Although there were a lot of guys who were moving off to Canada or England to get into the fighting, I didn't feel that urge. It wasn't until Pearl Harbor that I understood that we were going to be deep into the war and that most or all of the guys my age and in good health were going to be drafted. I decided that I just couldn't wait; I had to join, to get in and fight for my country. Hindsight says I could have waited and probably should have waited, but youth is impetuous; and so was I. So, immediately following Pearl Harbor, I joined. 1942 was the year. I didn't have to be drafted like a lot of those other ones, I was ready to go. And so I did.

After I got in and found what it was all about, I just decided that I would stay in and make a career of it. I served a total of twenty-nine years in the military, and was there during three different wars. I went to Vietnam twice and to Korea twice.

When I enlisted in 1942, I chose to join the United States Marine Corps. They had the reputation for leading the fighting and I decided that was where I belonged. I was what they call gung-ho to do my duty and serve my country. Of course, I wasn't alone, there were thousands and thousands and thousands who felt the same way, and many others who were willing if not eager to serve.

That's how we won, everybody doing their part including those here at home.

Even though I was eager and physically fit, the Marines didn't want to take seventeen-year-old boy, at least, not without the parents' consent. I had been born on the first of September 1925 and had just become seventeen so I begged and persuaded my mother to sign for me so that I could get into service. She was reluctant, happy, proud, sad and worried all at the same time, wondering what was going to happen to her son. She was also certain that I would not be able to pass the tests and that I would be sent home. But I fooled her, passed with high marks.

I was looking forward to fighting the Japs or the Germans, wherever they would send me. I wasn't worried, not at all. Didn't even cross my mind; not at the time.

The Marines kept us so busy during boot camp that we didn't have time to miss anyone, although later I would miss my mother most. Especially when I was overseas. I wasn't married at the time and didn't have any children, so that wasn't part of what I was leaving behind. I did get married later in life, and have one son. Guess he is smarter than I was because he is married and not in the military.

After the war was over, I returned to the States and got out of the Marines for a couple of weeks and then did an inter-service transfer into the United States Army. I had decided that I was going to make a career out of the service and felt the Army was the best match as they were trying to downsize the Marine Corps. In addition, the Marine Corps didn't have a recruiting office anywhere near where I was when I made the decision to re-enter the service, so the choice was rather easy. Either join the Army or go hunt for the Marine Corps; I chose the closest. Altogether, I served a total of twenty-nine years in the military, Marine Corps and Army combined.

One of the medals that they presented to me was the Purple Heart, given for wounds suffered in combat. It was on the islands of Palagie that I was injured. It was necessary that these islands be taken before the Allied Forces could invade Sicily. I was hit by shrapnel in my arm and shoulder. That's the only Purple Heart that I earned because afterwards I stayed away from them. I had learned how to duck.

During World War II, I was an infantryman and fought in a lot of the battles, at least it seemed like a lot to me. I fought in the Battle of Guadalcanal, which took place from August 7, 1942 through February 9, 1943. That's where I went shortly after basic training. Then on the atoll of Tarawa where fighting continued. After that, we moved on to the island of Saipan where we fought in June and July of 1994. There was the 2nd and 4th Marine division and the 27th Infantry division – my unit – and needless to say, we beat the Japs again. And we kept on fighting. Nobody quit, and in fact, when we were wounded, as I was, we would just get fixed up by the medics and then we would return to the front line. There were a lot of guys killed and many more wounded, some very badly. Still, for the most part, if you were not killed or completely disabled, you would fight on. There wasn't any quit in any of the Americans. Not in the officers, not in the men. We just didn't know how. We didn't have time to let any wounds affect us, we knew that we had to fight on and win. To lose or to quit was not an option. I think it was a part of what was bred into our generation. I had three buddies that gave us signs saying that we were courageous.

Another medal that I earned was a Bronze Star. I didn't think it anything special, but the commendation reads that another solder and I together held off ninety-seven Japanese soldiers, killing a lot of them and saving a lot of American lives. He and I both received medals. Frankly, it means more now than then, along with several other combat and theater medals and ribbons that a soldier in combat might well earn.

One thing I do miss now is that I haven't kept in contact with any of my friends that I made during the war. Just drifted apart, I guess, and lost touch with everybody. You get close to one another during combat, but afterwards you just move away. 'Course, a lot of them have passed away by now. I understand they have erected a memorial wall back in DC with a lot of names on it, but I just have never been able to go there to see for myself. I'm told that it is a wonderful memorial but it's not likely that I will ever see it.

During my tour in Korea, I was a member of the United States Army and served as an infantryman. Kind of a habit, I guess. I was in the fighting at Pusan during

August and September, 1950 when the North Koreans were constantly attacking, trying to push all of us, the US and the UN soldiers and Marines back into the sea. We were able to stand them off, although they kept on coming. Eventually, we were able to push them back but we were mostly in a defensive stand at Pusan. We were under pressure until there was a counter-attack by US forces on Inchon, which caused the North Koreans supply lines to be cut and the attacks on us stopped.

After being able to advance from Pusan, our forces drove into Seoul and were part of the retaking of the capital of South Korea, making the North Koreans retreat as we advanced. We had some of those big guns to help us, guns from Navy ships. And we were glad of it. Big boys, made a lot of noise when they went off, but the big artillery shells had quite an effect on the enemy when they exploded. I believe that had a lot to do with our having survived.

I was in Korea for two tours, 1950 and 1952, I believe. The Army would keep us there for a year, or almost, and then rotate us out, to either Japan or Okinawa, or some other rest area. Some of the soldiers were even sent home for a couple of months and then brought back. As I wasn't married, I never was given the choice of going Stateside.

After Korea, there was a short break before I went to the next war. That was in Vietnam. I don't know if it's anything to be proud of or not, but actually served in three wars altogether. I guess that it says something about mankind if you can have three wars in my lifetime, and if I wasn't too old, I could have served in the two Gulf Wars. That would have made five. Isn't that something?

Actually, I served two tours in Vietnam, much like I did in Korea. I was in theater for about a year, and then maybe seven months out of the war zone, and then returning to the front lines for another year. Guess I had gotten smarter because I transitioned out of the infantry into artillery. This time, I got to shoot the 'big boys', firing .105s and .155s. Made a hell of an explosion when they went off. I don't remember exactly where we were at any one time, because we were mostly in a combat zone outside the cities in the rural areas and the jungles, but we were all over the place, moving almost every day.

After my second tour in Vietnam, I returned home. I saw much of the protests the public was demonstrating, but it really didn't affect me at all. I knew that I was a good soldier, having done five combat tours in defense of my country. I was most proud of what I had done, and so was my son. He knows that his father did his duty.

If I had to do it over again, I would do it all over again. I don't know if I would change anything except maybe having fewer Americans killed or wounded. I would also like to see more help given to the veterans that were wounded in defense of America, wounded by gunfire and traumatized by the experience of killing and being killed. And the families ... they need it the most. They need all the help they can get. There is never enough. They gave it their all and they need help; now. That's the main reason that I am willing to talk about it all now, I've always kept it to myself. I didn't really want to remember everything, and in fact tried to forget it all. I saw things that I never wanted to see and certainly don't want to remember. But now, I'm told that it might help other veterans and I want to help my fellow servicemen. We are all veterans of the military forces that were doing their best to preserve the freedom of the American people. We made our sacrifices and now it's America's turn to take care of us. Not so much me, but all of our great people who were willing to fight and die for this nation.

Estes, Clarence A.
Sergeant, United States Army
1960-

Sergeant Clarence A. Estes served in the United States Army for twenty-four years before retiring. Originally from St. Louis, Missouri, Estes now lives and works in Jefferson City, Missouri. Although retired from the Army, Sgt. Estes continues to work with several branches of the military in conducting Military Funeral Honors services for Missouri veterans.

The program became effective under a bill signed by Governor Carnahan of Missouri in order to create a National Guard Trust Fund and appropriate funding to provide military funeral honors for veterans as a final tribute as a testament of their services to the nation. Sgt. Estes works with organizations such as the American

Legion, Veterans of Foreign Wars, American Veterans, Marine Corps League as well as the Army National Guard to provide these services for these valiant citizen soldiers, sailors, airmen and marine veterans and their families.

*****

Since I'm originally from the town of St. Louis, I am a true-born son of the "Show Me" state. Being born in 1960's, I wasn't old enough to participate in the 'flower' movements and don't believe that I would have had I been born earlier. I did join the military, the United States Army to be exact, when I was nineteen, entering service in 1979. That was after the Vietnam period and before the Gulf War onslaught. I actually decided to join the service because of my young son. I wanted to have a good life for him and felt that it would be wise. Further, I wanted to find a life and to find myself as a person. Those gave me sufficient motivation to enlist in the Army and to remain a soldier on both active duty and in the Army National Guard for twenty-four years.

I guess you could say that I was a 'tweener in that I served most of my time between the Vietnam War and the Gulf War, or Desert Storm. While I didn't see combat duty, I did a significant amount of travel. First stop was in Korea. There was a lot of team spirit in the early 1980's and there were still a goodly number of combat troops stationed in Korea as the situation was and remains unstable, with North Korea seeking reunification with South Korea. A lot of people spent either two weeks or a full year there. I was there in a support position, providing help and assistance to the troops stationed there.

Korea was only one of the places I traveled as a support staff member. I served back-to-back one-year tours in Alaska, sometimes in the M.P.'s or else Construction Engineers. After those two tours, I came back to the 'lower 48', working with recruiters, actually getting people in to join to help form their career. I loved doing that for three years straight. Following that tour as a recruiter, I then returned to the National Guard, where I completed my military obligation for the balance of career. During this time, I spent some time in Panama, Honduras and in Bosnia. Throughout this time, I was once again serving in a support role of helping the military men and women maintain their status of being ready at all times to engage the enemy and to defend the nation.

Now I have what is perhaps my most rewarding duty in a job that is probably not the most sought after. I actually do all the military funerals for the state of Missouri. It is a program that I honor and love doing on behalf of the State of Missouri. These services are offered under a program signed into law in 1999 by Mel Carnahan. I have done over two thousand five hundred funerals for the State and it is very, very important because those guys and girls who served before me did an excellent job to keep us safe here in the United States. That is one reason why I actually perform these duties, not only to give them back what they gave me as to my military career, but as life in general. I want to give that next soldier, that next family the honors that they actually deserve.

I'll have to admit that it was very hard in the beginning. After you do the first, versus twenty-five hundred, it never changes; it's still the same. I still get cracked up or have some emotional feelings every time I hear the sounds of "Taps." "Taps" is very, very big and the last viewing of anybody's personal life if they ever served in the military. I really get cracked up on each and every one; every service is different. After twenty-five hundred, no service is alike because there is something personal about that family or about that individual if I knew him or not, it's very, very personal. I take a big sigh of relief when I actually present the flag to the next of kin.

One of the hardest things is to lay to rest soldiers from the recent wars. Especially the young ones. The ones that, I would say, didn't want to go back or had some personal problems Stateside and actually didn't want to go back. Those were very, very touching to me because of the obligations that the individual actually signed up to do. But you can't really get into that, you can't really get yourself wrapped up into that, you are actually performing your duty at that time.

And there is the respect. Number one, respect goes a long way in our personal life. To actually have and show that respect for the next individual whether it is a male or a female. And the honor and the importance of doing military honors and actually guarding and standing for all the different traits: honor, respect, loyalty are all wrapped in the effort. We all have those traits in ourselves.

We do the honors for all branches of service, and for veterans of all wars. And we work with all organizations.

When I'm asked about inspiration to serve in the military during the difficult times following Vietnam and before the American public regained their respect for the military with the Gulf War, I answer that being an individual and believing that I could do something about it, helping, was a big reason. Lending a helping hand and being a part of something big led me on and gave me all of the inspiration I needed. When I put on the military uniform, I was moved in a certain way. And I'm sure that I was not the only one to feel that way as

I'm sure that many of my buddies felt the same thrill and excitement. That was the biggest thing, just to help out and be a part of something very, very big; bigger than myself.

One of the benefits of joining the military is that you meet a lot of good people and make a lot of new friends. I make it a point to stay in touch with as many as I can. For example, I will see one of them at one of the services we do or I'll just call on the telephone and say, "Hey, let's get into a football game or a baseball game, or just have a chat, to have some type of contact, to keep that spirit going and to find out what they are doing with their lives. Anybody who has been in service knows that the spirit in today's military is very high. In fact, the recruiting rate in all branches is over and above the expected range at this time. Earlier, it was lower when the war was going on, but their strength is back up and the camaraderie is still there ... which is very important – to keep that enthusiasm up throughout the United States.

Of course, part of the reason why there are so many volunteers and why they are so enthusiastic is the educational opportunities that are available to the military. The Montgomery GI Bill that provides for education is huge and has been going on for years. Young people are coming in and saying, "I want to join the Army," knowing that after their service they can go to almost any college or university in the country and much or even all of the tuition costs will be paid for by the country they served. That's becoming even more important as the costs of getting a degree is increasing every year and some of the kids would never be able to go to college without the military. And, while this may be one of the prime motives for joining, there are a lot of these kids who find the service much better than they expected and they decide to make a career of it. That's what will keep our military strong.

There are some things you miss when you enlist in the military, especially if you serve overseas. I know that I did, I missed my kids most of all. But there were other things, everyday things that you are familiar with such as the cutting of the lawn, being able to run down to the corner and get a hamburger, multiple stations on the cable T.V., the different friends you went to high school with, the ones you played ball with, neighbors: these are some of the biggest things. But you keep memories of all this with you and it sustains you. Sure, in depressing moments the idea of quitting and going back home crosses your mind, but it's just a fleeting thought, comes quickly, goes quickly. Military people, for the most part, are strong individuals and quickly form families with the people around them that are serving the same cause. Keeping the spirits up becomes an important part of daily life, so they make it a part of their lives to keep each other's spirits up. For me, that was much of the drive that caused me to serve for twenty-four years.

If I had to sum it up in a few words – 6, 8, 10 – I would have to say the best part may well have been the love of your fellow soldier, the family you form in the military, the support of people back home; more than a few words but all very important. And there's the thrill of looking forward to retirement.

Earlier I said that I didn't serve in a combat zone, however I did travel to Bosnia, where war was being conducted. Before the war, Bosnia was a vibrant country engaged in Olympics and other world affairs. But with all of the destruction we saw and the deaths, a different understanding about war occurs. I believe the reason why we go through a lot of war situations that we have no control over is an effort to make the world better.

That was, and is, one of the aspects as to why I served and I think that is what all – or most all – of the Presidents go through, their attempt at trying to make the world a better and safer place. That is why they send the military branches into the different countries, trying to make the world a better place and safer for all of us. The mission of the military was to make the world less dangerous and a better place for all people and after fixing things, to get back home as safely as possible. Getting back home with all our people: to us, that was huge.

When I was in an area such as Bosnia, or Korea, or Panama or Honduras, the things that brought good feelings were the children, the little kids from those countries. Here in the United States, we expect our kids to be the next generation, to run the country, to become President one day. For the kids of the foreign countries, that may not be possible, so the thought and the inspiration that the kids we were helping may have places to go get an education that are safe and secure and that they may live to be the next generation and that we had something to do with that is exhilarating and exciting. We gave them an opportunity for life, a safe life that they didn't have before. I think that was the biggest thing, to see the smiles on the kids' faces as we gave them care packages, or when we were building something for them; schools, houses, something that was safe. That was the biggest thing for me.

I am often asked if, considering it all, I would do it all again, and I answer, "Yes, absolutely. As a matter of fact, tomorrow." Of course, considering the time change, there are a few things that I might do differently. And with the experience that I've had, I would change a few things, but overall, I'm proud of what we do, all of the military and I would do it again, over and over. Everything, including the funeral services. In fact, I plan on continuing doing that until the day I retire.

I believe that I am setting an example – a good example, I hope – by continuing to do the services and showing honor to the families that justly deserve and have earned the honor because of the death of someone in their family. Whether from combat or natural causes, these men and women still served our country and need this as a final closure for them. One thing: we don't contact the family, they must contact us. That is, unless it is a combat wound that caused the death.

There are organizations around that help. One I would like to specifically acknowledge is the Freedom Riders. They help us and support us in a lot of different ways. They have chapters all over the country; guys on 'cycles who either served or have a family member that served. I think it's very important for the community to actually see something like ... to say, "Hey, those guys aren't just bikers, they are actually supporting something that is very honorably to their city or their country." Most of the biker clubs that are out there are some of the most loyal, down-to-earth, God loving, God fearing men and women. They care about this country probably more than most people realize. They are awesome. So, I think that it is very important that people know. I like and respect that organization and others like it; that really moves me.

Both before and during – as well as after – my military service, there were a goodly number of people who were instrumental in shaping my person, many more people than I have the time or space to acknowledge. However, there are a few who do stand out and one of those was a guy back in the 1980's, Mr. Tringally – if I spelled his name right – who was my mentor. He was the person who actually showed me the ropes as far as what I should do to make my career last. And there was another man, just recently retired, Colonel Shelly. I had known him from the time he was just a second lieutenant until he reached the rank of full bird Colonel. Another impact on my life was by Sergeant Major Jones. He was a heck of a soldier, often a very funny man, but he took care of his troops. And that was the most important thing, especially when you are overseas and abroad. In different foreign countries, Sgt Major Jones made sure that the lower NCO's were taken care of and he would bring them back home safely. That was important when you were away from home. He fought to keep the moral up ... he was the guy who made you laugh and believe, and he was the guy that brought you back home again, safe and alive. There are many, many more, but these especially stand out in my memory of special people who kept me highly motivated. Leadership was the common trait that each of them exhibited to a high degree.

One of the most often questions, if not the most often asked, is if I can remember the first funeral service that I did. I'll respond, "Of course. How could I forget it? Even after two thousand five hundred; and counting." It was very, very cold at the Jefferson Barracks National Cemetery, in St. Louis, Missouri. We normally do twenty-five to twenty-six services per day. They would be back to back, every fifteen minutes or so, at the National Cemetery. That was the procedure at that time and it is still the standard procedure today. Again, it was very cold outside. When it's your first venture or your first operation or your first trek, the sayings are usually the same. "You have to get started ... you have to bust your cherry, so to speak ... you have to take the wool off your head ..." and other sayings to remind you that you are so fresh and new at it. And you are nervous; very, very nervous, because you don't want to screw it up. Not for yourself, but for the family of the deceased; they deserved the best. Oh yeah, I can vividly see in my mind right now the very first one ... and how cracked up and speechless I was ... I was actually shaking when I presented my first flag to that individual. I don't think the family noticed, as most of them were crying and shaking as well.

You don't really forget any of them, but on occasion it became even more important to me when I did a family member: my uncle That was possibly more moving to me. I drove down to Jefferson City, Missouri from St. Louis and brought my whole team to the cemetery for this service. Indeed, my own kin – it was very moving and stressful, you bet. When I was handing off the flag to a family member, the emotions that ran through me, and undoubtedly the person to whom I was handing the flag, were quite extreme. It was touching ... a bone-chilling type of feeling that I would never forget. Not only me and my family members, but the team family members that we actually performed the duties for. It's still touching in some kind of way that brings something to your heart to say, "I can't stop. I have to do my best, the team has to do their best to make sure that family sees the last, best performance honoring that veteran, and I do that each and every day, in every service I do. I keep that thought in mind. I try to stay as sharp as possible. I'm on time and that is what the military put into my mind, to be on time, to stay sharp in what I do. I think every veteran has some of that in their soul in some kind of way, shape, form or fashion.

Let's face it, these families are hurting and struggling all at the same time, and for me and my team to be able to be there and hand them the flag and to show them America, the United States appreciates their services; that is huge to a family. And it has to touch anybody observing, no matter related or not. A lot of those families see us – or me – as the last person that gives them and their deceased loved one the respect they deserve. So, I know that they are going to be thinking about me and see me in their mind a lot, and I want to leave the best impression in their thoughts that I can, an impression showing honor to their sacrifices.

I have received so many, many thank-you letters and cards, from coast to coast from family members that have actually visited Jefferson City or St. Louis or Kansas City to see our Arms Honor Team perform. I have received so many thank-you letters from so many family members saying, "Hey, this is the best team we have ever seen ... and that individual I just buried would love that ..." I am personally glad and honored to do what I can because I am actually putting some type of honor or respect on that person who passed away.

We have several memorials for veterans whose family members are already gone. The State of Missouri is trying to come up with a program ... implement a program for a person in a nursing home, for example, that doesn't have any family. So, we are trying to get that Memorial program enacted throughout the state to honor all these people that are in homes that doesn't have any family. We do have a Memorial Day, but it's not as huge as it should be, so I think it is a very good idea that the State has come up with this plan that they are trying to implement to actually honor these guys and to find the records of those individuals that have served and to give them their respect ... and honors.

There are a few motorcycle clubs that will go to a coroner's office and urns that hold the cremated ashes that are from veterans that nobody has claimed. And they will pay respect to that veteran and they do it the right way, the way that it should be done. And to me, that says it all right there.

Sometimes, I'm asked if I would change the way we do the service. Actually, I believe that it is put in its right place, it's the right way of doing it. We try to be as perfect as possible on each and every service. Even our

VFW and American Legion that actually support us; to keep their organization going is very important to me and we try to perfect those guys so they can keep their organization going, whether it is the American Legion or the VFW Club.

Another honor is that I have been invited to become a member of the Elks. Naturally, I am thrilled and excited and was quick to accept. And it is to take place quite soon.

My story may not be as exciting and entertaining as stories you may read about active combat and all that, but I – we – me and my team, like others, serve what we believe to be a vital function. Much like the medics, we serve to heal the wounds suffered by the families of our deceased veterans, mental wounds that are often as grievous as bullet wounds or shrapnel. I believe one of the most important things is that we keep this organization going to serve the funerals. I think that all of the other states are getting a grip on how the program should be run; such as it is at the Arlington National Cemetery. Not everyone can be buried at Arlington; there just isn't sufficient space. So, I want this program to be around for myself when I pass, and for all my younger brothers and sisters that are in all branches of the military. This program must go on. That's the most important thing to me because I want that person to give me the same respect that I gave to all the number of services I did, and that I am going to continue to do. I have no idea how many that will be, I can't put a number on it. But, I would like to say that I would like to do them for as long as I can do them and as long as I can stay fit, and I'll try to stay as sharp as possible. If those VFW and American Legion guys can go on to eighty or eighty-five or ninety and pick up a weapon and fire them … I want to be just like those guys. I just hope that when I pass, others filled with the same respect that I have will take my place. Many people say they want to, but not everyone is able to deliver. They admit that they would be emotional, even cry. I can only respond that I am emotional at every service, and frequently cry. Trust me, there are a lot of cases where I've been touched so deeply that I have shed my tears. But you have to move on, you have to be strong, you have to be stronger than the next person. But, it's very touching. I get the service done, and then move on; but never forget ... never.

Without sounding like I'm bragging, I must say that I have given over two thousand five hundred flags to families, have done over twenty –five hundred services, more than anybody in the state of Missouri.

I said that I try to stay as fit and as sharp as I am able. And so does my team, and I believe most other teams do the same. Every state has its own teams And, I'd welcome the challenge of trying to teach teams in other states to do it the way we do. I'm certain that there are differences in every team. We have eight teams in the state of Missouri and all of those teams are trained thoroughly in the guidelines. The procedures have to be performed in a certain way, according to the regulations. Not all of them do it exactly the same way, I'm sure, some of them put their own twist on it, they perform slightly different. All with respect, of course. Sure, I would like to train them all, but in the same sense, their teams are their teams. Still I would love to have all of those teams put the effort, the honor, the loyalty into each and every service like I do and like I feel. I'm sure some of them – maybe even most – of them do.

A team is composed of a number of members. Minimum requirements in our State are four members, but there can be as many as ten. I have performed with as few as three others and as many as nine. And we have performed in all types of situations and in all climates; rain, snow, sleet, hot sunshine; all of it. But the climates is not the worst of it, frankly, it's the kids. That is the hardest thing, when I see a kid out there with his mother or father and I have to hand the flag to a child, it is one of the most difficult things I ever have to do.

I have run through different scenarios where I have imagined myself being in the same situation as the family and as the deceased. I go into a lot of cemeteries and I read a lot the markings. And I have served at a lot of places. And each service or each location, I asked myself, "How much longer do I have on this planet? And will I get the same respect?" And that's another reason why I want this program to actually get stronger, to have it go on for life. Of course, my team members feel the same way, otherwise they wouldn't be doing what they are doing, they wouldn't be able to go on.

As I said, twenty-five hundred and counting. And I will continue counting so long as I am able. I owe that to the brave men and women who have dedicated their lives and in fact given their lives on behalf of their – and my – nation. They have earned my respect, and they are due all the honors that a grateful nation that has remained free because of their efforts can bestow upon them. I am most honored to be an instrument of that gratitude.

Fulks, James A.
Colonel, United States Marine Corps (Rtd)
1946 –

James A. Fulks served as an enlisted man in the early stages of the Vietnam War, rising to the rank of Sergeant. Graduating from OCS school, he returned to Vietnam as a Second Lieutenant. Rising through the officer ranks, Fulks was promoted to First Lieutenant followed by his promotion to Captain and then to Major. Next rank was Lieutenant Colonel and then full Colonel.

Colonel Fulks served in Vietnam and then played a vital role in the Persian Gulf War known as Desert Storm as commander of Task Force Grizzley.

His personal decorations include the Legion of Merit with Combat Distinguishing Device and Gold Star, the Meritorious Service Medal, the Navy Commendation Medal, the Navy Achievement Medal, and the Combat Action Ribbon with Gold Star

*****

I'm a native of 'The Treasure State' although most people now refer to Montana as 'Big Sky Country." I first saw light in a little town up on the Canadian border by the name of Bad, Montana; a long away from everywhere

Born in 1946, I guess that I am what they call a 'baby boomer'. During my younger days, for about as long as I can remember, I had the military on my mind. It comes from that era, my family ran a hunting and fishing resort in Montana. People would come up and go hunting and fishing. I can remember sitting around a campfire with my dad who was a B-17 pilot together with a former Marine aviator that fought in World War II named Colonel Crockett, who was retired at the time. Those two men would go at it about who was good and who was bad between the two of them. Dad was an Army Air Corps aviator—the Corps eventually spawned the United States Air Force. Colonel Crockett was a Marine pilot during all of the Pacific campaign. When he was talking, I was completely fascinated with his stories about the Marines, and I started studying the Marines when I was in high school because the memories had just stuck in my head after Colonel Crockett had told all those exciting stories around the campfires.

I really haven't told my story before but I realize the importance of trying to help our veterans and their families, so I am willing to talk about most everything that I did in service. However, understand that I am talking from memories and the story may be a little disjointed and I am likely to jump back and forth as we go along.

I served twenty-eight years, from 1966 until 1994. I served two tours in Vietnam; first in 1967 and then again in 1969. After Vietnam, I then served in the first Gulf War in 1990 and 1991. At the time I was in combat in Kuwait and the Saudi Arabia theater.

Now that I am in civilian land, one question that I'm asked a lot now in these civilian communities is what gave me the courage to serve in the military during these times, especially Vietnam and the Gulf War. Of course, I'm dealing with civilians all the time, many of whom have never served, so I expect those kinds of questions. Actually, my answer was and is that my motivational factor was the opportunity of leading and being with the young military people. It absolutely makes my day. There's nothing better than coming up to a machine gun crew while they are going through their training, being an 'A' gunner, laying down, talking to some young Lance Corporal who's eighteen or nineteen years old, asking him the same kinds of questions that is often asked of me. Motivates the hell out of me. Crawling in the motor pool while some 'grease monkey' is changing the oil in a Humvee, and asking him, "How's your day going? What's going on? How was chow?" The young Marines absolutely just motivate the hell out of me. It took me twenty-eight years before I got away from them. And once I got away from them, I said, "I'm done. It's no longer any fun." Still, it's the young marines, their motivation and their total dedication. They would to anything. You'd order them to jump off a cliff and they would say, "Which cliff?" And off they would go. They are absolutely amazing; then and now. They haven't changed. There is no old breed, there is no new breed; there's only the United States Marine Corps breed.

I began my military career by enlisting in the Marine Corps in April, 1967 as an enlisted man. Deployed to Vietnam, I served as a helicopter crew member in HMH-462 and attained the rank of sergeant by the time I finished my first tour in Vietnam in 1968. I had an opportunity to go right out of the country at that time. I was in Phu Bai, Vietnam, and had orders to go to Officers Candidate School. I suppose it was because I was just a young sergeant at the time, I was kind of ambivalent about the Marine Corps as a whole, didn't really think about being an officer, and didn't particularly want to leave Vietnam. In fact, I was thinking about extending my time and taking another tour.

I had gone into HQ and there was this old Warrant Officer, a W-4. A W-4 in 1967 was an old World War II vet, and this guy had a gristled face, gristled body, chewed tobacco, and was a W-4 admin guy. I don't know how in the heck he got into admin, but ... I went in and asked him how I could turn down these orders. And he said, "You don't, Sergeant. What's your problem?" I said, "Well, I'm not sure that I want to go to OCS and become an officer." And he said, "I've got one thing to tell you. It's easier to pin them on than it is to sew them on. Go to the club tonight, get drunk and get on the friggin' airplane tomorrow and go back there."

I flew back and, literally, two days later was in Officers Candidate School in Quantico, Va. It was what was called the 52nd Special OCS class in 1968. Seventy-five percent of that 52nd Special OCS class were prior enlisted men. We had everything from Gunnies (Gunny Sergeant) down to PFC's. And it was ... it was quite an experience. Yep, I was a sergeant when I got commissioned and a Colonel when I retired. So I hit them all. Of course, as a former enlisted man, you know what the enlisted men go through. However, sometimes you can have too much empathy. There's an old saying, "The mission first, and then the troops." But you can do both. You really can do both.

Of course, when you are away, you miss your family. On my first tour, I wasn't married and my brother was in the army. As a matter of fact, we found that we were both in country (Vietnam) at the same time. They weren't supposed to allow that in those days. And although I didn't realize it, my mother was a complete wreck. On my second tour, I was married and to our great pleasure my daughter was born while I was there. We were up in the Que Son Mountains, freezing our a... tails off. We were assigned to the Ameri-Cav division and hadn't been re-supplied. They had changed the frequencies of the radio communications, so we couldn't radio for supplies. It was a whole mess. I was the Company Commander for Bravo One-One and I remember when I got the message, a cryptic on this little canary yellow sheet that had been called in. I was a second lieutenant at the time. The message would be like, 02 then they would spell out your name – Julia Alpha Foxtrot – Daughter born November 4, 1969 and I thought, "Oh my god. All I want is something to eat."

Now when I tell my daughter that story, she just rolls her eyes at me. But it was often then that you literally went six, nine, sometimes ten months and never had any contact with your family. It was what was expected. Now, in our technologically rich era, it's interesting seeing the troops with the internet, and Skype, and email and the constant contact that families have. I think it is more of a distraction than it was for us. I mean, you'd get a letter, read the letter, and then okay, go back to business. Actually, it's hard to say that you really miss your family when you are totally focused during combat on the lives and survival and the making of decisions that are going to keep your troops alive. It's only during the quiet times that you can really think about back home.

During Desert Storm, I was Colonel – during Desert Storm and Desert Shield, I was Colonel, but I was still washing my utilities in a bucket. One of my fondest memories is sitting there with General Myatt as we were washing our utilities, talking strategy. Can you imagine, sharing a bucket, a two-star general and a colonel? In Desert Storm, one of the things I missed most was fresh vegetables. In Vietnam, you could, although you really weren't supposed to do it, it may have been a heinous crime but we would take some vegetables out of some farmer's field, and eat them. Made sure we washed them first. But, fresh vegetables, of all the odd things to miss in Desert Storm.

I can remember when Steve Martin and his wife, Victoria Tennant, came over to do a USO tour and he, Steve Martin, came in, and we're sitting there having lunch with him and his wife. They were running behind schedule and were hurrying. One of the things that I didn't know was that both Steve Martin and his wife Victoria Tennant were vegetarians. They put all these fresh veggies on the table. We had been in the field, the 1st Marine Division, had been in the field, eating on mess-hall wraps and MRE's (meals ready to eat) for a minimum of four months, living in the field, the entire division. Well, I'm sitting next to Victoria Tennant having lunch and she is sitting there eating carrots as we are talking. She's sitting there snapping these fresh carrots and snapping celery and cutting these juicy red tomatoes. To die for.

And here's this hungry, aggressive, class-act Marine Corps group sitting there eating our MRE's. And Martin and his wife are running late, they have to get up and go. And so, they get up and leave, like, "Thanks for lunch, it was great meeting you guys." And all that. I turned to Victoria and said, "Victoria, this may sound odd, but are you going to finish your vegetables?" And when she left, there were about three of us that jumped in and started eating her fresh vegetables. There were cucumbers and pickles and ... It was awesome. Didn't even wait until Victoria was out of sight. I really missed fresh vegetables.

I have been asked if there was ever a time that I felt like quitting, like just chucking it in and stopping and coming home. There has never been such an occasion; I loved the military. I'm also often asked if I have ever been afraid. And I have to answer truthfully, I don't know. I don't know if I was afraid or not, I was so focused on what I was doing. My job as a platoon commander, as a company commander, and as a regimental commander in my three some odd years in combat, my job was to worry about those thirty-six, those two hundred and thirty, those five thousand marines that worked under me. And I never once gave a though about my own safety. I never gave a thought as to what was going on in my life; my whole focus was making sure that they had what they needed to do the job. Because I'm going to give them a hell of a job to do. And, for the record, they never once failed me. Always rose to the top. That sounds like a cliché answer, but that was exactly the way I felt. I never once ... I don't think about myself, I worry about them.

One of the most difficult chores as a commander was to notify the next of kin. Writing such a letter was very difficult, because you want to personalize it, you want to make sure that the family knows what their sacrifice, the family's sacrifice, meant. I remember those young marines that didn't make it back. It's heart-felt, the agony. I think about them every day, and the odd thing about it is that there are no names, there are just faces. I can see every one of their faces. I don't know what their names are, I know who they ... For the longest time, I didn't go to the – I was stationed in D.C. – but I didn't go to the Vietnam Memorial. The Wall. I remember the first time I did go to visit it. I was a newly promoted Lieutenant Colonel. We had something going on down at the mall. I was stationed at Headquarters Marines Corps. That day, I was dressed in my dress greens, which was very unusual because you didn't see Marines in dress greens unless they were going somewhere special. I can't even remember what the event was, but a friend of mine, Major Mike Coleman, who served under me – he was an aviator, a Marine aviator ... you know how you can tell a Marine aviator? They wear gloves, so that they don't break their nails. That's how they work. Anyway, so my friend – I don't want to call him my best friend – but my friend, Mikey Coleman was with me and we stopped. Mike had been in the Army, a helicopter pilot, and had inter-service transferred into the Marine Corps after Vietnam. He had been in the latter stages of Vietnam, so he wanted to go see one of his buddies that had been one of the latter guys in the Army that got killed when his helicopter got shot down. I'll have to admit that my thoughts were, "This isn't going to affect me."

Mike wanted to go look for his friend that got killed. Well, I got up there around that wall and I was there for three and a half hours. I couldn't leave. Three and one-half hours. I kept going down by the dates, and I started ... your hand going down that wall and you started touching the names that you knew and those faces came alive. It's a ... it's a very tough thing.

General Barrow told me this one time ... I worked for him at Paris Island. He became ... he was kind of my mentor. Amazing man. Absolutely integrity beyond reproach. And he told me one time, he said, "Jim, always make every decision in the Marine Corps like you are going to have to look yourself in the mirror when you make it. And as long as you can look at yourself in the mirror, you made the right decision, so get on with your life. Get on with your mission, whatever it is. And the

Marines will take care of the rest." So, tough one, very tough.

Let me tell you about one of the names that I do remember. This kid was a Cat-4. Do you know what a Cat-4 is? They had them in Vietnam. When you go in and take your military entrance test, they rate you as a Cat-1, Cat-2, Cat-3 and Cat-4. If you are as low as a category four in taking that intelligence test, you can't come into the military. During Vietnam, in 1968, McNamara—he was Secretary of Defense at the time—did what was called "McNamara's One Hundred Thousand." They inducted into all services; soldiers, sailors, marines and airmen, one hundred thousand applicants that were Cat-4's. And I had one of them. At the time, he had been meritoriously promoted twice in Vietnam. He was the section leader of my machine gun section when I was a company commander, and his name was Oney Painer and he was from Wheeling, West Virginia. And his mom worked for the Wheeling Marsh Stogie Plant that made cigars in Wheeling. I didn't smoke, but I chewed those cigars. He would get a carton of cigars every month from his mom—never failed—and he would always come up and give me a couple of them and I would chew on them. Maybe light them during the day to keep the mosquitoes away.

One night, Oney was taking—this was the kind of guy he was—he was taking a watch for the machine gun section. He was a sergeant, and sergeants didn't have to stand watch. He didn't have to do it, but he was just that kind of kid. Remember, this was one of those kids who supposedly were not smart enough to come into the military. Unbelievable section leader. You never had to worry about where those machine guns were when Oney Painer was with you. They were set up correctly. They were the first to be in place. As soon as you stopped, you would hear someone digging in; it was the machine gun section. And it was run by Oney Painer. Well, Oney was standing watch and somebody lobbed – we figured it was one of those kids that were hanging around during the day – well someone lobbed one of those Chi-Com grenades in. It was like a tuna fish can, but instead of being wide like ours are, they were tall. They were mainly like a flash bang, but they had these hot metal pieces. That hand grenade went off and tore off the top of Oney Painer's head. It scalped him. When you get a head wound, you bleed like a stuck pig. We thought that he was gone.

They medi-vaced him out country, and this is one of the things that you never hear about again. You never know what happened to those young men. That's why you have to go to that Wall because some of them die from their wounds, and otherwise you never knew it. Anyway, I kind of kept track of Oney Painer. I had my command, when we were back in the rear, find out where he did go; he went to medical hospital, ultimately discharged out of the Marine Corps. You know that if he gets discharged he is probably okay, at least still alive.

I can remember the first time as a young captain I was at Paris Island. That was in reality my first time on the East Coast, and I was going up to Washington, D.C. I said to myself, "Wheeling, West Virginia can't be that far off Interstate 95 and there can't be very many Oney Painers in the Wheeling West Virginia telephone book." So, I took a day off and went over to Wheeling, West Virginia, and sure as hell – course, there were fifteen Painers in there, this was West Virginia, but I tracked down Oney Painer, Oney is an unusual name. I tracked down Oney Painer; married, three kids, working in construction, doing good. I went in, patted him on the back and told him that he was one of the best Marines that I ever ran across. Unbelievable. Oney is doing fine. I'm sure he appreciated my coming. We had a fine reunion. I met his wife, I met his kids. It was just wonderful. I just wanted to go in and thank him for doing his service. I don't know why he stuck in my head. Probably because he was such a good marine. They were all good marines, but this guy was absolutely something special. Mainly because we had absolutely no expectations of him because he was supposedly one of these Cat-4s.

I don't know why I'm telling this story because I could tell a hundred stories about another Cat-4, by the name of Vernon, that we had who was a disaster waiting to happen, but no, we need to focus in on Oney. Oney Painer. He was special. Incredible guy.

Although I did suffer wounds, I never applied for a medal of any kind, not even the Purple Heart. In the 1st Marines, I believe it was Division Y, but in the 1st Marines Regiment in 1969, during my second tour in Vietnam, there was an unwritten rule that if you were an officer or a staff NCO, you didn't put your name on a casualty report unless you were medi-vaced from the field. So we would get in an engagement, shooting it up with the bad guys and you would perhaps get some shrapnel in your legs or your body, or you step on a piece of shrapnel, or you had some mortar shells coming in or a hand grenade goes off and you're mixing it up and you get burned or scraped or whatever. Okay, if I write it down on a casualty report and it says on the casualty report that I wasn't medi-vaced from the field, then that casualty report goes in, and you get a Purple Heart. Well, in Vietnam, when you get your third Purple Heart, you had to leave the field. You had to go back stateside; you couldn't stay in country. And so, there was, as I said, this unwritten rule in the 1st Marines for the officers and staff NCOs that unless you were medi-vaced, in other words unless it was serious enough that you had to go and seek medical attention in the rear, that you didn't put your name down on that casualty list. Now, the troops; yeah, you put down every one of those guys, even a slight dingy. We had one, Hippy was his name. He had this long hair—we always had to get on him about his hair—and he had this wonderful smile. He was right out of the flower children of the late '60's, and that why his name was Hippy. He was a mortar man, .60's mortars, and he just loved life. I have no idea what his name really was, but to us he was Hippy. I remember one time – he had pierced ears – and he still had the holes in his earlobes. Every now and then we would catch Hippy putting something in the holes to keep them open, because he was afraid that he was going to go back to the streets of San Francisco, the flower power and all that and he wouldn't be able to get his ear-rings back in. So we were constantly riding his ass, I mean, just good riding, because Hippy was a good ... he was a good Marine.

I remember one time that we were moving down in the Son Han River, a major river that went through an area they called the "Arizona Territory," just south of Da Nang. There were just booby-trap after booby-trap, just one after another. And if you didn't know what you were doing, then you were going to lose about half of your company. We had a booby-trap go off – we usually moved a platoon in a column, and a company in a wedge. Usually, your mortars are right behind your company commander in the middle of that wedge. Someone, I can't remember who, set off a booby-trap. It was a booby-trap with one of those Mark M-26 hand grenades which is 360 little pieces of copper wound inside a hand grenade and those things go off and are very effective, flying out in 360 degrees, with hundreds of little pieces of copper about a quarter of an inch. One of them hit Hippy right in his earlobe, and sliced his earlobe. He was bleeding; you do bleed when you cut your earlobe, but not very much. We had all pulled back after the booby-trap was set off because you are aware that you have five seconds or so after the grenade is activated, so I don't think that anyone was seriously hurt in this thing because of the time lag. Anyway, Hippy comes up as we're doing our casualty report and said, "Hey, man. Oh, Skip. Man, I'm hurt. I can't pierce no more." The shrapnel had clipped him right on the bottom of his earlobe and sliced his earlobe. Everybody laughed and laughed and gave him a lot of shit and the medical corpsman told him, "Naw, it ain't no wound. Just get out of here. I'm not going to work on your earlobe; it will fix itself as it was already pierced." Sort of like a self-inflicted wound. Hippy was doing it all in fun, but no, I had to write it down and put it in the casualty report because he was in fact wounded. Hippy ultimately was wounded three times and was medi-vaced out of the country and that was one of his wounds. It was legit. It could have taken out his eye, it could have taken off his ear, it could even have killed him. But that was the policy. You had to take care of the troops. If they got hurt, then you got them on that casualty report. As an officer, I couldn't have put my name down if it had happened to me.

    First time that ... ah ... got my attention was ... it was Operation Pipestone Canyon. It was in June, 1969, in the same area that I was talking about. They called the first area south of Da Nang along the La Tho River "Dodge City." Okay, this was where you have combat in the streets. Only there were no streets. Everybody had been moved, all the villages were gone, but it was like an open free-fire zone. Once you crossed the river and got into Dodge City, there were supposed to be nothing but bad guys. Then, south of that was "Going Away Island," in the Arizona Territory. Well, this Operation Pipestone Canyon was the entire 1st Division along with some regular Army soldiers was moving down. I was company commander for Bravo Company One-One. There was another reason why you don't put your name down for a Purple Heart, I still have it on my dog-tags—religion: O.T.S.S. Only The Strong Survive. It's an old Elvis Pressley song. Throughout the whole company that was standard motto. Everybody had it. "I need a set of dog-tags." "What do you need dog-tags for?" I don't know if you've ever seen them make dog-tags, but we had this little machine that we just put in the leather and it would crank out a set of dog-tags. Everybody wanted O.T.S.S. on their new dog-tags as a religion. The chaplain was freaking out. Anyway, we had set up right on the river as we were going down, and we had gotten some activity the night before. This was a major infiltration route for the North Vietnam Army to move in and attack in the Da Nang area. We had the company set up; four manholes, interspersed. A nice little hill overlooking ... about a hundred yards off the river. And that night we got hit ... and we got hit hard. One of our holes ... after we had pulled in our L.P.s, (listening posts) the enemy got in there and hit the hole with two hand grenades. We had one dead, two seriously wounded and one that was still firing. We had to call in ... I called back to my 'batman' (a soldier or airman assigned to a commissioned officer as a personal servant or assistant...Ed). My batman was this incredible kid, skinny; a reedy little emaciated black guy named "Heavy" Holcomb. Heavy had been through his own extension in 'Nam and Heavy had been through the 881, the heavy North Vietnamese attack. This guy had senses like a cat. I swear that if the NVA even thought about shooting mortars—and that was who we were fighting—it wasn't the Vietcong, it was the regular North Vietnam Army. If they even thought, if they were just sitting there talking and say, "Hey, let's shoot a few mortar rounds at the Marines," Heavy would know it, and he would start moving, looking for cover. The guy was like a cat. He had nine lives and senses like you couldn't believe. So, Heavy was my 'batman' and in our company, my batman served as a messenger. In those days, we didn't have a radio for everyone, not a personal radio that we could talk to everybody.

So I grabbed my senior medical corpsman, my radio operator and we ran down to the hole because it was just in front of us and we had heard the grenades going off. So, we run down there and I call the battalion, and ask what is going on. They don't know. We get down there and I call for a mortar round, an illumination flare so that I can see what is going on. The mortar round goes off and as it is going down, we jump into the hole. I called back to the 1st Platoon that had the command post and Heavy was with them. So I told him, "Heavy, get the reserve squad and get down here right now. And tell those mortar men to fire another illumination round."

Well, the next illumination round goes off and when that flare opens up, I look down the hill and we have probably forty NVA soldiers on line assaulting our position. It looked like something out of an infantry training school. They are on line, advancing up. So, what would a company commander, at night—I had a rifle, but I didn't have it with me—a company commander, a senior medical corpsman and a radio operator carry for weapons? .45 pistols, right? So I pull out my .45 and I say, "This ain't going to get anything," so I reach out and I grab a rifle, a rifle with a magazine in it. It belonged to the wounded Marine, and I started shooting at these guys. I tell the corpsman and the radio officer to grab a rifle, because there are three rifles lying there. I tell them to start shooting the NVAs. Lo and behold, it was one of the policies that we had, that the squad leader always kept a magazine at night that had tracers—I hadn't realized it was the squad leader's foxhole that we were in although I should have known—they keep a magazine with tracers in it so they could spot targets for the marines. So I grab the rifle up and start shooting and I've got nothing but tracers coming out. And so, at that moment in my life, every one of those forty NVAs were shooting right directly back at me. Now, multiple mortar rounds were going "whoo, whoo, whoo." It was bright as daylight out there. And I felt that every one of them was shooting only at me. Now I know that was not the case, but ... Then I'm down under the parapet, trying to get as low as I can while I'm still shooting.

A hand grenade comes flying up. Again, it was another one of those cheap-ass Chi-Com hand grenades. To make a long story short, the grenade goes off and shrapnel literally hits me in the knee, burns through my utilities and burns ... I've got this beautiful half-dollar or silver dollar-size scar right on top of my knee, still. But it was a burn. You hardly know what's happening when you're out there shooting. Matter of fact, the illumination round goes down and Heavy Holcomb comes running up and flops down right next to me, with his M-16. I said, "Heavy." He says, "Where do you want me to shoot?" The troops called me 'Montana'. Heavy says, "Where do you want me to shoot, Montana?" I said, "Just start shooting."

Well, his M-16 is right beside my ear. So he starts blazing away and I didn't notice until a day or so later that the ringing was still in my ear. But I can't hear anything ... I still can't hear a damn thing out of my right ear.

The burn on my right knee I didn't notice until the next day. I looked down and saw this hole in my utilities. I looked through the hole and there's this big red burn, which is now a scar.

The second time was in the Que Son Mountains. I believe I've already talked about this Ameri-Cav Division. It was in late December, 1969. We were down there in the middle of nowhere. We had assaulted up this hill and we were taking sporadic fire. It wasn't like we had over-run an NVA position but we were taking fire from our flank. I was right behind the lead platoon. Our base of fire was on the far side, and we were moving up. All of a sudden we got fired on. We took the hill which is where we were going to dig in that night and all of a sudden we were taking all this fire from the far left side. As I'm walking up the hill, I'm kind of paying attention, talking on the radio. We're getting air support on station, the artillery was registering positions, the Marines are setting in, the Gunny is doing his job, getting the casualty reports. Like I say, there didn't seem to be any NVA on this hill, but you never know.

So, the troops are all setting in, and the next thing I know I did a flip in the air and I'm laying on my back in the middle of the perimeter and I'm like, "What the hell?" and I get up and say, "That's interesting," dusting myself off, kind of embarrassed. Started giving orders and getting things done. We are sitting around later that evening talking. It was still light out, and we were all set in, the whole company was set on this hill now; everybody was in their place. I'm sitting there talking and I'm giving the platoon commanders a report on what's going on and what our positions are and who's got what. Then, one of the platoon commanders, R.C. Allen—nicknamed "Moon Pie,"—Moon Pie Allen looks at me and says, "Skipper, what's wrong with your foot?" I said, "There's nothing wrong with my foot." I looked down and the whole front of my boot was blown off. A round had come in and exploded. The laces of the boots are overlapped and a round had come in and hit the inside flap of my boot and blew the whole front off. The round had hit with such an impact that it had flipped me up in the air and shredded the front half of my boot.

There was a little bit of blood on it, but not much. It had just broke ... er ... scraped the surface. And I'm going like, "That's interesting." Then when I put two and two together, I realized that sure as hell an AK-47 round had come in and knocked me on my ass. And I hadn't even realized it. Sometimes it just happens. You just don't realize it, it's just gone. Those are the kinds of things you don't put into the casualty reports, at least not for officers or staff NCOs. Those things happen out in the field. But, that's it. That's all. Nothing exciting. Just good fun. Still, there are those that are close. And the close ones you remember. And you're lucky if you do.

The event with the boot. Think about it. If it had been a little lower, then it likely would have taken my foot off. And then I would have serious blood loss. And the damage it would do. Everybody has something like three hundred bones in their foot. The damage that could happen to a foot is just unbelievable. So, I'm very fortunate. I did think about it – for about two seconds.

Neither event had much of an effect on my life now, although during the summer when I wear shorts, my legs tan quite well, everywhere except for the scar on my knee. It doesn't tan, which leads to questions from some people. Gives me a chance for some cool war stories, but otherwise isn't really helpful, nor does it limit me in any way.

When questioned about my state of mind, which is often, and would I do what I've done again, I feel excited. Of course I would. In an instant. The opportunity to lead Marines into combat is—and this is what I learned from the Colonel Crockett that I've talked about—without a doubt, the opportunity to lead Marines in combat is the highest honor that can be bestowed upon an individual. And I would never, ever miss out on that opportunity. I know that of my college fraternity—I went to college in Utah—we had forty-two members of one hundred and six members in my college fraternity—forty-two of the one hundred and six volunteered to go into the Army or Marine Corps. It was just one of the things ... That was what you did in 1966. There was a war on and we've got to go and save the country from the Godless communists. Now, we're buying their oil and their ... whatever. Levi's and rock and roll. Now, they are making our hats. And they own the New Jersey Nets. They own a professional basketball team. Of course, those were different communists. Those were supposed to be the Russian Communists ... that were supposed to be the bad guys.

I'm reading a book now, about ... Donald Rumsfeld's book, "Known and Unknown," that just came out. I'm reading it, and Rumsfeld was in the Navy and he's going through that era about the build-up in Vietnam. He was elected to Congress in 1962 out of Chicago. So he was in Congress and voted for the Gulf of Tonkin Resolution, and served two terms in Congress and then he went to work for the Nixon administration, when Nixon took over. But it's interesting, putting those pieces of history together. He really hit on a point for us Vietnam veterans that we need to remember which was that the consternation of Vietnam was hippy; it was all free love, flower power, and smoking dope and riots. But if anybody remembers the early part, there wasn't—and I think I am correct in this—there wasn't a negative article in the New York Times against the war in Vietnam until, like, 1966. The Marines landed in 1965. There were about thirty or forty thousand Marines for a year in Vietnam and there was no negative publicity. All we remember of the 1960's is that part. We don't remember that, 'boys are going off to war' and 'our country is being challenged being challenged by communists', there was a communist challenge in the Bay of – the Cuban missile crisis in 1962. 1964 we were heavy into Vietnam. 1966 we are still very much pro-Vietnam, pro-war, to go save what they called the "domino theory." To thwart the spread of communism going into all these little countries. That is why we went into Southeast Asia. So many people forget. There was a reason why we were there. All they remember is the latter part of the '60's, a total dichotomy in the decade. From Eisenhower, Kennedy, Johnson and the build-up in Vietnam, and like I said, the Cuban missile crisis, Kruchev pounding his shoe on the podium of the United Nations Council, saying, "We will bury you." Don't forget that part. There was a reason why we were there. Sorry, didn't mean to rant on, but I love my country.

During the first Gulf War, I wrote the 1st Marines Division's attack plan to attack into Kuwait, which was a part of Desert Shield. At the time, I was a G-3, the operations officer for the 1st Marines Division, which I want to emphasize was the largest division in the United States Marine Corps with twenty-seven thousand people. We had two mechanized regiments. We had two straight-leg infantry regiments. I'm talking about three thousand men in each of those residents. We had one helicopter-borne regiment in the 1st Marines Division. Now, when you want to lay the wood on somebody, when you want to put on the steel and you are going to go get somebody, you want all your ballplayers on the field. You don't want to start the football game with only ten players on the field. The quandary was how to get the infantry on foot involved in this mechanized desert warfare.

Well, one thing to do is to go back and read some of the desert warfare in World War II and also in World War I; there's a mission called 'infiltration'. Infiltration is infiltrating under the guise of darkness into enemy's area. So I designed the 1st Marines Division attack plan to start with infiltration of infantry on foot through Hussein's minefields of death. 'Cause we can do it. We've got the technology; we can get through those minefields. And now, if we can get infantry deep into the rear of the enemy, that is going to secure the flanks of these two mechanized armored forces going right up the middle, because we've already cleared the flanks. The one thing that ... Tanks can't hide from another tank, for the most part. We've got air power. But, what tankers fear most is infantry with anti-tank weapons. Because you can be anywhere, pop up and hit the tank in the side and knock him out. So the idea is to screen the flanks of these mechanized units. There are three tank battalions. Not platoons, not companies, one hundred and seventy-two tanks that are attacking. One hundred and seventy-two tanks, three hundred and some odd Am-Tracks, three hundred plus lightly armored vehicles are attacking right up the center. So, how do we secure the flanks? Well, we designed an infiltration machine. We had Task Force Grizzly, which was based around the 4th Marines Regiment on the left flank; we had Task Force Taro, which was the 3rd Marines under John Admire, infiltrating from the other side, through the minefields to secure that first forty kilometers.

Three days before the ground war was launched, Task Force Grizzly, which I commanded, had twice the distance to go as did Task Force Taro, which had the shorter side. It was just the way the border and the minefields went. So we went in three days prior to G-Day, and a 'movement-to-contact' of twenty-seven hundred Marines was 2nd Battalion, 7th Marines; these were my battalions, the 4th Marines Regiment, Task Force Grizzly. 2nd Battalion, 7th Marines commanded by Lieutenant Colonel Roger Mawyer and 3rd Battalion, 7th Marines commanded by Lieutenant Colonel Ken Hannigan, who just so happens to be married to the daughter of the former Commandant of the United States Marines Corps.

The two commanders had been with me for some time. Roger Mawyer had been a classmate of mine at amphibian warfare school, Ken Hannigan had been a series commander for me at Paris Island. That's one good thing about the Marines Corps, you very rarely ever command troops you don't know. Anyway, our mission was to infiltrate. We had a 'movement to contact', about forty kilometers into Kuwait, some distance across Saudi Arabia and then cross the border into Kuwait and move through that minefield barrier that Saadam and his Iraqi troops had laid out, and dig in so as to be unseen by morning. All of this infiltration was going to take place at night.

So, we moved to contact, all twenty-seven hundred Marines dug in, gone to ground. You couldn't see us, we were out of sight. No vehicles, no trucks, no nothing. How did we move our weapons? We pulled them along on carts, machine gun carts right out of World War I. The carts were fabricated for us in Saudi Arabia. That night – daylight go to ground – that night get in that minefield. And how does a Marine get through a minefield? He gets on his hands and knees and he probes with his bayonet, and he goes klunk, klunk, klunk. And when he hits a mine, he knows it and then he marks it with a dim pin-light, facing towards the rear so that the enemy can't see it. And so, you go through and you mark your minefield. Well, as we got into the minefield that night, there was some confusion and there was air support running in what I thought was way too short of fire support coordination line. My Marines were in danger and I didn't want them in that minefield. They were running air, which was not being controlled by us that night, so we pulled them out of the minefield. We didn't get through the minefield that night. So, go to ground again. The next day, we started in that evening, which was now G-Day minus two. Ground war was going to start on G-day. I'm sorry, it was now G minus one. In an earlier reconnaissance, Task Force Taro had found a route through the minefield. Their mines were all marked and they were ready to go. We still didn't have our route marked for us, so we get in, we have one night to get through there, we start that evening and this is the evening before the ground war is going to launch the next day. I get a call from General Myatt that says they had just got word that they are conducting some political activity going on and "you can't go into the minefield."

I'm going like, "my mission is to get through the minefield and that's the way it's designed and you've got to be kidding me." So, to make a long story short, numerous conversations going back and forth, I was very upset about the whole deal, because I was right up with Ken Hannigan, who was doing the breech through the minefield, and I had to go back, because I didn't have a radio up there with me because those radios broadcast half way around the world. So, I had to go back, and I'm talking about one hundred miles back to my main command post and have this conversation with my boss that I don't want to have. I tell my boss, "You can't do this to us; we are halfway through that minefield." Just then, we get a call from Unit 37 that said, "We have some Iraqi prisoners that have surrendered. We are half way through the minefield and they tell us they will show us the path through the rest of the way."

So I tell them to go. "Give them penlights and have them mark through the minefield." So I call back and I tell Jim Myatt that we could turn around, but that we were through the minefield and had captured about three hundred Iraqi prisoners. I told Jim to call back and ask for forgiveness. So this goes all the way through the line, all the way from Myatt to General Boomer who was the commander of the Marine Expeditionary Force and then to General Norman Schwarzkopf, who was the Central Command commander. They said, "Don't do anything that's not reversible. Don't start the war early because what's happening is that the Russians have some late political thing to cause a cease fire and require the Iraqi to pull out." Well, as you know, it was all b.s. and what happened was that I was told that I could put a reconnaissance force on the far side of the minefield to secure that side of the minefield. Well, fortunate for us I decided a reconnaissance force was an infantry battalion. So I sent Ken Hannigan's 37 through the minefield. Now, this is ten o'clock at night. We have to be through that minefield and on the other side. We think we have the route through the minefield marked. But the situation worsened. The Iraqi had put an anti-personnel minefield. I don't really care anything about anti-tank mines. As a matter of fact, one of my men won a Silver Star by running through a minefield pulling a cart. Anti-tank mines won't go off under such a light weight. Well, behind these Iraqi troops, the Iraqi had put in an anti-personnel minefield so that their soldiers couldn't retreat. We knew nothing about that minefield; we had no intelligence at all. We spent the whole rest of that night, literally on our hands and knees, probing through that minefield that we didn't know existed. Most minefields are one hundred feet in depth. We hit it at an angle and had further to go through that minefield, on hands and knees, probing for mines. But, at first light, we were probably fifty-eight or sixty kilometers inside Kuwait, had moved and remounted.

When the war was over and they came down and said, "We want to see the first tank, the Marine tank to put in a museum. The first Marine tank that went into Kuwait. We want to see the chemical suits of the first Marines that went into Kuwait." And they wanted to see the first Am-track. They were thinking that the tanks and the Am-tracks that went into Kuwait and these first artillery pieces were these mechanized forces that were the first to go into Kuwait. When Task Force Ripper first started off in way back in Saudi Arabia attacking up toward the border, the war was on. It's six o'clock in the morning. It's daylight. It's G Day. Boom!. Fire the red flare, the war is on.

We blew a hole through those two minefields and the first tank through that field was our track-width mine plow behind an infantry regiment. The first Am-track was the Am-track that blew it and then plowed it with the track-width plow. Then an entire general support: one self-propelled .155 artillery battalion, 511 commanded by Jim Soclaven came in through that breech that the infantry regiment Task Force Grizzly had put in. We had self-propelled .155 artillery pieces fifty kilometers inside Kuwait on G-Day. An absolutely incredible mission that our Marines executed so, the old saying is: when you wake up in the morning and you are headed to the officer's club and the enemy is sitting there firing small arms and mortars at you when you're going to the officer's club for breakfast, then you know you are in trouble. And that's exactly what happened to the 3rd Iraqi Corps headquarters at the Al Jaber Air Field. When Ripper started their launch, we had infantry weapons firing into the 3rd Iraqi Corps headquarters.

The Marines were absolutely superb, and General Schwarzkopf mentioned it in his ... The Marines Corps were so fast and got so deep into Kuwait, the Army never caught up. Schwarzkopf mentioned it in his brief, and said there was a breech and that the war map into Saudi Arabia will be studied for years to come as the way to conduct a mechanized assault. And that's the story of Task Force Grizzly, which was based on the 4th Marines Regiment which I had the extreme fortune to command during that mission. It's extremely rare that you get, at that level, the opportunity to design the mission and then go execute it. Usually, you just sit back and listen to the radio to find out how it goes, but I was very fortunate to have won the confidence of the troops to be able to design that mission. Which people didn't want us to do; they didn't think that infantry could operate in that environment, but I said, "Pfft. If we can't operate , nobody can. We are the lowest priority target on the modern-day battlefield, and if you launched us and the enemy wants to come up and shoot his weapons at us, if he wants to attack us with armor, that's just fine."

This is what I told General Boomer when he came down and talked to me the day before we launched. I said, "What better strategy than to have his armor attack me, the infantry, on the ground, when you control the air? The guy is not going to get ... Day one, there's not going to be one tank that gets anywhere near me. As soon as his tanks are up and moving, I've got every aircraft in the 3rd Aircraft Wing flying protection over me. I'm the only war going on. That's exactly what you want to happen, for him to attack infantry with armor, when you own the air. It's right out of the German's defeat in the battle for Moscow in World War II. The Germans lost their legs and couldn't control the air, and all of the sudden the little T-34 Russian tanks comes up and starts wiping them out, because they controlled the air."

Anyway, I'm totally excited about it; it was an incredible mission and incredible execution by the Marines of Task Force Grizzly.

Unfortunately, not all of the Marines came home alive. The sad part of is that we lost eleven Marines out of Task Force Grizzly over that period of time. Most of the casualties were from incoming .155 artillery fire and 122 millimeter rockets that were fired at us after we had moved into a position to get ready for an assault on Al

Jabber Air Field, which was going to be house-to-house fighting. Al Jabber Air Field was like their ... it would be like attacking the Air Force Academy in Colorado Springs. That was their Air Force Academy, there at the airfield. Underground bunkers, buildings, everything was underground and it was hot as hell. Underground bunkers, houses, family houses, clubs; I mean, it was a regular city out there in the middle of nowhere. Task Force Grizzly's mission—after Ripper passed by, going north toward Kuwait City—was to go in and secure that airfield, for the following medi-vac. The first plane to land there before we secured the airfield was a Harrier that had gotten shot with some flack, and he had lost his engine—Harrier is a single-engine aircraft. The pilot called us and said that they had to land their airplane there. We said, "Have at it. We don't know what else is here, but there's an airfield there." So, the first plane to land at the Al Jabber Air Field was a wounded Harrier that came in there. He was glad to know that we were there, I'm sure. If he comes in and we're not ...

We were getting ready to launch our attack and an interesting thing about it was the oil smoke from all the oil wells that had been set off was so bad that we had extreme difficulty—forget about helicopter activity or evacuation, you can't see where you're going—the smoke was so bad that night that you couldn't see your hand in front of your face. So we had to run guys out and we had to run g.p.s. and the guys that were wounded suffered and some of them succumbed to their wounds because we couldn't get them out of there fast enough, because they had travel by ground transportation, they had to go on ground. There was just no other way to get them out. And we couldn't wait because they were all on triage. It was very unfortunate that we did lose some Marines doing that. But, there could have been more.

When I'm complimented on the good job that we did, I recall a book that was written by Rick Atkinson about it all. I don't remember the title right now, but the author was spot on. It talks about it, and my explanation of the whole thing follows that same line. Actually, it was a failed strategy, because if you look at the strategic importance of Kuwait in the Middle East, it's nothing. Our mission, according to General Schwarzkopf, was to destroy the Republican Guard, and I can say that we ... the Army in the left hook didn't close the gap and the Republican Guard fled and got out before they closed the gap above Basra. We pushed them too far north, the Army didn't get there in time, the Republican Guard escaped and we had to Saadam for another ten years. Then wound up having to go in there during Iraqi Freedom and some ten years or more later and do something that we could have done right then and there. It's unfortunate that it turned out the way that it did; that we had to go back and do it again. But the concern, and I fully understand the concern, was that the coalition would fragment if we actually attacked into Iraq. And so, we bit off as much as we could at the time.

I'm aware of such programs as Remember the Wounded Ride, Operation Military Embrace, Wounded Warrior Project, Semper Fi Fund, and the ... er ... the mind is a terrible thing to waste. But there are other such organizations formed to help the veterans who have sacrificed so much for our country. I'm going to get on a political soapbox here for just a second. It is very unfortunate ... it's great that we do it, it's awesome that a lot of them are behind it with their volunteerism and their help. Not just ex-veterans, but there are people involved with many of these programs who have no kinship connection to the military. They are doing the right thing with both their volunteerism and their funds. And it's kind of a travesty that our American government doesn't take care of it. Doesn't take care of it at all. I don't want to bad-mouth the Veterans Administration, but all these programs should be involved in the Veterans Administration and making sure that these families of the wounded; the service member and his family are taken care of until these men and women are back fully integrated into civilian life. That is what the government is supposed to provide for its military, it's not supposed to leave it up to hands of some awesome heroic people that are doing yeomen's work to get this done. It should all be assembled under the government mantle of taking care of the troops. Including the troops AND their families. Because the family is an integral part of the rehabilitation of any wound, whether it's mental or whether it's physical. We have to deal with the family. And we can't take Lance Corporal Smockatower and put him in the Balboa hospital in San Diego, California and expect his family to go live in a high-cost of living area such as San Diego without any money. Their families have to quit their jobs and go help take care of the wounded and help in their rehabilitation. That should all be part of the Veteran's Administration responsibility, the integration of the wounded veteran into society. This work that these non-governmental organizations must be done, because the government programs are not there.

The veteran and his family are not looking for a hand-out, they are looking for a way to take a wounded veteran and integrate him or her back into society the way that we want it done. We can't just turn our back on these folks, because they are the backbone of what makes this country great. They sacrificed their life or they sacrificed their mental health or their physical health to go do what our government asked them to do. And, to be honest about it, I'm upset that the government doesn't see it, that they have to take care of them. Here, we've got volunteer drivers. We are in a rural area here in Steamboat Springs, Colorado. Craig's got a Veteran's Center and we've got a Veterans Services officer, and he volunteers to drive. But Craig is an hour's drive away, and the closest hospital is in Grand Junction. Well, he gets a van, comes in and picks up the veteran and drives the veteran to Grand Junction. Grand Junction is three and one-half hours away. Is that paid for? No, it's not. It's a volunteer driving. The van is probably a GSA van, but ... it's just little, simple things like that, of getting a veteran to his appointment is ... this should be as easy as ABC, this should be soup to nuts, everything should be covered. The veteran, if he didn't volunteer for service, if he didn't go into combat, if he didn't have that service-connected wound wouldn't be going three and one half hours to a medical facility in Grand Junction. And we wouldn't have our liberty, our freedom, our individual rights. So, go figure ...

I'm most grateful for the thousands of young marines that keep the leaders going straight, but the comradeship of the Marine Corps, and it doesn't make any difference ... we know the difference between officer and enlisted, but in the Marine Corps that innate inherent built-in respect allows us to go have a beer and enjoy life, and then if we have to go to war, we go to war. So, it's the thousands and thousands of troops that I have been associated with and commanded over the years that made my life easy. One of the two people that were tremendous influences on how I think, how I operated and how I commanded and led my Marines was General Robert H. Barrow, who I believe has since passed away; a great, absolutely incredible individual who left such an impact on me with his integrity and his role – his single focus in life as a Marine officer was to take care of Marines and make sure they had the tools necessary to do their mission. Robert H Barrow was a company commander Alfa Company One-One, 1st Battalion, 1st Marines in Korea. In the landing of Seoul, in the taking of the town of Seoul. The Regimental Commander was the infamous Chesty Puller. Barrow comes up over a hill and looks down at a railroad station in the main section of Seoul. His mission, as a company, was to take that train station. Well, they are looking at, they are looking at the intel and they are looking through their glasses. These guys have been in combat for about two or three days. Barrow tells the story of looking down at that railroad station and the thing was bristling with automatic weapons and North Korean soldiers. China wasn't involved in the war at that time. Barrow and his company have some six hundred meters of open ground to go through to get there, so he calls in for air support and artillery fire, saying, "I can't attack there."

Chesty Puller, as the story goes, hears about this commander who is not attacking as planned, is not aggressively going after the enemy and comes driving up the hill and demands, "Who's the company commander? Where's the company commander?" Barrow stands up, all six feet, four inches, big, tall southern gentleman with the slow voice and says, "I am, Sir, Captain Robert H Barrow, company commander, Alpha Company, 1st Battalion, 1st Marines."

Here's the situation, Puller goes up and could see through his field glasses that the station was full of North Korean troops, well dug in, heavily armed, bristling with machine guns, etc. It was unbelievable that he would think about crossing that distance and engaging the enemy without artillery support. To make a long story short, Puller went back and called support, and said, "Give him anything he wants."

Barrow lost three-quarters of his company and won the Navy Cross because he took the station, with the air support and with the artillery support. He surely would have lost his entire company and himself if he had attacked when he was told to attack. And this is the story that he would tell, this was getting up and looking at yourself in the mirror. He often said, "It would do me no good to send the Marines without the tools to do ... they would do the job, but give them every chance to succeed by giving them the tools." Barrow went on to command the 9th Marine Regiment during Operation Dewey Canyon in Vietnam during which he would kinda look the other way; the enemy was in Laos, they are not in Vietnam. You go and take the battle to the enemy. He was decorated with the Distinguished Service Cross because he did what was the right thing to do.

The second strongly influential person in my life was General Tony Zinni. Tony Zinni and I have worked together numerous times and he was just one of those guys. He became commander of Central Command, got out as a four-star general and became one of the few people in the military and out of the military that said, "Think about what you are doing before you go into Iraq. I headed Central Command and you think the Iraqi people are going to rise up and welcome you; and they are not going to do it."

He turned out, as we all know, to be right. Four thousand dead soldiers, marines, sailors and airmen later, we discover that Iraq is not going to be an easy place to take. And that is just the kind of mind that Zinni has; he just put it out there, while all these other generals were lining up and saying, "Oh yeah, this is going to be easy." And "We've got all this high tech." and so on. It meant nothing in that kind of conflict, as we have found out.

General Zinni and General Barrow were two of the consummate professionals that taught me to not only appreciate Marines and their inevitable sacrifice, but more importantly, to think outside the box, to make sure that the Marines and the sailors under my command would have what they needed to get the job done. Those lessons stayed with me during my whole career. And, hopefully, the Marines that I had influence on or that I touched their lives, I left a positive impact that was what I was about, too. Taking care of them. Doesn't mean I'm not hard, doesn't mean that I'm easy, but it means that I'm going be there right beside you in the hardships and make sure you have everything you need.

My final comments are that we are not doing everything that we can do to get these guys and their families back into society, so anything that can be done, should be done. Let's do it.

Semper Fi!

Lyle D. Gessford
Major, United States Army (Rtd)
1943 –

Deployed to Vietnam in 1968, Lyle D. Gessford was assigned to the 1st Battalion, 12th Infantry Regiment, where he was part of the Red Warrior Mission. The Red Warrior Mission statement for Vietnam read, ***"To close with the enemy by means of fire and maneuver in order to destroy or capture him, or to repel his assault by fire, close combat and counterattack."***

In March, 1968, then Captain Lyle D. Gessford was designated Battalion S-2 Officer, in essence the battalion intelligence officer.

The battalion commander has specific information needs relating to the unit's area of operation and specific tactical interests. The two critical categories of information available to both the battalion and brigade commander are intelligence and combat information.

The S2 is responsible for collecting, analyzing, and disseminating information about the enemy and the area of interest. The S2 also prepares the collection plan designed to support the staff-developed decision-support template.

In August, 1968, Gessford was appointed as company commander to Delta Company, a position he held until he was selected as Battalion S-1 Officer in late August, 1968.

The S-1 is a vital link in the commander's staff as he supervises the health, morale, and general welfare of the battalion. The S-1 serves as the principal adviser to the commander, supplying the commander with the tactical information needed to wage combat. Gessford served as Battalion S-1 Officer until his tour of duty was completed.

*****

First, let me say that like most other military personnel, I am proud to have served my country. The fact that my two brothers had served in the military, but only during the draft, may have had some input into my decision to join the Army. One brother had served during the Second World War, but in truth, there was an underlying desire to fulfill what I considered to be a 'manly' thing to do. An obligation, if you will, to do the right thing and to serve our country may well have been the spark that lit the flame that propelled me toward military service. The support of my family was a welcome blessing.

I actually joined the National Guard while I was still in high school in 1960 and stayed in the Army until August, 1980, twenty-one years of military life, on some form of active duty. I was a mostly green lieutenant but learned and rose in rank until I retired as an Army Major. As I entered the military, I believe that I realized it was a good opportunity for employment and now I feel that it was at that time I made the decision to make the Army my career. My feeling was that this was a great opportunity to serve my nation, so my choice was easy to make. And one that I have never regretted, not even for a second. If I had to do it over, I would do it again in a heartbeat. Possibly the one thing that I may have changed would be that I would have extended my time in the military so as to be of more service to my country and my fellow soldiers, but there are no regrets.

In 1966, with the advent of Vietnam, I went on extended active duty as a National Guard officer first, then as a reserve officer on active duty full time.

I served two combat tours in the Republic of Vietnam. First, during all of 1968. During my first deployment—or tour of duty—I served as an infantry company commander within an infantry battalion of the 4th infantry division, as well as the Battalion S-2 intelligence officer. I also served as Battalion S-1 officer, the primary counsel to the battalion commander. After my first tour, I came back to the States for additional and specialized training, an advanced course in leadership and tactics. After that training, I was sent to helicopter flight school. After graduating the helicopter flight school course, I returned to Vietnam in 1971, where I served as an infantry commander until early 1972.

When people ask me what was my inspiration and what gave me the courage for serving for extended periods during difficult and trying times as the Vietnam period certainly was, I can only respond that above and beyond the fact that I was—and had chosen to be—a career officer—yes, I had actually elected to be a career officer, and I had been ordered to that particular theater of operation; there really was something much more than that. The over-riding factor was the issue that I strongly believed, in the beginning at least, that the United States government—my nation—was doing the right thing in Southeast Asia and I was going to help stop the spread of communism. I later probably changed my views as I matured. I have definitely changed my views now about what we were doing in Southeast Asia and why we were doing, it. I don't think my thoughts today would have affected my going to Vietnam because as I said, I had chosen to be a career military officer and it's not a military career officer's prerogative to decide what his government should or shouldn't be doing. The military, soldiers—sailors—airmen—marines —we are all part of the execution phase of the decisions the government makes. I always believed—and still do—that if I were so strongly against the war, that my choice would have been to get out and try to do something about it from the other side. But I didn't do that. I elected to stay on active duty and serve my nation the best way that I could; as a military officer.

The major difficulty with military service in a foreign theater is that it often disrupts or displaces a family. The separation from family is perhaps the strongest trauma that affects the military. And during the time I served, it was even more difficult. I had a wife and two children at the time of my first deployment to Vietnam, and a wife and three children at the time of the second deployment. Unlike the situation the soldiers are fortunate to be working under today, there was no email, no Skype; there were no computers, there were no cell phones. We went to Southeast Asia and I received letters whenever they arrived, and they weren't always in order. All of the military suffered the same conditions and rarely saw our families.

I saw my wife only one time before I had finished the two separate tours and finally left Vietnam and came home. That occasion was on an R and R (Rest and Relaxation) in Hawaii. Sure, it was difficult for me. But I suspect it was probably more difficult for my wife and my family. Because they had two roles to play; they had mother and father roles to play ... my wife did, and I know that other wives did, as well. Also, the children were without an active present father. That's not an unusual situation at present in today's environment, but in those days—the early and mid seventies— it was difficult for kids to be in school and not have a dad that went to ball games and have no dad to go to their dances and do those kinds of things That was probably the most difficult and trying part of it.

Compared to that traumatic situation, the combat part was piece of cake, so to speak. Especially now that I look back on it and think of the separation part: that was difficult; hard on the soldier, devastating on the family.

Even so, I can't say that there ever was a time when I actually wanted to quit and come home. Not just quit ... that was never an option. We were there to do a job. I must admit that I wanted to finish the job and come home, but I don't think there was ever a time that I actually felt like, I'll go home, I'll quit. I'll do anything else. Like I said I had chosen the military as a career and I was determined to give it the best that I could possibly give it. And there was the comradeship.

Being at war and serving in a war zone, there is always the likelihood that you could come under enemy fire. Injuries or even death is always a distinct possibility. And I was one of those who were fortunate enough to only suffer a wound. At the time of my injury, it was like I was in a situation...an "Oh damn-it" moment. I don't really remember what I felt, not at that time. I think back now and I can go through my mind and the sequence of events that happened and how it all came about. It's probably clearer now than it was at the time. When you are in combat, you don't really think about how it is going to affect you unless it keeps you from doing your job. At that time it was just a matter of getting patched up and get back to my unit as quickly as I could. That was my concern. That had to be my concern. My thoughts weren't that "Oh my god, I was gonna lose an arm" or "Oh my god, something was gonna happen to me. Or anything else. I just wanted to get back and finish my tour so I that—so that we—could go home.

I was commanding a rifle company that was securing a fire-support base north of the city of Kontum. We were under fairly heavy probing attacks testing our strength for two or three days. Then it became a complete outright attack. The attack started in the middle of the night by a North Vietnamese full battalion-sized unit. They even hit us that night with flame throwers on the perimeter, so it became a pretty intense battle. I had put a group of soldiers at an outpost that was about a thousand meters away from the fire-base where I was located. That outpost got over-run by the North Vietnamese fighters. My soldiers were able to scramble into a bunker, one of five bunkers that were there, and they were able to hold on until morning. At the break of day, the ground attack had kind of diminished for the time being. We took a fire team—actually, we took most of our company over and relieved the individuals that had been pushed off the outpost and recovered them. We lost a couple of people in that skirmish and actually had one of our soldiers pay the ultimate price in that attack by diving on a hand grenade and saving a lot of lives. That soldier subsequently received the Congressional Medal of Honor.

The following day, we came under heavy bombardment from this North Vietnam Army's battalion-size unit that was completely surrounding our fire-support base. They were attempting to fire—actually was firing—on us with 75-caliber recoilless rifles. They were trying to knock out the artillery of the fire support base because that artillery was one of our main defenses that were enabling us to maintain our position on the fire-support base. The N.V.A. had successfully hit one of our howitzers, which knocked it out. Being on the lookout for such a sign, by chance, I happened to see where the fire came that hit the howitzer. I saw the smoke rise out of a hillside about five hundred meters or so across the ridge. I had spotted the puff of smoke and the flash that occurred at the rifle's discharge and was able to direct our return fire onto the position where the rifle attack had come from. Almost immediately, there was a big secondary explosion and we knew we hit the site and destroyed its weaponry. We foolishly began to celebrate, forgetting that the enemy was still viable. Dancing on the bunker and raising our hands and hollering and shouting and doing all those foolish things that shouldn't have happened; we were dumb. Then, from another site down the ridgeline about four hundred or five hundred meters, a second recoilless rifle fired again. That was when I was hit. The round from the rifle exploded behind us. Shrapnel from the round hit my arm, the back of my leg, and back of my head.

Even more unfortunately, we lost my forward artillery observer at the same time and, in addition, his radio operator was killed. Both of those guys gone at the same time. You can say that I was fortunate. My wounds were severe enough that I would need to be evacuated, but I was not able to leave the base until the following day because of heavy volume of enemy fire that was coming in. They just couldn't get an evacuation helicopter in, it was just too dangerous, but I was subsequently evacuated the following day.

Considering the physical and mental trauma that many wounded veterans and veterans who were under fire but not bodily injured, I consider myself most fortunate. Physically at present there is no residual damage to my body that I know of, at least no more than getting old and decrepit. The medical personnel and the doctors patched me up pretty good and I was able to come back to my unit and serve with my unit exactly one month from the day that I was injured. Of course, from time to time, I think about it. Like I mentioned earlier, I think it's probably much clearer today than it was at the time that it happened. Sure, I do think about it. Certainly, I do remember it. Even so, I don't have what I consider to be any mental hang-ups from it, no long-lasting mental images, no nightmares. I don't feel that I in any way have any residual damage from it.

From my part, I would like to thank the doctors that helped me get patched up and got me back into service. I think I'm very, very fortunate. Although I was wounded, I was just wounded physically. I wasn't wounded mentally or socially, I wasn't ... it was just another day at the office so to speak. My recovery was swift and complete. It was over before my family even knew it happened, pretty much. Being able to go back to my company and take command of my company again was probably the greatest encouragement that I received. Because that gave me a reason to get back in the fight so to speak It's kind of like being knocked down in a football field and the coach takes you out and makes you sit on the bench for awhile. Well, you feel bad, you're letting the team down.. But then all the sudden he says, "Ok, Gessford, get back in the fight." And you feel good again even though your arm hurts or your foot hurts or whatever caused you to have to sit on the bench, now you're back in the fight and you actually feel good again.

Taking into consideration my injury and sacrifices, the things that have happened in my life, the places I have been and the things I have seen, the comrades I made and the people I served with, I am very happy with my decision to join the military. I would make the same decision again. I would probably even stay on active duty longer.

Although I am no longer on active duty, I still feel a close kinship with the military, especially those who have seen action and suffered wounds—bodily and mentally—on behalf of our nation. My wife and I are both active through the Benevolent Protective Order of Elks, avidly supporting our military. I presently serve as the State Veterans Chairman and we've recently become involved with a fantastic program called Operation Military Kids. It's a program to support families of deployed soldiers, mainly National Guard and Reserve. It's extremely rewarding to be able to step back from where we were when we fought in Vietnam and the lack of support that was given to our families and to our children, and now to be able to step up and help families ... kids and wives. To help them perform the day-to-day tasks that they wouldn't have to do if their spouse was home.

And I'm sure that the 'wounded veteran'; who is home, back in the U.S. after being wounded in combat, going through the trauma of recovery and getting a high degree of medical support at least from the active duty military or the VA, is one thing, but what's missing is the fact, the understanding, the knowledge that the family of that soldier is suffering as much, if not more, than the soldier himself. The soldier knowingly and willingly took the risk. The soldier was wounded and he knew it was a distinct possibility when he went into the service and mentally, he was somewhat prepared for the possibility. I'm not saying he was completely prepared for it but he was somewhat ready for whatever might happen. But the wife and the kids ... they were not prepared for it ... they might have thought they were, but they really were not prepared for it. They weren't prepared to see Dad come home with a limb missing or a limb heavily damaged or worse; and then having to continue to try to have a family without the support that the soldier himself gets.

It's a wonderful thing that there are now these organizations who recognize the situation and the difficulties, and are stepping up to help not only the soldier recover and return to an active life, but help those families who are suffering. Socially, mentally, physically ... help those families continue a life of being somewhat normal. There are several that help a good bit, but it's not enough; there needs to be many, many more.

The final thing I might say is that in the focus of my career less than twenty-four months of it was spent on active duty and in what I would consider a combat environment in harm's way. That's a pretty short part of your entire life and your entire career to give to your country and your fellow American citizens. And yet those other eighteen years were equally as rewarding as they could be. There were great things to be done. We were doing things not in a combat environment. The cold war was on. We were protecting Germany. We were protecting all of the NATO nations and it was just rewarding. The highlight may have been the two years in combat. That's the ultimate. I've heard a lot of soldiers say the ultimate is to be in combat. Well, no...that's not the ultimate. The ultimate is to be a good soldier. The ultimate is to serve your nation and feel like when the day is done, that you've done a good job doing it. And that you have done your very best.

And the blessing is the gratitude of a free citizenry and a nation at peace and at liberty. The appreciation and the respect is all that any soldier can ask for.

Henderson, Reed H.
Sergeant, United States Army
1922 –

Cited for bravery and gallantry in action on more than one occasion, and among other awards that ninety-one year resident of Preston, Idaho, Reed H. Henderson received were the Silver Star, the third-highest military decoration that can be awarded to a member of any branch of the United States armed forces for valor in the face of the enemy. The citation is that for "Conspicuous Gallantry in Action During WORLD WAR II in action against an enemy of the United States ... **Henderson, Reed H.**"

The fourth highest combat decoration that can be awarded to a member of the United States armed forces is the Bronze Star. The citation reads "while serving in any capacity in or with the Army, Navy, Marine Corps, Air Force, or Coast Guard of the United States, after December 6, 1941, distinguishes, or has distinguished, himself by heroic or meritorious achievement or service, not involving participation in aerial flight—while engaged in an action against an enemy of the United States ... **Henderson, Reed H.**"

The **Purple Heart** is a United States military decoration awarded in the name of the President to those who have been wounded or killed while serving on or after April 5, 1917 with the U.S. military ... 1945- **Henderson, Reed H.**

The World War II Victory Medal is another award given to those who served during wartime. The decoration commemorates military service during World War II and is awarded to members of the United States military who served on active duty, or as a reservist, between December 7, 1941 and December 31, 1946 ... **Henderson, Reed H.**

Battle of the Bulge Commemorative Medal was designed to honor U. S. Armed Forces who fought or supported the Battle of the Bulge 1944-45. The medal shows combat infantry and armor with aircraft arriving in support stopping desperate Nazi attacks ... **Henderson, Reed H.**

A United States Army Combat Service Identification Badge (CSIB) is a metal that uniquely identifies combat service with major U.S. Army formations ... **Henderson, Reed H.**

And there were others, including theater badges for Europe and for Africa.

Henderson, Reed H.

*****

Henderson, Reed H. Present and accounted for, Sir. Native of Swan Lake, Idaho, but now I'm living in Preston Idaho. Born in 1922, I guess that makes me about eighty-seven, trying to make it to 88. I served in the United States Army, 28th Infantry Division during World War II.

I didn't volunteer, I just waited for them to draft me. Not that I had anything against the Army, but I would just as soon stayed home. Still, they called and I went. It was just a job to me. Actually, I was drafted one year too soon. Another year and I probably wouldn't have been injured. I'm not really sure exactly when I was drafted, but I believe it was either 1942 or 1943. I served eighteen months in the Army, and saw action in Europe: Germany, France and Belgium. when I was drafted. I wasn't much to complain but if I'd had my way I'd been home. I had left the good old farm and I missed it and the work we had to do each day. It was a dry farm, we raised cattle, hay and a variety of crops that was enough to work us all good, kept us out of mischief.

I was the only member of my family that served in the military at that time, the rest of the family stayed on the farm. I'll have to admit that I wanted to come home lots of times, but I knew I had my obligation to fill. And they were telling us how bad the Germans were.

After basic training, I was allowed to spend two weeks at home, and then I was scheduled to go overseas. We assembled in Baltimore and then were sent up to New Jersey. From there we went by ship overseas. Our first landing was in England and after a short time we went to France. From France the next stop was Belgium and finally we were sent to Germany. We would go to one place and fight for awhile and then get out of there and go someplace else. Yep, that was quite a roundabout; lot of fighting and shooting and dodging. Man could get killed, or at least badly hurt. Sure enough, I was.

I was injured by a hand grenade. An enemy soldier snuck up on our foxhole. There was a kid named Gentry in the foxhole with me. I don't recall his first name, but he was from Iowa. He was a pretty good kid. There were only the two of us in the foxhole, as it would be harder for the Krauts to hurt too many of us at one time. We had only been there two days when it happened. The Kraut threw a grenade into the foxhole. I grabbed the grenade and tried to throw it back out and just as I went to throw it out, that's when it went off. Blew my hand all to pieces. That hurt. Guess that I did save his life, in fact, I guess I saved both our lives.

Anyway, I was bleeding and I had four or five miles to get back to the company command post and another trip of twenty miles to get from there back to a medics outfit. We spent most of the night chasing around hunting the medics. I was about give out when we finally got back to the medics. I was definitely under the weather because I had lost too much blood. Yep, I was weakened down too badly to do much of anything else. It was a close deal. They got us back there and after trying to take care of me they got me on an old ship and said, "Go home." And so we done it. We went. Yep, and it wasn't none too quick either. Can't say that the wound made me hate the Germans or the war any greater, just kind of had to realize that wounds happen and you just have to go along with it. At least I was still alive and there were many who weren't.

Back home, the only bad thing I had ... the only problem the damage to my hand caused was in my ability to tie sacks on the combine. That was just too rough. I could do pretty near anything else. That was about the worst. Work didn't bother me a bit; it was just getting around to it. But, there were some difficulties as I just had one hand to use. Driving the horses was a hard deal. Couldn't guide them properly with just one hand. Yep, my brother Tom, he had to drive them horses and I had to do the bagging. But we got by. You can always get by if you really mean to.

I was injured in 1945, and the war ended the same year. Too bad it didn't end a little sooner.

Yeah, serving in the Army was quite a deal. I was in the 7th Army overseas. I wouldn't trade it, I don't believe, for anything. It gave me the feeling that I had done my part, that I had made my sacrifice for my country and for my family.

Only problem with growing old is that your memory starts slipping. After this many years, you can't remember it all. When you get old you lose your mind and you think a lot about it, but I guess that comes with life. I would give the kids of today a word of advice. Stay away from the Draft Board.

While I was in 7th army overseas, I got to see parts of southern France and all along the Rhone river. It was very pretty country but they sure were mean to us. I was on the edge of the Battle of the Bulge. We didn't get deep into it. Talking about bad memory, I barely remember the nurse that took care of me. Pretty? Oh, she was. Of course, all of the girls looked pretty to us back then.

Here on our farm, we used to have a lot of cattle and a lot of horses. We used to do our farming with horses, using horses and mules to pull the plows and the wagons. That was before we had a tractor. Then we got a tractor, a Deere John … no, we got a Caterpillar tractor first, and then a John Deere; and then another John Deere. I don't know what they have down there now. My old John Deere is in California now. They took it to do some training. I gave it to the man and he hooked it up to a trailer and away they went. Went down to Homeland, CA That was a good tractor, that was a really good one. We had 440 and 160 and 160 and 320 and 760 enough to keep us busy. Just a little busy.

Getting back to the Army, there were some awful good guys in there, awful good guys. And there's some of them others too. You had them one day and the next day they were gone over the hill. I don't know where they went when they went a.w.o.l in Europe. They might still be battling over there, as far as I know. Yep, it was a long time out there. Oh, they had a way out of it. It was easy enough to get out of service. They could get out of there and come home. Probably, they would use another name or something to get on a plane and come home. Yeah, they had quite the deal of it. As for us being brave and doing my duty, most of the guys were and did; I was just one of them. Yeah-a lot of awful good guys in there, and a few of them others. You just couldn't trust none of them nowhere. You might send them out on patrol and they would go around a bush and that would be as far as they'd go. That would be where they would end up. Didn't really want to go, but had to obey the government. But it's over. It was good to get home.

I haven't seen any of my former comrades; I don't think that any of them were from around here. In fact, I don't see many of the people from my younger days, most of them are dead and gone.

I guess my last comment will be that I did my job, served my time, paid my price and am proud of what we did. And it's a good thing we went. Otherwise we might be speaking German or Japanese, and I'm just too damn old to learn.

Hohm, John A.
Sergeant, United States Army
1923 –

The fourth highest combat decoration that can be awarded to a member of the United States armed forces is the Bronze Star. The citation reads "while serving in any capacity in or with the Army, Navy, Marine Corps, Air Force, or Coast Guard of the United States, after December 6, 1941, distinguishes, or has distinguished, himself by heroic or meritorious achievement or service, not involving participation in aerial flight—while engaged in an action against an enemy of the United States – **Hohm, James A.**

The Purple Heart is a United States military decoration awarded in the name of the President to those who have been wounded or killed while serving on or after April 5, 1917 with the U.S. military ... 1950 – **Holm, James A.**

The Army of Occupation Medal is a military award of the United States military which was established by the United States War Department on 5 April 1946. The medal was created in the aftermath of the Second World War to recognize those who had performed occupation service in either Germany or Japan. The original Army of Occupation Medal was intended only for members of the United States Army, but was expanded in 1948 to encompass the United States Air Force shortly after that service's creation ... 1950 – **Holm, James A.**

The Parachutist Badge, also commonly referred to as "Jump Wings" or "Snow Cone", is a military badge of the United States Armed Forces awarded to members of the United States Army, Air Force, Marine Corps and Navy. The Army Parachutist Badge is awarded only to those military personnel of any service who complete the US Army Basic Airborne Course at Fort Benning, Georgia. It signifies that the soldier is a trained Army Parachutist, and is qualified to participate in airborne operations ... 1946 – **Hohm, James A.**

And like so many others of our brave men and women, Sergeant Holm received a number of other lesser medals and ribbons for his valiant serviced, but space limits their description.

*****

Yep, I'm John August Hohm, born and bred on a farm a little bit south of Jefferson City, Missouri, in the year of 1923. That makes me about eighty-eight years old, going on eighty-nine. And like most of the people at my age, my memory is a little spotty. I really appreciate the opportunity to tell everyone about myself, but if I kind of jump around, I can blame it on my memory. It's like me, it's getting old.

I didn't like the idea of being drafted, so I just decided to up and enlist so that I could choose a little. I decided to enlist in the Army and eventually made the rank of Sergeant. I had enlisted because of World War II. I had a brother who was in the Army, actually the Army Air Corps. That was before they had the United States Air Force branch that we have today. Anyway, I didn't like the Navy and didn't like the Marines and about the only thing left was the Army, so I enlisted. Basic training took place in Aberdeen, Maryland, at the Aberdeen Proving Grounds– at least the early training did, but there was more training later on. I was sworn in at Scott Field in Illinois, I think it is now called Scott Air Force Base in Bellville just outside of St. Lewis. I had a neighbor who decided to join with me, so the both of us went in at the same time. In fact, our serial numbers are just one digit apart, mine ends in the number five and his in the number six. We stayed there for three days, with only the clothes we had on our back. Then we were sent to Fort Sheridan, Illinois, on the lake for a couple of days and then we were transported to Aberdeen Proving Grounds in Maryland to be outfitted and for basic training. It may have been hard for some people, but to me it was a piece of cake. 'Course, it was hard on some of those city kids, but most of them got through it okay. That was some sixty years ago, so I remember very little about it and don't believe I can even recall the instructors. Guess they must have been decent folks, because I can always remember the bad ones. I made it through basic training in great shape, went right on through it with no problem.

After basic training, we shipped out to Japan on the ship Admiral H.T. Mayo, the largest ship on the west coast at the time. Once we had arrived in Japan, we had to wait on board for three days before we could dock because of a huge storm that was raising Cain. I was one of the lucky ones, I didn't get seasick at all. It took us about twelve or thirteen days from Seattle, Washington along the northern sea route to Japan. We finally docked at Yokohama. Japan was different, there were a lot of people, and they were all trying to look over the rail to see what going on. I'm sure they thought we were going to crash into the dock as the seas were still running heavy. But we didn't, we landed without any problems.

At Yokohama, they were recruiting for the 11th Airborne. I don't think I had ever heard much if anything about the Airborne, but I signed up and became a paratrooper. We went up northern Honshu to Hachinohe, where you jump off to go to Hokkaido, the next island. Then after that we went down to Sendai to take basic training and parachute training. I was in the 511th Parachute Infantry Regiment. Following the parachute training school and after we had made qualifying jumps, we went to Hachioji, Japan to a place called Camp Haugen, named after the commander of the Regiment, Colonel Orin D. Haugen.

At Camp Haugen, we continued practicing and training and doing basic duties, while we were just waiting. I believe that at the time, the leaders were worried more about the Russians than about the Japanese or even the Koreans or Chinese. Our commander did make use of us, and we were all transitioned into glider training, making the necessary six qualifying flights.

I'll have to admit that the first time I jumped out of a plane, I thought it was fun. It was really exciting. You have to remember that I was a farm boy before. Altogether, I had twenty-six jumps. Then, on the 8th of August we were at Yenomi, Japan, making another jump when a friend of mine and I got our chutes tangled up in mid-air. Yenomi had been an emergency landing field for the Japanese fighter planes during World War II, and they had built the runway with large steel mats. Those mats were still in place with grass and weeds growing up through them, about four feet tall. If I had landed on the ground, it is probable that I wouldn't have gotten hurt. Most of the others made the jump okay, but this guy from Montvale, California—who had a most unusual name: Joe Smith—and I collided in mid-air, causing me to flip over and land oddly. Anyway, getting the parachutes entangled caused us to fall, and I fell awkwardly, landing on my a.. can on one of those mats. I fractured four of my vertebrae and my tail bone was badly damaged and one arm was almost torn off, but that was during peacetime and so, no purple heart. That put me in the hospital. I was in the hospital for quite a while, and when I was released, I was returned to Hachioji, back to Camp Haugen on limited duty. A little later on, it was time for me to get released from service, so I headed back home.

When we finally arrived back in the States, I spent Christmas aboard ship. Then when we got home, I took my discharge from service on January 6, 1948. That finished my first active episode.

I spent the next six weeks in a hospital in Wadsworth, Kansas, followed by outpatient treatment for my back. Although I had been injured and was somewhat restricted, I was able to join the 339th Military Intelligence Company, Team I. This was part of the Army Reserves, and we would meet once a week. The group was what was called a 'closed unit', only sixteen people in the unit. We were learning to read and write German. It was known as a 'German Constabulary Unit', intending to put people into Germany that was fluent in the language. My father could read and write German fluently, and I was coming along pretty good.

Our instructor was a German professor from Lincoln University in Jefferson City. He had a lot of bad luck. He had two sons, twin boys. One of the sons was killed in Korea early in the fighting and six or eight weeks later the other boy was killed in a car accident. The old gentleman was down in the dumps, I guess, and couldn't continue. So, our unit kind of just blew up and the next thing I knew I was transferred into an infantry unit down in Fort Hood, Texas. That's how I got in the Korean deal.

At Fort Hood, they gave us refresher basic training and there were a few new guys who had to go through the whole thing. I guess it was kind of rough on them, but some of us were old-timers. There were about eighteen or so guys from this area and we had a heck of a time, lot of fun.

From Fort Hood we went Camp Stoneman, California and from there we went aboard a ship. We made a stop in Hawaii where we dumped off a bunch of civilians and twenty some cars and trucks that went with them. We sailed on to Yokohama, Japan, where we offloaded.

I was at a local beer hall with some friends one night and saw a bunch of Navy guys. I found out that I was going to be on the same ship that they were. They wanted somebody to sign on early for Korea, so I signed on early. One of them, a Chief Petty Officer, asked me if I wanted a job. I said I didn't want to work for the Navy. He said it would be an easy job and it would get you a meal, just making coffee eight hours a day, and no other duties while I was aboard ship. And that would give me access to the food supply. I would eat with the first class petty officers and have it easy. And he repeated that I wouldn't have any other duties. Otherwise, I would be like the rest of the guys and have at least eight hours duty each day. Easy choice. They made some pretty good pastries so I ate well on the trip to Korea. That was a fun trip while it lasted. It took us about eight days to go around the southern tip of Korea and then we landed at Inchon. We got there about 2:30 in the morning and crawled down some rope ladders, got on landing barges and went on in to Inchon. We had to wait for the tides to come in so that the landing barges could make it to the docks.

They had some cans set up with heat under them, like garbage cans with little cans of heat under them. They also had a bunch of little cans with beans and wieners and other stuff that I can't remember. I drew a can of beans and wieners. That was all I received for rations. We were twenty-two miles from Seoul and we walked all the way with just those rations. That's all that we had to eat on the march.

I was a Browning Automatic Rifle gunner and carried a .45 sidearm as well. The BAR weighed nineteen and three-quarter pounds. Additionally, I carried a filled canteen, a back pack, a camera, a pair of Japanese Navy field glasses. All that stuff weighed about ninety-five pounds. Then I was assigned to the 2nd division. From there on, I didn't have a map and most of the time didn't know where I was. We moved around quite a bit. I don't know how far north we really got, but we were all the way up on the Han River and then in a lot of mountains.

Then on January 6th a Chinese mortar round got me. I was setting a perimeter guard around our company when a Chinese mortar round exploded just beside me. The temperature was thirty degrees below zero. I don't know how bad I was hit, or at least, I didn't at that time, but they kept me overnight in a MASH unit and then they flew me to Fukuoka, Japan and then the next night they flew me to the Osaka General Hospital. That was a little experience, anyhow. Korea had been different than anywhere I had been before. I suffered wounds to my hands, feet and stomach. Additionally my fingers froze up. That was how I earned the Purple Heart.

I was mainly a perimeter guard in an infantry company, Company, 38th Infantry Regiment, 2nd Infantry Division. Our main job was to guard a bridge. A tunnel led to the bridge and across the river, and our job was to guard that bridge and keep the North Koreans from using it. Like an Indian scout. I had my BAR and a .45. I was walking in one night about midnight and we came in on a dirt road. And it was cold. There was an intersection and beside it there was an outcropping of rocks. And there were some bundles or as we call it on the farm, shocks of barley on the side the road, so I picked two of them up and went over to the rocks. I put one bundle down and sat on it and put the other at my feet, trying to keep them warm. Several mortar shells went over. One of those shells hit a telephone line above and dropped beside me and exploded. I didn't think much of it, but the next thing I knew I was just laying there. Someone picked me up and took me over to an old Dodge 4x4 and took me to the MASH hospital. We spent some time in the hospital there.

They had a place named Nara, Japan. It was a place where there were a bunch of shrines, a place that was never bombed. The Army had a place there they called a Recuperation Hospital for anybody that had frozen hands or feet. There was something that was just like a picnic table, with tin buckets and a round basin; tin buckets because this was before they had plastic buckets. We would sit at the table and put your feet in the basin and your hands in a bucket. There was some purple stuff in the basin and the buckets to fight infection. Two times or so per day we would soak our hands and our feet. Well, they got us out of it alright. My hands did okay. I came back pretty good. I wore a back brace for quite a while, but I'm doing pretty good at this time. I'm in my eighties. I can't play much ball anymore and I had to quit bowling. They told me that with my rear end, it would be best because it could really mess me up. I used to love to bowl. But I used to like to drink beer, too. However, no root beer and no Shakespeare, though.

We had quite a few casualties in our division. From one hundred and sixty-eight men and officers, we were down to twenty-six able-bodied men. A lot of the casualties were victims of frozen hands and feet.

In Korea, our mail was as sporadic as heck. Caught up to us only every now and then, and the letters were seldom in order by the date they were sent. My mother sent me a box of cookies for Christmas. Because we had moved around so much, the cookies didn't catch up to me until Easter. The cookies were still good, though, and we all enjoyed them. I was glad to get out of there, it was too damn cold.

There were a few other things. There was this little, thin guy in Korea that was my assistant BAR porter and he would carry the ammunitions, extra ammunitions and things. Once in a while there would be beer available, normally just one or two 7.5 ounces. He would give me his beer and I would give him my sweets. After I left, I got word that he had been drilled right between the eyes. That kind of got to me a little as I thought that if I had been over there maybe things might have been different. One of his favorite jokes was that "this invisible man married this invisible woman, and their children weren't much to look at either."

Another instance was when this guy, a friend of mine by the name of Olin G. Marlow, came over from the 82nd Airborne to the 11$^{th.}$ He said he had drank so much cognac it had knocked all his teeth out. He had two of sets false teeth and kept one set stored in his wall locker. At the time we were having stand-by inspections by Captain Stringle, a heck of a good guy. He open Marlin's locker and there sat a set of false teeth just smiling at him. He wasn't supposed to laugh or even crack a smile, but couldn't hold it back and of course the rest of us couldn't either. I don't believe that I will ever forget that.

Marlow was one of the older guys; everybody called him 'Pop'. He was our supply sergeant. He couldn't type or anything like that but still he was a good supply sergeant. I could type and take shorthand, so I helped him out quite a bit. We got along pretty good.

I had an interesting career. I had fun and I had some tough times. I was in Korea for thirty-two days and lost forty-six pounds. We were low on rations and it turned cold. We were only getting two meals a day and those were scant meals because supplies were short. One of our trucks and trailers that were carrying supplies went over a cliff as we crossed one of the mountains. The driver and the guy riding with him jumped out and made it to safety, but all of the supplies they were carrying were lost. Of course, that didn't help. But, I wasn't the only one. Everybody lost weight as we didn't have enough food, and the temperature got as cold as 32 degrees below zero. That wasn't the most fun time.

I had over four puncture wounds, and if you had more than three, you were not allowed to return to Korea. I was fluent in shorthand and I could type, so I was scheduled for reassignment in Yokohama, Japan. I was transferred to Headquarters Company Southwestern

Command. I was assigned as chaplain's assistant. He was a Methodist preacher, a major, and I was a Catholic. We made a pretty good combination. That was back in my beer drinking days. And in his too, I believe. I remained there until October and then was sent back to the States. I had gone to Korea on five different ships, but I flew back home from Korea. Made the trip so much faster.

Back here they had started the 816th Field Artillery unit, and I joined. I was the supply sergeant while I served with them. I stayed with that unit for a number years until I finally retired out of there.

I had a five hundred percent disability rating and about six years ago, I was finally able to get a decent disability retirement income from the US Government. Took me quite a while, but I just wasn't going to take no for an answer. They take pretty good care of me now.

Even so, I had a lot of fun and made a lot of friends. Still got some friends scattered all over the country; 'course we're a bunch of old codgers now, although most of them are dead. But we still have a lot of fun. With my buddies, I served in two war zones: World War II, and in Korea. And after sixty years, it's still going on, as far as I am concerned. Of course, they don't call it a war; they call it the Korean Conflict. Same thing to me, they still shoot you.

I had missed home on the farm. And I missed a girl, a long time friend. I was engaged to her, but she married someone else while I was gone. Other than that and my family, I didn't really miss much at all. There was never a time that I would have just quit and returned to the States. I am a hard-headed Dutchman-German and was in the Airborne and figured that if anyone else could do it, I could also. In addition, I got in pretty good shape, keeping up with the younger kids. It was a twelve and a half-mile boundary around the perimeter of the airfield, and I felt that if those kids could double-time around the field, so could I. And I did. I wouldn't change it for anything.

Although my injuries did have some effect on my live, like I said, I'm a hard-headed old guy and come hell or high water, I'm going to go on. After the military, I went back to the farm where my father and two brothers were still running a pretty big farm. Sure, I know there are some things that I just can't do. Working on a farm hasn't helped and makes it necessary to do some things and make some adaptations. For example, on a big John Deere tractor, I can stand up and drive. I can't set down and drive, but I could have made some adaptations. There are a few things that I just can't do. It's a different ballgame, but I know what I can do and what I can't do. I don't feel sorry for myself because there are a lot of people in the same boat ... or worse. That's the way I figure it, I just happened to draw the hand I drew.

As to whether or not I am happy with my decisions to join the military, I will tell the world that I wouldn't take a million dollars for it. But I don't want too many more nickels worth. Right now I am one hundred percent for the draft. There are too many people getting a free ride. There is one certain class of the people who are doing all of the grunt work and I don't appreciate that. I believe that everybody should serve some two years in the military. That would eliminate a lot of the problems in this country right now, and I think there are a lot of people who would agree with me. You would learn a little discipline and you would know what a little sacrifice was for one thing. And more than that, it would be a good deal for our youth. They would get a heck of an education out of the deal, for one thing. The military right now is really a great deal, I think. I was invited to speak at the University of Missouri, but I just wasn't in shape to make the trip. Anyway, I'm not quite sure what I would have said. I believe I may suffer from A.D.D.

A lot of people ask me if there are any special people that I would like to say thank you to or to expression my appreciation, and there certainly is ... or are. Do you ever watch MASH on T.V.? The first thing you see is the helicopters. And if you are in a hot fire zone or wounded or in danger, that is the most welcome sight you will ever see. It means that you are safe. Then there are those people who take care of the people who are unable to take care of themselves, the wounded veterans who have sacrificed so much. It takes a special breed of person, caring, to take care of people like that who can't even wipe their own rear end. These people are there for those in real bad shape. I say that I drew a bad hand, but in comparison, I really didn't, these other veterans who are just waiting to die did draw a bad hand.

There was one guy had a birthday and we gave him a card with a five dollar bill. He was a lucky person and won a bingo pot with $257 one time and the next month another pot with $125. He's a jolly guy. His birthday was on the fourth of July. I said, "Mr. Walker, you had a birthday on the fourth of July, didn't you?" He said, "Yes." I said, "I always knew you were a firecracker." He really enjoyed that bit of humor.

Like I said, I came from a farm. When I joined the Airborne, I believe that everybody around me thought that I was nuts. We had people down line in my family that had been in service before and they didn't know much about the Airborne. They thought that anybody that willingly jumped out of airplanes was mentally short. Mom would write and send me papers. And there are a few things I remember clearly.

Back then, we were appreciated. When we were stationed at Aberdeen Maryland undergoing training we would go to Baltimore, which was a half-hour away or to DC which was roughly twice as far. I can tell you that Baltimore was a fantastic service town, they treat you the way that service men should be treated.

All in all, I have had one hell of a time down through the years. And I'm looking forward to making it to one hundred. When I'm asked if I am still driving and why, I say, "It beats the hell out of walking."

I am also most proud to announce that I am an active Elk and was the chaplain for a period of years. The Elks stand for all that is good in America and I feel humble that someone nominated me, and to my surprise, I was accepted on the first go round.

One additional benefit, having a Purple Heart, my car license is only ten dollars. Otherwise it be thirty-seven. And there are a few other benefits—some small, some large—that a grateful nation has given us. And we have given back to America and to the American citizens. In spades.

Ingels, Gregory C
Sergeant, United States Army
1949 –

The fourth highest combat decoration that can be awarded to a member of the United States armed forces is the Bronze Star. The citation reads "while serving in any capacity in or with the Army, Navy, Marine Corps, Air Force, or Coast Guard of the United States, after December 6, 1941, distinguishes, or has distinguished, himself by heroic or meritorious achievement or service, not involving participation in aerial flight—while engaged in an action against an enemy of the United States – **Ingels, Gregory C.**

NOT JUST ONE, BUT TWO:

The fourth highest combat decoration that can be awarded to a member of the United States armed forces is the Bronze Star. The citation reads "while serving in any capacity in or with the Army, Navy, Marine Corps,

Air Force, or Coast Guard of the United States, after December 6, 1941, distinguishes, or has distinguished, himself by heroic or meritorious achievement or service, not involving participation in aerial flight—while engaged in an action against an enemy of the United States – **Ingels, Gregory C.**

The Purple Heart is a United States military decoration awarded in the name of the President to those who have been wounded or killed while serving on or after April 5, 1917 with the U.S. military ... *In the theater of the Republic of Vietnam for wounds received in connection with military operations against a hostile force ...* 1969 – **Ingels, Gregory C.**

- ➢ National Defense Service Medal
- ➢ Republic Vietnam campaign medal
- ➢ Combat infantry badge
- ➢ Army commendation medal (2) with valor
- ➢ Reason for citation ACM with v= Republic of Vietnam for heroism in connection with military operations against an armed hostile force in the Republic of Vietnam as directed by the Secretary of the Army under provisions of the AR-672-5-1 and the USARV message dated July 1966.
- ➢ Certificate of appreciation for the faithful performance of duty – (General Westmoreland)
- ➢ Certificate of appreciation for the faithful performance of duty – (President Richard Nixon)

*****

I seriously thought that my assignment to Vietnam would last much longer than it did. I'm Greg Ingles from Iowa, Kansas, and figured that I would get drafted sooner or later, so I decided to go ahead and join the

Regular Army, knowing that my tour would only be for two years and if I were sent to Vietnam it would only be for twelve months or so. Although a lot of people thought that I had a lot of courage to enlist, especially with a war going on, I'm not sure of that. I won't say that I wasn't scared, but then I was quite young.

As I assumed, I was indeed sent to 'Nam in 1969, at the age of twenty. Almost immediately after I completed basic training, I was deployed directly to Vietnam where I was injured some sixty to seventy days after I arrived in country. I arrived on around the first of April, 1969 and was wounded in mid-June, 1969. Didn't take them Vietcong or North Vietnamese long to take me out. And it didn't take the Americans long to get me to medical facilities, either. I didn't get out of service at that time; I served my full term of two years although much of it was in the hospital. I don't know how I healed up like I did, because in Japan the doctors wanted to amputate my legs and I told them no, that they would have to kill me first ... no way I was going to give up my legs, especially both of them. Eventually, I returned home and left the military and I became a mail carrier and delivered mail for thirty-six and one half-years after that, all on foot. Guess you could say I made the right decision. To me that was awesome. It turned out, in the long run, it turned out pretty good.

My war to save America was going to be the Vietnam War. I knew that others had fought for the United States to stay free and strong and now it was my time. My buddies and I decided during basic training that we were going to be 'point' men (the lead or forward man on a combat patrol). That's how I wound up injured, stepping on a mine.

Most people who step on a mine do lose their legs or get killed. On this one weekend, we lost three of our point men that were killed on that weekend. Monday was my day to be point and that is the day when I got hit. One other guy got one piece of shrapnel in his leg from the mine I stepped on, my sergeant.

People often ask me how it happened and I can remember quite well. We had a new captain that had taken over our company. He was not an old hand in Vietnam, but he was a Captain. He told me to set up a perimeter around this rice paddy. In a combat zone a perimeter includes a trip flare, a wire that will go off if anyone hits it. Every experienced point man knows that you just do not walk down a trail next to a wood-line because they are usually mined. So, I stepped off to the side of the trail to install the perimeter and that new captain said, "No, I want it right down that trail." I knew better but it was a direct order from a captain and I was a private. I made it about ten feet before I hit the mine.

The medic came around and another guy came running up, and I kept yelling at him to get down and stay down. We were under fire and it had started to rain. Heavily. This guy that I had saved his life stood over me and he held his helmet over my head. I said, "You get your butt down now!" The medic came running up and asked me if I were in pain." I said, "No, not really." Actually the shrapnel in my legs and arm had killed all of the nerves for about two or three months. I said, "I'm not in pain." He said, "You dummy, you get a free shot of morphine and you had better take it." "Oh, okay." So when I got on the helicopter. The pilots of the helicopter knew they were coming into a hot LZ (landing zone under enemy fire.) so they didn't actually land, just bounced and the guys threw me onto the helicopter and then they just kept going. So, as I was leaving, I was legally high, so I just flipped that new captain off.

They had me at the hospital in Dong Tan in short order and I bet it wasn't much more than fifteen or twenty minutes from the time I was injured until they were wheeling me into surgery. They had done their jobs. I always admired those helicopter pilots. They would come in under fire and pick up those wounded guys. They were great. They saved a lot of lives. They saved mine.

There were other close calls during the time before I was injured. On my first day over there, we were crossing a stream one at a time on a rope because the stream was so swift. We ran into an ambush there and our medic was killed that day. The enemy was shooting at me, but I guess I was fortunate.

There was another time when they called me up and told me to carry a wounded man across a rice paddy about a quarter of a mile, out in the open. I low-crawled most of the way out there carrying this wounded soldier. Eventually, I had to stand up and lift him up so that I could throw him into the helicopter. I was passing him up to a medic that was standing in the door of the 'copter. Just as I stood up, a bullet went by my head, nicking my earlobe. That bullet went right into the medic's mouth. I don't know if the medic lived or died, I never found out, but the wounded guy that I carried over there did make it. There were a lot of things that happened over there. We got ambushed several times.

We came close to getting run over by the enemy one time. But, we had the best artillery f.o. (forward observer, a person attached to a field unit to coordinate the placement of artillery fire...Ed) as far as I'm concerned in the Army. The enemy had us badly outnumbered and they were assaulting us and trying to kill us all. The f.o. called – I'm pretty sure it was the Navy boats, the big ones like the USS Iowa or some like that – and those big guns started laying down heavy artillery. He had them fire a marking round that fell behind the enemy and then he had them start walking the artillery back toward us. And when he got it back toward us, it was awfully close, not very far from us at all. But, let me tell you, those Navy ships were accurate. We could hear those big guns firing all the way from the ocean back to where we were and that was at least sixteen miles. They – those Navy gunners – really saved our butts.

And then there were the helicopters and the helicopter pilots. We would have died for them. They saved our butts so many times. A lot of us would have died if it hadn't been for them. One time we were out on patrol and in the middle of an enemy ambush in a rice paddy. One of the helicopters went down. The guys had so much respect for the helicopter pilots, we just formed up a line and charged, right in the open. We didn't care. They took care of us and we took care of them. We were able to rescue those pilots. A little payback.

A lot of what we were doing in Vietnam was trying to save each other's lives, not so much to kill other people or anything like that. I don't know if I killed anybody or not. I just didn't try to keep score. In truth, you become so close to your buddies and those in your squad and your platoon that you go all out to save each other, too. And that was what we were doing. Even so, we lost a few. The night before I got hit, the point man stepped on a mine and was blown in half. At the time we were hiding from the North Vietnamese or the Vietcong. We hid in a stream and I had to sleep on the body bag holding the remains of the point man in order to stay afloat. At least, I didn't have to see him.

I hope that I saved a few lives, my guys and the others. I never became 'kill-crazy'. We did have a scant few who did, but I tried to take live prisoners. I didn't kill them. And any of the prisoners that I captured lived while I had control of them.

When I first went over, I guess you think all these gung-ho things, that you are going over there and 'bang-bang', shoot-em-up and everything, but when I got there, I realized that I wanted to live, but I didn't want to take anybody out either. If I could capture them I would and I would try to do it without shooting. I believe that is what separates Americans from some of the other people in the world. We really weren't major killers, I guess, for the most part.

I was only nineteen or so at the time, but believe I quickly developed a sense of maturity far beyond my years in the short time while I was there. All of us guys were young over there. And we all matured, quickly. Or we died. I understood that we were being asked to do things such as serve in combat, something that only about one percent of the population ever sees. I'm not sure that I could do it again today. I had a lot more nerve at that age, or perhaps a lot less common sense. Now I realize the enemy shoots back.

The guys had a reunion this year, but it was all the way back in Ohio and I received a list of names and phone numbers in the mail. I didn't really think that I could afford to go to the reunion. Not that I was hurting, but I did have some bills come in at the time that needed to be paid, but the primary reason was that when I looked at the list of names, some of my closest buddies weren't even on the list, so I kinda held back on it. Should have written some of them.

There is a mobile Vietnam War Memorial that they are taking around, and I have seen it. I'm not sure that seeing it helped. Actually, I was overwhelmed by all the names. I was glancing around and then told my friend, John, who was there with me that I wanted to leave because I was afraid that I would see a name on there that I didn't want to see. They had a records place that you could go into and give them a name and they would tell you where it was on the wall, as the names are not in alphabetically. John and I talked and decided we didn't want to go in there because we were afraid that we would find somebody that we didn't want to know was hit or dead.

The layout was nice and the display is totally impressive. They had different stands where you could talk to people and remember. However it was just a little traumatic. I didn't want to start the nightmares again. There were just too many names on there, something like fifty-eight thousand one hundred and eight. Just too many, just too traumatic. The Wall just freaks me out a little bit.

When you are overseas, you are among your buddies, but there are things that any soldier misses, and I was no different. One of the things I missed most was my girlfriend. I told everybody, "They can say anything they want about foreign girls, but there is nothing prettier than American girls." So, I guess you actually miss the people as well as the good things we have in this country.

I wanted to get back to the States alive. And especially when I found out that they could save my legs. It only took me two or three months to walk again, and my legs came back almost to their normal status by the time I finished my duty. I had a medical profile and didn't have to march or anything like that if I didn't want to, but I had been a long-distance runner in college. The company was having a mile run, and I really wanted to run during that contest. I was wearing combat boots at the time. The guys got out on the track, and I kinda snuck out there behind them. And then I lapped the entire platoon. This was after my injury so I guess you can say that my recovery was sorta complete.

While a lot of the credit should go to the doctors that worked on me, there were seven doctors in Japan who said that I would never walk again. However, then I got lucky. I was sent down to Fort Leonardwood, to the hospital there, and this doctor – he was a doctor of course, but he was a also therapist – he said, "Who told you that you wouldn't walk again?" Then he said, "I'm going to tell you something, young man. You've got thirty days convalescence leave coming for getting wounded overseas. But until you walk out of here, walking straight, you are not going on that leave." Then he took my foot and moved it to one side, and grabbed hold of my leg and then started twisting and massaging. They had told me I would be club-footed, that my left heel would never touch the ground again. He said, "Not so, I'll take care of that." And then he really started.

I was screaming and hollering and yelling and cussing and fighting and cringing and crying and ... calling him all sorts of names. But that son-of-a ...

I went back afterwards and I thanked him profusely because he did straighten out my legs when those other doctors only wanted to cut. He came close to performing a miracle. I could walk and I could walk pretty darn good, too. And it has been that way ever since. So, yeah, I am thankful for the doctors and the medics and the nurses, but most of all to that therapist, wherever he is now.

When I was in the hospital, I was having some pretty bad nightmares, but things got a little better after I was released and went back to civilian life. I receive sixty percent disability now, so I can't say my injury didn't affect me at all. Actually, the fear doesn't come until afterwards. At the time that it happens, you are too busy to think about it. However, the last month that I was in the hospital, I'm not sure that I slept any at all. If I did, I would wake up in the middle of the night and ...

With the injuries I suffered, I'm asked if I would do it all over again. I must respond that I might. I just might. At the age I joined, you are at least semi-fearless, at least for a while; young, bullet-proof. But now, looking back, I believe that our country might have been able to avoid that war. Actually Ho Che Ming came to the United States first. He was a hero to the United States during World War II, so I don't know – I'm not a politician – and I don't have that kind of say anyway. But to serve for my brothers and sisters and other Americans, I'm not in the least ashamed of having served and what we did. And I would serve again, but I would want the war to mean something, not just an exercise in futility like Vietnam.

Combat does something special for friendships. You get close – really close. There isn't much you wouldn't do for your fellow soldiers. It was kinda like, they had my back and I had theirs. I must say that I appreciated all of the people that I served with.

There is something else I would like to say. I used to hear people talk badly about the V.A. hospitals. I had the very best care in the V.A. facilities. I know of other people who feel different and many of them may have reason, but there are a lot of us who used the facilities were well treated and served properly. There a lot of good people there, and I have had a lot of good care from them.

There are things I really don't want to talk about, but I have agreed to have a list of the medals and awards that I have received for my service to the United States of America as part of my story. I really don't think I did anything special; actually, I just did what I considered my duty as the best that I could.

I am blessed and I am alive because of two that watched over me: God and my buddies that served with me during my time of extreme peril. And now that I have had the opportunity to ease my pain a little, I must admit that yes, America is worth the sacrifice and yes, I will do it all again. God bless America.

Jensen, Dennis D.
Lieutenant, United States Army Air Corps
1949 –

The war in Vietnam during the 1960's was one of the most evil wars in history. Ill advised and ill planned, the war was primarily a political war that none the less claimed an extremely high number of American military. Not all were caused by enemy gunfire, many were caused by the defoliants that were used in an attempt to destroy the hiding place of the Vietcong and their allies from North Vietnam.

Decorated with the Purple Heart medal for participating in a military operation against an enemy of the United States of America, Dennis Jensen is one of those unfortunate soldiers who suffered additional damages by the misguided use of what we now know as a deadly poison: Agent Orange.

*****

Lieutenant Dennis DeeRay Jensen, United States Army Aviation and proud of it. Originally, I'm from Genoa, Utah, born and raised there. I now reside in Preston, Idaho and have lived here a little more than 20 years.

Even when I was in high school I believed that it was our duty to fight for our country. It was mostly the reason I joined the military because there was a war being fought in Vietnam and I thought that winning the war was crucial to our country. And so did another six of my partners from my high school. We decided that we were going to over and fight for our country. Although we may well have been drafted at a later date, we felt that we should just go ahead and enlist. So I joined the United States Army and was what they refer to as R.A., Regular Army. I was a soldier from 1967 until 1970, and I served in Vietnam from 1967 to 1968.

People today ask me what gave me the courage to join the Army during the time that Vietnam was heating up and some of the American public was beginning to doubt our purpose for being there. Certainly it was because that in my home-raising era, it was proud to be an American. I was taught that I should be proud to be an American. To fight for our country was an honor and a privilege and that was the feeling that caused me to join. My father had been a sailor in WWII, serving on the United States super-dreadnaught battleship, the USS Pennsylvania, of the United States Navy. The ship had been badly damaged during the Japanese surprise attack at Pearl Harbor, but she had been refurbished and she was noted during the Guam campaign for being the ship that fired the most ammunition during any one single campaign. The ship had been torpedoed again by a Japanese torpedo plane as it lay at anchor in Buckner Bay.

Dad's patriotism and his philosophy was just something that was taught to us when we were children; that it was an honor indeed to be allowed to enlist in the service of our country.

It was in that era, around 1967, when the war in Vietnam really got going, beginning to heat up. In early December of 1967, North Vietnam and the Vietcong decided that they were going to take back over Saigon and they tried to overrun it. Estimates from captured documents were that there were more than forty-seven thousand North Vietnamese Regular Army soldiers that came down through Saigon to fight along with an unknown number of Vietcong. It was a real hard time, a rough time, a time of hand-to-hand fighting, a time of a lot of action. There were a lot of people that died during that fighting.

When you're not in battle, there is a lot of time to think about things, including those things left back in the United States. And there is time to miss certain things. I missed my family perhaps most of all, and I really missed my girlfriend. She was special. In addition, I missed my home quite a lot. However, there were a lot of things that I had seen which were good. The country was different, of course, really different. I was a farm boy my whole life up to that time, so it was interesting for me to go to a lot of different places in the US and take the different trainings that I took; and then to go overseas and see a third world country up close and in person. It wasn't anything like the films. I'd never seen poverty in my life. Not poverty such as existed there. Of course, I've known what being hungry was and stuff like that, but I'd never seen anything like this. Nor the things I couldn't even imagine. It was different. And it was frightening.

Even at the worst moment, deep inside, I knew that I would not quit, would not even contemplate quitting. There was no giving up and there was no possibility of just throwing our hands up and walking away. American soldiers just do not do that. We do not abandon our own. Even so, there is time for reflection, time for consideration, but there is not time for second-guessing. It's necessary to just keep on keeping on.

There are times when you are laying among the dead or stepping over the dead bodies, in that moment of where either you're going to live or die ... with prayer inside you and knowing that you're going to meet your maker and the thoughts of home is ... well, those are the things you think about. When there is nobody else left and you're the last one in your unit that is alive and there's just nobody to help and there is nobody to help you, you just hope and pray that they come and get you. I've been shot behind enemy lines and everybody was dead but me. It sounds crazy, but in that moment of despair, I realized that I was going to live and that I was coming home. I had that quiet, calm voice somewhere deep inside me that was telling me that I was going to make it and I had no more worry after that. Even at that moment, there was no thought of quitting, of giving up, of surrendering, of just walking away. There was belief sometimes when you can't understand it and just happens.

Sometimes, there were new people that would come into our gun platoon, and in short order, the MPs would come in and take their locker boxes because they never even made it back from their first sortie. They were already dead and gone and you didn't even get to meet them even though they were part of your outfit. It was a little different view. The life expectancy wasn't much as a gunner or a crew chief in the gun ships.

My MOS was 67 N(ovember) 20 which was helicopter mechanic and crew chief. I became a gunner first, then crew chief and gunner. Mine was basically the armament. I took either the left or right side of the helicopter with an M-60 machine gun and day and night we flew. Mission after mission. In the time I was there, I don't know how many missions, maybe a thousand missions or more. In just the short time that I was there.

We flew ... we were all over Saigon during the night. As far out as Black Horse; and from Bearcat where I was stationed clear up north along Highway 1, all the way from North Vietnam and back down. So we frequently patrolled Hwy 1. I worked with the 101st, with Marines, worked with the Navy, worked with the Navy SEALS. From Cambodia to Thailand; we were all the way through. Of course, we were always busy. Anyone who was in a firefight or had some action, we were called in. We would come in and strafe the area. We would try to clear the enemy out or clean them out. Basically, that's what we did. Those M-60's, we'd just burn the barrels out of them. And some of them, you just couldn't imagine. Sometimes you didn't want to imagine, but that—that's what war is. You don't want to think about it, but still your thoughts ...

When I got back, it got a bit hairy because I thought about ones that I killed and I wondered how many moms and dads, how many brothers and sisters had I ..., but then how many people did I save? I killed nine of them one afternoon. They were kinda setting up an ambush. We were just letting infantry off the slick-ships and the slick-ships were leaving and I happened to get a glimpse of them. And so I opened up and by the time it was done, I killed nine of them that were there. I was the only one that shot. And the thing was, I wondered about their mothers and fathers and I thought, why them? For years it kind of bothered me...and dreams, you have dreams and you just never forget. I had a psychiatrist ask me, "Well, how many did you save?" And it made a realization to me, that no one can sort this out but God. I don't know, but maybe there was somebody there that I saved that might have had his child or his child's child might have had a child that could have created a vaccine that might have cured something or was somebody special , and that this was supposed to happen and I was just a tool; and that was basically it. I was put in a lot of positions where that happened just because I was in a gunship and that's what gunships do. It's nothing like today. I can't even fantasize what they do today with all those big black-hawk helicopters. We were just a little four-seater with six thousand pounds of ammunition and armament. We were the blah. We looked like liquid lava at night when we'd fire those mini-guns, just spray hoses and the liquid lava from all the tracers. But of course you had better believe that the Marines loved us when we came in and sprayed the enemy. I don't know how many we saved, but that is what we did.

The first time I was shot down, and the first time I was wounded, was outside Saigon, by the Firestone Plantation. What they were growing were rubber trees and we had been flying night patrol. As we came in, I heard the bullets come through the turbine engine. I heard the turbine come apart and then the pilot came over the radio, saying, "Mayday! Mayday!" just as we were going down. I remember looking out of the helicopter and thinking, "Boy, this is the first time that I've been shot down, and I don't know nothing about it." I was looking at the trees below us, they were all in a row, if you know what I mean, and they looked like carpet. We were high enough that the trees looked just like a large piece of carpet. But, we were falling. I heard the pilot say, "Fire detection," so I looked out the rear of the 'copter and the tail boom is on fire. And down we were going. And I'm thinking, "What do I do? What do I do?" I looked over at my crew chief and he reaches out and grabbed the pin holding his armament. So I grabbed the pin holding mine; it has an exploding bolt which drops the armament. And then he grabs his M-60 ammunition and he throws it out. I'm thinking, "Man, what are we going to do when we hit the ground. There's enemy." And then he grabs his M-60 gun and throws it out, too. And I'm thinking, "Nope, that isn't happening to me." So I unbuckled the belt and left about a hundred rounds of ammunition in the belt that was feeding my machine gun and then I pushed the gun and belt under the co-pilot's seat. I wedged it in with my foot. Then I got up into my area and wedged myself in there tightly, and I remember thinking, "Boy, it doesn't look like we are falling all that fast." And as we are coming down, now I realize that what I was seeing wasn't carpet, it was trees. Just before we hit, I heard something say, "Take off your monkey strap." So I unfastened the monkey strap and wedged myself there in the doorway. There were these big web belts so I tied myself in there as tight as I could get. And the next thing I realized was that I could see these trees going by so fast. They were like twenty-five apart and I couldn't even count them, they were going by so fast. The next thing was that we hit. And it was like I was blacked out.

When I came to, I was face down in the dirt, but I was buried in the dirt, actually buried. I guess that I hit so hard that it interred me. And when I came up out of the dirt, the back of my arms were on fire, so I was throwing dirt all over me trying to put out the fire caused by the JP-4 fuel. I looked around and the helicopter was all on fire. I don't know how long I had been knocked out, but I went over to the helicopter, and I went to the co-pilot's door and opened the door. When I first neared the helicopter, the crew chief was underneath the helicopter and the flames were just above his face. It looked like the landing skid was over the top of him and his face was up in the helicopter, and I didn't know if he was going to live or not. I was a little dingy or something from being knocked out, but I got to the co-pilot's door and opened up. Both the pilot and the co-pilot were already gone. So, I backed off and looked at my crew chief. The skid was actually across this ditch-like thing, and he was in it with his face in middle of that helicopter. So I reached out and grabbed him and pulled him out. Now, this old boy weighted about two hundred and forty to two hundred and sixty pounds. They had already warned him that if he gained any more weight, he wasn't going to fly anymore. I grabbed him, threw him over my back and then went into a dead run with him. In fact I hit the concertina wire (perimeter wire around a military site...Ed) coming into where the Americans were. I stumbled, but picked him back up and threw him on my back, and it was like I was packing a rag doll. There was just nothing to it. Guess I was jacked. I got him to the ditch line there, and I can still see him out there.

As we lay there, there was this infantry troop approaching. They were a "fire team," and were walking out in the open, just firing almost everywhere. At the same time, here was our helicopter out there in the opening, on fire and burning. The fire was "cooking" off ammunition rounds, the heat causing the cartridges to explode. I was screaming at them to get back, because this ship was still full of ammunition. We're talking about some six thousand pounds total weight and probably some two thousand rounds of mini-gun ammunition stored beneath the two seats between us, and lodged under each mini-gun. Anyway, it was popping and ricocheting everywhere. And here I was screaming at them, and it was so bright, because the helicopter was made out of magnesium, which is like a flare, and you could see them standing out there in the field and just walking around and shooting, carrying M-16s and machine guns, and they are walking up to this fire, and here is this ship "cooking off," and ... anyway, I took a round, a ricochet to the top of my head that knocked me back into the ditch.

They put me in a Medi-Vac and then they medi-vaced me to the 249th Medi-Vac hospital. I spent thirty days in there, and believe me, the things that I saw in there was just unbelievable. It was more or less that we helped each other with shaving, feeding and personal care. There was anything from arms blown off, legs blown off, bullet wounds, just everything. My pilot, he stayed there a lot longer than I did. They had him in a sandwich wrap and had knocked out a tooth or so, so that he could drink using a straw. They had him in a bundle so that they could roll him back and forth. It was a heck of a deal, you break your back in seven places.

James, my crew chief that I had packed out, had busted his left arm and had compacted his spine. My spine had been compacted as well. Altogether, I was in Medi-Vac for some thirty days before I went back to my base camp and I was put right back into a helicopter, and back out flying. We just couldn't keep enough gunners going, so ... I flew through Tet (Tet Offensive, 1968 ... Ed.). That was when Christmas was. I made it through Tet, and we were the gunners on the gunships that did the shooting out at the race track and in the middle of Saigon.

It was just a free-for-all there at that time. At night, there wasn't a base camp that wasn't under attack. It was pretty hairy. We lost a lot of ships.

The last time I was shot down was out in the Iron Triangle, an area between the Saigon River on the west and the Tinh River on the east, about twenty-five miles north of Saigon. We had two thousand Vietcong infantry cornered at a ditch line and they had been fighting all day, it was just a back and forth battle. We couldn't even get close, because a lot of the guns they were using were anti-aircraft. We finally got them cornered against the river, and our leaders ordered in everything we had. It was like a hundred helicopters. Each helicopter was loaded with seven infantry each; two pilots, two gunners and seven infantry. Plus there were thirteen or fourteen gunships. We flew to the other side of the river to catch them in an ambush.

Well, this ambush we were setting up for them had already been set up for us, with five to seven thousand North Vietnam soldiers. They had already been dug in. So when we came in ... when the slicks came in, they just stood right up out of the ground and shot us while we were still in the helicopters. Not one helicopter made it out of that trap.

As we were flying in, we were the second helicopter to strafe the back side of the formation, and the enemy was so thick that it didn't matter where I ... wherever I looked, they were just pointing up at me, shooting. Wherever I was shooting, they were just all over. Sometimes I could hit two with just one round. It was just a human wave assault on these helicopters. And we came through that wave of enemy fire, then just as we pulled up to circle and come back around to re-strafe, they hit us with anti-aircraft fire and we went over behind enemy lines and that's when we crashed.

When we crashed there, I had the monkey strap on me and it shattered my pelvis and broke my hip. I don't know how many bullets we took, but I had one that hit me in the left leg, just above my ankle. Anyway, I lost both my pilots, and my crew chief - my gunner. In fact, I don't know how long I was knocked out that time, because when I crawled back to the ship, it had already burned out. The pilots were lying there, still in their seats. The meat came right off their legs and fire was coming out of their bones. I had never known that people could burn like kindling wood. This is new for me. I had seen people in napalm and stuff like that but ...

Well, later that night, they brought in the fighters, and they dropped the napalm over top of me. I could see the eggs drop over top of me and hit the jungle, and those Vietcong would just come out of there on fire and screaming. They would just lay there and burn until they were just burned up. I don't know just how many bonfires I had around me.

I crawled into a place where they had been harvesting rice, and I covered myself the best I could with these rice husks to where I could just barely see through it for the night. And they came out, and just walked right through, right by me, never saw me. It was on the third day when I saw a helicopter that morning and it was way up high, and I was just trying to lift my arms, but I couldn't hardly raise my arms at all. I remember that a Vietnamese came up and stuck a gun in my face, and pushed my head to the side, and I thought, "Why don't he shoot me? Why don't he get this over with?" I opened my eyes and I saw him go off into the tree line. He was a North Vietnamese Regular .. a member of the Army. I guess I was covered with so much blood and dirt that he didn't see me as an American when he came upon me. So, anyway, I was still alive.

They put me in a poncho, there were six of them. They put me in a poncho and they pulled me back to a safe zone. In that safe zone were lines and lines and lines of bodies. They were all my company ... and the infantry that was with us.

There were a lot of times that I wondered, 'cause, later on, after being held in Japan – I was held because I couldn't do anything anymore – and then I went to Fitzsimmons General and then I came home, and it was amazing. The things they said on T.V. about Vietnam were that maybe we had one or two killed and a few wounded, and that we had killed maybe ten or fifteen of them. I flew into a lot of places where everybody was dead. Just everybody laying around, they didn't even look right, because of the way it was. It was ... there were a lot of things that happened that, until the war was over, no one knew about. It was like ... ah ... two weeks ago, I was ... they said that I had "Herbicide Exposure." From Agent Orange. So, here it is forty something years ago, and I'm dying from Agent Orange. They did a liver biopsy on me last week. It's amazing; the horrors of it all and things like that.

I don't know, but I'm still proud of what I've done. But, if there is a way to make peace and not war, it's better. And that's the way I feel. But I'm proud of what I've done. And we went over there and we did our job.

You look at those boys from World War II. You look at the way they fought, hand-to-hand, and everything else. Well, the same way as we did. A small war doesn't seem to mean as much today as it meant way back then when it was World War II. When we came back from Vietnam, a lot of us were treated badly. And it was a sad thing. It should never have been like that, because although I was only eighteen, I was still a man, and my belief was to fight for my country. You ... I just had to do it. I just hope that the veterans will never be forgotten.

Today, I've got a friend down here. He is ... was a sniper over in Iraq. And the things that ... it's just the same things; war is really bad. And, like I say, if they can talk peace, then that's great.

But you have a lot of good veterans out there. I don't know how many I counted on last Veterans' Day up in Boise at that Memorial Cemetery, but there are a lot of them buried there. And a lot of them from Vietnam. I think about the real heroes. Just because I've got a Purple Heart, just because I've got a Bronze Star, just because I've got an Air Medal, just because I've got a Combat Medal, just because of other soldier medals, all those combat missions, that doesn't make me a hero. Those boys that laid down their lives, they were the real heroes. It wasn't us that made it out alive. I mean, we did alright. We just came back to testify. That's what we do. We tell you that that war was bad. It wasn't a good thing. We did what we had to do, and that was to walk in the line of fire. Takes a special type of courage. When you pick up your buddy or you look at him and you just wonder, and there's no tomorrow for him. I can tell you about him. There's a lot of brave men there. Or a lot of brave kids who became men. Anyway, that was my war, Vietnam.

When asked how my injuries affected my state of mind, I have to admit that I was just crazy for a while. I don't know how other veterans are or anything else, but it's just like this; if I got into my pick-up and backed up out of my brother's house and ran over the baby, I would never forget it. It was the same way when I killed my first man, I'll never forget it. I'll never forget it. And even later on, when there were so many of them I couldn't count them, I still don't forget it. A week ago, I woke up and I was over a lime green jungle with bright yellow smoke coming through it, and I was thinking the same thing then as I was in Vietnam: "All these Australians are down there, a whole company they put in there and they are fighting hand-to-hand over the radio, and they are popping yellow smoke and we are to shoot on the top of them." I was also thinking, "Am I killing them or am I killing the enemy?" Yeah, it had a lot of effect on me. A week ago, this is what I was dreaming. Another dream: here I am on a bridge, and there's a Vietcong in front of me and he's being shot. The thing is, I know this Vietcong because I'm the one that killed him. And I look up into the helicopter and there I am in it. The next thing is that I'm standing behind myself and here's the machine gun and I'm shooting it, and I'm seeing him right now. What I'm going to do is that I'm going to shoot him. I'm shooting him and when I roll him off the bridge into the water, I'm going to sink him. You never shoot a man once, because he doesn't die from one bullet. You shoot him until he's dead, so he can't kill nobody. But in that instant, I'm back down on that bridge and I watch him roll off into the water and I look up at myself and I say, "What an atrocity." and I reach for the .45 pistol on my hip and I put it to my head. I pull the trigger, but I don't hear the gun go off. Still, I hear the empty casing hit the bridge and roll. But I never carried a .45; I carried a Smith and Weston .38 Special. Then I wake up in bed and I sit up and I'm just covered with sweat.

Day after day, month after month, year after year I'm crawling through a river of water with my helmet down in it and it's so thick with oil that I'm choking on it. But, it isn't oil; it's blood.

Until you've done it, you just don't know. Until you wake up in sweat like I have, and you say, "Well, did you have anything happen to you afterwards? Is there anything ..." And you say, "Yeah, I went nuts."

I came back to the United States and it seemed like I had spirits around me. The people that I killed, some of them never left me. It finally got to a point where I said, "This is enough. When I get over to the other side, if there is a qualm, then we'll fight about it then, because I'm a man." Then I was left alone by them, but I still have my dreams. Regular? Is that regular? I don't know. I only know that by killing, I saved people. It's just crazy isn't it? Yeah, you just don't know. But, I believe that I saved a lot of Americans. And I could shoot. I was good. I was raised with a gun in my hand from the time I was a little kid. And when we went through basic training, in the two companies, when we went down for our 'shoots' (marksman test ..Ed), I outshot everybody in the two companies. And that was my thing right there. There wasn't anything that moved that I could see, or pick out, that I wouldn't be able to shoot. When you are firing a machine gun, you don't actually aim through sights on a barrel, but because of my ability, with the second tracer, it would be in there. I would just put it out, and it would be right on the mark. So, that was my calling. That's what I did.

Like I said, I'm alive and I'm here to testify.

Even so, my injuries did affect me when I came home, I didn't have a job. I couldn't keep a job. I married my high school sweetheart, but that petered out, too. I couldn't trust anybody, I couldn't hold onto a job. I'll tell you what it's like. Imagine that you are working on an engine. You take this tool down and you tighten it up. And then you set the tool down. You go back over and you reach for that tool and it isn't there. So, what do you do? You look for it and you look for it. And pretty soon you're aggravated. I look around, I look around and I can't find it anywhere. And that was the way I was. It seemed like I walked in circles. I worked on job after job after job. I just couldn't shake them.

So ... I know there were a lot of them just like me. And I know that today there are a lot of them that are in bad, dire needs. Seventy percent of your homeless are Vietnam veterans. Almost half of them or more have Hepatitis C; some of them have never been out of the hospital. There were dues to pay with that war, too; just like any of them. I'm sure those boys that were in Korea, those boys that were in World War II; they were the same way. They didn't ... they didn't forget. They didn't have an easier time either. I didn't think I was any different than any one of them. And thank goodness, I found help when I did. I never did trust a psychiatrist or anything like that, I wasn't going to go into group therapy; the only people I trusted were people the same as me, a Vietnam vet, someone that knew the language and what was going on, 'cause everybody else didn't know, and we hadn't been treated right when we came back, so it was really ... like I said, even today there are a lot of our veterans out there in dire need of help. Thank goodness I finally just dropped my resistance and said, "Listen, I've just got to do something," and it has helped. Hopefully others will do the same. I'm praying for it. I was single for 23 years. Like I said, I just couldn't keep a relationship. I raised my three kids, and I got married here about a little over five years ago and I'm just totally in heaven. I just love my wife and we have a good relationship. We have a church life; we trust one another. All those things I didn't have before, I have today.

When I'm asked if life has been hard since I've been back, I have to say ever since I have been back. Sometimes I would just like to throw my hands up and run away. At least, that was the way it used to be, but it isn't now.

I'm often asked if I am happy with the decision I made to join the military. My answer is short. You can't change what is. Can't change what is. Like I said, I'm proud that I am a veteran.

Our veterans need assistance. Anything to do that would help our veterans. Anyone that has been a volunteer in DAV has helped. That is the mission. I've been over to the Disabled American Veterans here in the state of Idaho, over there working in the hospital and stuff like that. And everything that we've done when I was Exalted Leader here at our Elks Lodge and was able to work on the committee for the Disabled American Vets has helped. And I've really enjoyed it.

But it's not enough. Like I say, there are a lot of veterans out there that need all the help they can get, and more. So thanks to all the organizations and all of the guys who are bringing attention to those needy veterans. They are bringing a lot of things together now, and it's just wonderful. But the need ...

When I was in Fitzsimmons General Hospital there in Denver, I was in a ward where there were mostly amputees. There were a lot of lieutenants in there that used to giggle at each other, because they would have these hooks and hand pieces that replaced hands that they had lost to grenades exploding or being shot through the hand and being blown to pieces, or whatever, but I'll never forget that click of that leg, of clicking back in with one leg gone. They would swing that leg and click it, swing that leg and click it. I would wake up at night to it, hearing that sound, locking in and ... Those veterans are still one-legged or still one-handed. Some of the don't have any arms. Some of them don't have ...

When they pulled me in the first time I was shot up, they stopped me in the middle of the hallway. There was a black soldier and he was leaning up against the wall, and there was a nurse next to him. She was holding him there. And he had about four or five blood transfusion iv's running into him. He was wrapped in bandages all over and they were covered with blood. His eyes were black and that was the only way that I could tell that he was black. I looked at him and he looked at me and it was like we were conversing. This was on the day before Christmas. He'd had a mortar round that landed behind him and blew off his legs and his arms. They were trying to keep him alive until after Christmas. You know that some people really do care. This situation just happened. But he died on Christmas, but they recorded his death as the day after Christmas so that every time his family had Christmas they wouldn't think about what it was. The things that happen to men in war are really bad. But the good that comes out of it—there are a lot of people saved. Now our veterans today, there are still a lot of them that have a lot of problems. There are a lot of organizations that can help and if a veteran like me goes out there and seek help, he probably can find it. At least some help. For example, I have hospitalization, I go to the Veterans and they found out that I have this Agent Orange. It wasn't me that went in for that, I had gone in to find out how come something wasn't right, and now I know what it is. And now they are trying to help me, they are doing all these other things to try and help me through this.

Those Vietcong don't have medical. Those people that were sprayed with Agent Orange or with weed-killer; they are still there. They have already died. They lived in it. So, I feel lucky. That's right, I feel lucky. I wouldn't trade a single helmet full of American soil for all of Vietnam. And not for any third-world country. We have so many rights and freedoms here, and it's so amazing; so much more than anyone in the world, and it doesn't matter if it's Canada or Mexico or England, or whatever. They don't have what we've got. And as long as we've got our veterans and our soldiers, we'll always have this. But, we've got to keep guard on our country, so we'll always have this freedom and never lose it. Never let anybody overtake us. We were a country that was made from freedom and for freedom. Freedom of speech and freedom of religion, things they couldn't have anywhere else in the world that we have here. And it's that same way today. If I don't like the President, I can say it. That's my freedom. You say that somewhere else. China. Go ahead and say that in China. Yeah. You see, they don't have what we have. God bless America.

Before I end my story, there is someone out there that I want to thank, someone that did something really special for me. One that I would like to thank the most for their help in the two times that I was shot down, shot up, bullet wounds, shrapnel and whatever, and that is the Red Cross. After three days, a friend of mine, who had gone to school with me and we had joined up together, was with the 9th division. He had heard that we were at the same base camp and he went out looking for us. Turns out that he had called home and said that I'd been killed, 'cause everybody had been killed. After I was flown back on the third day, the first thing was the Red Cross came in. They gave us everything we needed like shaving equipment, toothbrushes, food to eat and to do whatever, and they gave me a phone call home so that I could tell my parents that I was not dead, that I was alive. That was the Red Cross. I could thank all the nurses and all the doctors and I could thank everybody else that helped everybody, but we were just all there together. And it didn't matter, even if I didn't know you, I would shave you in the morning and I would help you brush your teeth, if you couldn't do it. If you needed bandages or cleaning, we just helped each other. It was the time of Tet, it was a time when everybody was being shot up, and there were so many wounded and so many killed, it was just unbelievable. They were trying to overrun us and show America that they could just kick us out of there. Well, they didn't. Later on, things happened and we moved out, but ... That's who, even today, that I think about ... the Red Cross.

Finally, the last and most important things I want to say to the American people: cherish your freedom. Cherish what we have here. I've already said everything. Cherish your freedom. Keep our country free. Watch who you vote for ... go out and vote. Raise your children right. And teach them what America is about. People don't know what it's like to live with a dirt floor. We have so many things here. So many that we don't ... we take so much for granted. And we are helping other nations. We are helping all over the world. A lot of that should be here at home, but there is a lot of that we are doing, a lot of good. That's as it should be, because we are a country like no other country. And I do love my country. And if I had to go and do what I have already done, I would do it again. For my country. That's what I would do.

So many different soldiers ... so many different things. But, we are all one nation. Under God. Indivisible. With Liberty and Justice for all. That is what we do. Absolutely. Amen.

Lengkeek, Peter J.
Sergeant, United States Army
1973 –

One of the great tragedies of the United States is the inhumane treatment that our veterans and their families suffer after their sacrifices on behalf of a great nation that should be so grateful for their services that America should open its heart and its wallet to provide for those who gave so much. There is another group to whom the United States owes so much, and that is the Native Americans. Time after time, treaty after treaty has been abrogated by the federal government and the Indians have been left to suffer the consequences of a voracious government that has forgotten or ignored the promises and vows that were made.

There have been many occasions when the members of an Indian tribe would enlist in the armed forces in time of war or need, serve honorably as warriors do, and then upon leaving the military be forgotten or deserted, left without aid, without help, without the benefits promised on so many occasions. It is little wonder that the status of the Native American living on the unwanted and barren reservations is that the welcome they had offered to the white man has resulted in disaster.

It isn't often that such an individual has the chance to inform the world as to the actual treatment of a former military man that has honorably served the United States and who is also a full-blooded Indian that has experienced the false promises by an unfaithful government, as well as the devious and devilish methods by which the United States has virtually caused the demise of the first Americans.

Here, in Sergeant Peter James Lengkeek is such a person.

*****

Yes, I am Peter James Lengkeek. At least, that is my white man name. I serve as one of the tribal leaders here. I sit on the tribal council. There are six of us that are the leaders of the reservation. We are each elected by the people in secret ballot voting and serve for two-year terms. We can, if the people so choose, be reelected. Being a tribal leader is a huge responsibility, something not to be undertaken frivolously. It's a 24/7 job, round the clock. Sometimes I get so involved and so busy that I even forget that I have a family. It's a tough, demanding job; the need here is so great. We do everything including protecting our sovereignty and protecting our borders, our reservation borders. Constantly the federal and the state government are fighting to get on this little chunk of land here. It's not like they want to make it out to be in books. In reality, it's a constant fight to protect our sovereignty, our jurisdiction; it's a constant fight for self-determination, self-governance. It's just a constant fight against both the federal and state governments.

The race relations between the Indian tribes and the people in South Dakota are very, very poor. We know that the State of South Dakota is the Mississippi of the North. Conditions are terrible here. I suppose that there are a number of factors that bring this on. A lot of our people ... race relations are so bad here and we get treated so badly when we leave this reservation in Chamberlain ... even the state capital Pierre is one of the worse places for an Indian to be. We get treated so unfairly up there that a lot of our people just stay right here, they won't leave these boundaries.

It's hard to get a fair shake anywhere, in anything. For example, the closest Wal-Mart store from here is in Pierre. It's probably a little over an hour's drive. For those of us that do have vehicles and do have the money to go there, that's where we go to do our monthly shopping. It's a 24-hour Wal-Mart and you can go there at three o'clock in the morning and it'll be full of Indians. That's when they decide to do their shopping because they don't get the dirty looks and people laughing, pointing at them, calling them names; despite our serving in the military on behalf of the nation. It's a sad situation.

This is the poorest County in the nation. It has been that way for years. At one time we had one of the highest suicide rates in the world. It's just that there is so little here. We suffer eighty-five to ninety percent unemployment. It's a daily struggle just for survival here for some, perhaps even most, of our people. Our only hope is educating the public about the situation as the average American citizen has a bad perception of the reservation and the Indian people.

We work very hard on economic development, self-sustainability and just trying to develop our natural resources. The wind here ... we're looking now at wind energy development—alternative energy development and all its realm, as well as natural gas and natural oil. We have a small plot of land here and we're trying to develop a tribal cattle organization, a tribal farm system. Being right on this river, we have some of the most fertile soil in the central United States here. We are sitting on a big flood plain and that's where a lot of these fields usually are; in a flood plain. Just trying to develop that land is a fight in itself. The State is constantly against us, the County is constantly against us. It's like that on every reservation that you go to. And there is a lot of misunderstanding, miscomprehension, false beliefs.

For example, when someone approaches our club, they will notice a sign on the door: "No Alcohol Allowed in This Building." That is something that we prefer not to be associated with; drunkenness. Even so, the alcoholism rate here is unbelievable. I was examining some old pictures one time not long ago and I was looking at our sixth-grade graduation picture. All of we kids were present there. There were twenty-eight of us in the class. I think that now there are only eleven of us still alive and I'm in my mid-thirties. A lot of those kids died because of alcohol poisoning, drinking and driving, car wrecks; that takes a lot of our people, just being stupid with alcohol.

Our bodies ... alcohol is very detrimental us, to our people. Our bodies have not yet evolved to handle that drug. We've only had alcohol available to us for the last one hundred and fifty years and it's devastating to our people. The same thing is true with salt and sugar; the things they put in food today are very detrimental. The diabetes rate among us is unbelievable. Even our babies are being born with diabetes. The life expectancy of the average Indian male here is only forty-five. And woman is just forty-seven or forty-eight. That's not just because of alcohol abuse; it's from all that stuff, everything. Our bodies just have not been able to evolve into processing these devastating ingredients. I've lost a few friends in their late-twenties from cirrhoses and things like that. It's really, really tough on a reservation.

The thing that the United States government can do to help our plight is to uphold their end of the bargain; the treaty. That's one thing personally that I have taken on, trying to make the government uphold their end of the bargain and give us what they promised to give us in the treaty. They took all of our land, they took everything from us and we haven't been compensated for it like they said they would. If they were willing to do only what they promised to do, then we could possibly get out of this hole we are in.

One thing that affects our people, unlike the white man, is historic trauma. It's like that old Yosemite Sam cartoon when he says, "I'll hit you so hard your grandchildren will feel it." That's what happened to us. These people here—the world knows us as the great Sioux Nation, but that's not who we are. Sioux is actually derogatory to us. Our real name is Dakota. We are the Southern Dakota, north of us are the Northern Dakota, west of us are the Lakota nations. The Teton Sioux is how the world knows us. But the people that are here on this reservation are the Houqua Tea nation, which means, more or less, meeting the relatives. We are a people of compassion and love. Our very name Dakota translates as to be or live in a state of peace and harmony.

Like I say, we are a people of love and compassion, but when time called for it we were also some of the fiercest warriors that ever walked this planet. Some of the most highly decorated US soldiers came from this very reservation. Right now, we have over thirty of our members overseas fighting on behalf of the United States. And that is the way it has always been; whenever a war starts, a lot of our people leave the reservation and join the armed forces. That's just who we are, we are a warrior society. Even before we were made American citizens, we still had one of the highest volunteer rates of any ethnic group that ever joined the military.

Originally, we came from Minnesota. Also, Northern Iowa and Wisconsin are our homelands. In 1862 the government put out an order that said to *"annihilate the Indian race or forever to push them from the borders of Minnesota"* and that's how we ended up here in this prisoner of war camp. And that is what it truly is.

Getting back to the historic trauma, our people today carry deep depression and we pass that from generation to generation. It's actually genetically imprinted on us now. We were hit so hard back in the late 1800's that it affects us today, as hard as that is for most people to believe. A lot of our people are severely depressed. They don't know where it comes from, what it is or even how to deal with it. So they turn to the bottle, or drugs and things like that to try and quell that lonely feeling that we have. In 1862, when we were exiled out of Minnesota, the people that were brought here were only women, elders and children because by then all or most of our fighting-age men were dead. Disease took a lot of our people; starvation took a lot of our people; exposure to the elements and the sheer brutality at the hands of the US government took even more. We were almost annihilated. Myself, I feel very lucky; that's a miracle that I'm even here.

Over there in Minnesota, that is where our homelands are. In 1862, our lands were constantly taken, taken, taken. We were eventually pushed onto a reservation that was ten miles wide and twenty miles long that lay along the Minnesota River and we were forced to stay there and to eke out a living. We weren't allowed to leave. By then, with the constant encroachment of the European settlers, all the natural resources were gone. There was nothing to hunt, nothing to gather; no way to make it for ourselves. They put us on this little strip of land and this is where we were supposed to stay and make our living. Like I said, the remaining resources quickly disappeared and our people were starving to death.

Our warriors, those that were left, just had enough of that and they started a war, trying to take back some of the things that had been taken from us through the treaties and the broken promises and everything. Of course, the war didn't last that long, because most of the fighting-age men by then were gone, they had died. So, this war started, which is called by many names: The Dakota-Sioux Conflict, The Minnesota Uprising of 1862 and a lot of names like that. The war only lasted a couple of months. There was very much confusion among us. Among the bands that were present was some in-fighting as some of the bands wanted to go to war to take back what was ours and some of the bands didn't want war. These latter were like, *"Just try to survive on what we've got, we don't want any more people to die."* It turned our people against each other. Besides fighting the US government, we were fighting our own people.

After the war was over, they rounded up all the fighting-age men that had taken part in the war that still lived and imprisoned them down in Davenport, Iowa. President Abraham Lincoln took thirty-eight of our leaders and he hanged them all at one time. One pull of a lever and thirty-eight bodies dropped. To this day, that's the largest mass execution the government ever carried out. That happened in Mankato, Minnesota on the day after Christmas in 1862. Then the government rounded up everyone that was left which were women, children and elders and took them down to St. Louis, Missouri and put them on riverboats and brought them up the river to where we are now. At that time, this was a prisoner of war camp. Here, again, we were forced to stay put under guard; we couldn't leave, couldn't hunt, couldn't gather, and couldn't provide for our people. When we came here, our people almost died off completely. So, for those of us that are here, it's a miracle that any of us are still alive. There's probably close to fourteen hundred people on this reservation now. And the population is not all totally Indian.

In the late 1800's and early1900's, they opened this land for settlement. Small as it is, they opened our borders and the settlers came in and took what they wanted; which was some of the best land around here. A lot – even most – of the best land on our reservation is not even owned by Indians. Most people probably think that the reservation is solid Indian-owned land from border to border, but if anybody would look at a color-coded map, it's like a checkerboard; Indian land, white land, Indian land, white land.

The things that make me go on fighting and struggling every day are my ancestors, and the elders, and the children here. To our people, traditionally, children are sacred and our name for children is "Wakiaga," and that means sacred people, sacred little people and they were always treated as such. Every decision that was made in the camp was made with the children in mind. Everything that was done ... our ancestors always thought seven generations ahead. The decisions that we make today, *how is that going to affect those seven generations down the line?* That's how our people always thought, seven generations ahead. That's how they made their decisions. And it's the same today.

When it was time to eat, the children were always ate first; that was our future. You always invest in your future. Our people don't believe that we inherit the earth; we believe we borrow it from our grandchildren. And it was the same with the women. The women are sacred also. They have that gift, to bring life into this world. They were also treated as sacred, honored as such. But, it's not like that today. It's completely opposite of that today. The children and the women suffer the most here. For most of the Indians on this reservation, it's a day-to-day struggle just trying to get the next meal together, trying to pay the electric bill. Especially in the wintertime.

Long ago we were a tight-knit people—we were close. We all took care of each other. We never had poor houses, we never had 'homeless', we never had jails. There was no reason for a court system. We all followed a natural law. And that is how our people thrived a long time ago, by following that natural law. We always took care of one another. In history books you see people talking down about us having two, three, four or five wives. How that came about was that if my brother got killed in war, I would take in his family, his wife came to me and his children, I would take care of them and raise his family for him. If my cousin got killed in a buffalo hunt, I would take in his family, took care of them, raise them. That was how things were done back then. But, today, it's not the same. Traditionally, we were highly resourceful, very adaptable, and extremely hardworking. And we were highly intelligent; we had to be in order to survive out there the way we did and thrive. We took only what we needed and we always gave back.

I did eight years in the Marines Corps and a couple of years in the Army after that. I don't tell other Marines about my time in the Army. Actually, I do, but I like to tease the Marines. A lot of us here came from military families. My grandfather was Woodrow Keeble. We finally got him his Medal of Honor. He was the first

Sioux ever to receive such an honor. It was incredible how he won it. We had to fight for years to get it. The guys in DC, when we were checking into it, were like, *"To tell you the truth, when it came to minorities, especially Indians, that were put up for the Medal, as many were, they just swept it under the rug. There just ain't no way that no Indian is going to have the Medal of Honor in the Army or wherever."*

But we fought and fought and fought. Finally, it was given to him, posthumously of course, but he won the Medal for his actions in Korea. He was like many of our elderly men who had fought in World War II and Korea. Even some of them fought in Vietnam. We have until this day the highest rate of volunteers out of any ethnic races to join the military. Many of us come from military families. We don't join the armed forces just because of the poverty here and we're promised "three hots and a cot." We join because that is who we are. Even back during the draft, they didn't have to draft our people; we were there—volunteering, enlisting, and ready to fight.

I joined in 1991 to serve during the war. A lot of us did. I was in the 3rd Combat Engineers. That period of time was great. I loved it. I have some great memories and only a few bad ones. After basic training, I was sent to Okinawa and was stationed there for a while. After that, I was pretty much sent most everywhere. I should have stayed overseas. I wanted nothing more when I was younger than to get the hell out of this place and put Fort Thompson in my rearview mirror and never look back. A lot of our people do exactly that; they get educated and they leave and never come back. And that's one of the things that's really hurting us, loss of young blood. Nowadays, I speak a lot to our young people, I'm heavily involved in anti-suicide and anti-alcohol and things like this that are detrimental to our people. I always tell them go out there, join the military if that's what you are going to do, get educated and come back and help us out here, you know. But with the extreme poverty and the conditions here; once they get out of here they never come back. voici

I have a sister and brother who live in Portland, Oregon. My sister is a doctor there and my brother who is getting to be a famous artist. Both of them are veterans of the Vietnam era. And they do not want to live on this reservation and put up with all the discrimination and slander and slurs that we who do live here have to endure.

Right now, I think we have thirty-two of our members overseas fighting. As far back as the War of 1812, when we were in Minnesota, we served. Our chief at that time, Wapasha, was made a general in the British Army. The War of 1812. Of course, we all know what was behind that. But the British came to our people and told us that if we would fight on their side they would give us back all of our land and, "Everything you could want, you can have."

Of course, they were lying. But they packed up three hundred warriors and the warriors rode east and fought there. Even in the Civil War, we had members that fought in that Civil War—on both sides—and throughout every war since that time, we have had people in service. It wasn't until the 1930's that we actually became citizens of the United States, but even before then we had a extremely high rate of volunteers in the military. So, it was nothing uncommon. We have a lot of veterans here, a lot of veterans. Sad to say, some of the Vietnam veterans are still "eighteen and still in the bush." We rarely get access to the needed help that's out there for everyone else. There is some help out there, such as the V.A. benefits, but it's hard to get access to that stuff and get the medical and physical help we need.

My dad was in World War II in the Pacific. Our military people, our veterans are known by the name of 'Akichita', that's what we are known by: 'the warrior society'. These warriors are highly respected here. There are some things such as ceremonies and different things that happen culturally and traditionally which won't take place unless the Akitchita are there to perform those things.

We are struggling hard while trying to keep our language. That is something that I am really fighting strenuously to save: our language, our culture, our tradition. Talking about that historic trauma, my grandmother, Rose Keeble, was a full-blooded Dakota woman and she was able to hold on to that language and some of those traditions and culture until she died. And what she had to go through to hold on to that was incredible, because the United States government wanted all Indians assimilated. This is how our people are today, standing around with their hand out, waiting for and expecting a dole. This is how the government made us and this is how the government likes us. We have to beg for everything that we need just for basic survival. That's all our younger generations know now and that is what I'm working so hard to get away from. It is the worst form of slavery. It has affected generation after generation. It is very hard, but there is hope there.

I was often with my grandmother when I was fourteen or fifteen. She would pick us kids up and would try to immerse us in that culture and tradition as best she could, but she was old even then. We were at a powwow north of here, up in North Dakota. We had just arrived there, got the tents set up and we got some bad news from back here about a couple of deaths in our family. One of them was my favorite cousin. He was thirteen. He had hung himself down near the creek. Two other really close family members had died in a drinking-driving car wreck, which frequently happens here. So, we packed up camp and we started coming back to Crow Creek here, and as you can imagine, it was a pretty solemn, pretty quiet ride. I was just sitting there thinking about it and I asked my grandmother, "Why do these things always happen? Why do we always do these things to each other? Why is tragedy always on our doorstep?" She didn't say anything for a long time. I looked over and there was a tear running down her cheek. Then she said in our language, "yo ki che cha." The only way I can interpret that, the only meaning is, "that deep imbedded depression. We keep passing it from generation to generation." "And where that comes from," she said, "was that long ago our people had a very strong connection with the Creator, a very strong connection with Mother Earth, with the natural law and the forces of nature, and a very strong connection with the Spirit World. And there was a very strong connection with our own people. All those things were taken away from us just like that, at the snap of one's fingers. That is what affects us today, and that is why we are the way we are today."

    Back in the early 1900's, there were boarding schools; Catholic boarding schools. They would come down into a community here. There was no registering, or taking your kids to register for school. They would just bust the doors down, walk in, grab the kids and then they would leave. They would put the children into these Catholic boarding schools. My mother was one of those who went through the boarding schools in the thirties. At that time it was illegal to be Indian. You were shot on the spot for speaking your own language or praying to the Creator in your language. My mother's mother—or rather my great-grandmother, her name was Two Arrows—this was when Fort Thompson was down on the river—she was probably seven, her sister was nine and a female cousin staying with them was eleven. She said that one day the door flew open and there stood a man in a black cloak and he had two Army police officers with him. They walked in and they grabbed the three girls, threw them in the back of a horse-drawn buggy and took them north. North up there was where that Catholic school was, the boarding school, and it still stands today. It was built in 1886. The whole purpose behind those schools was to assimilate our people. Teach us the 'white way', become farmers, the Bible and religion and all that. They took the three little girls up there in a buckboard – a horse-drawn wagon. That was the first time the girls were away from their parents so it is easy to imagine that they were very terrified. So, they snuck away, went around a corner and began praying to the Creator in our language. They were caught by a priest. Before the day was over, those three little girls were raped by nine priests and beaten by about fifteen nuns, using whips, sticks and rocks and whatever they could. The eldest girl died from the beating because she was trying to lay on top of the two little ones and protect them. So she died and they drug her corpse into the hallway of the school and left her there for a couple of days. And every day, all the children—the school was a military style—the children had to walk by that body and the priests and the nuns would say, "If you want to be Indian, if you want to speak your language and follow your heathen ways, this is what is going to happen to you."

A lot of our elders are still severely traumatized by those days and they don't try to teach us our language or our traditions because of that. When my mother was on her deathbed, she began speaking in Dakota. She was speaking to an unseen someone over in the corner of the room. We knew that it was near; her time of passing was coming. Her mother and her father and all her loved ones that were in the Spirit World were coming to get her and show her on to the Spirit World. I had some time alone with her, so I asked her why she didn't teach us this beautiful language, this beautiful way of life. She said, "I didn't want you to go through what I had been through. Your life would be much easier if you didn't know these things."

Of course, it was and is very hard on me and on us. That's what our people struggle with today, that lack of identity. Our young people relate with the African-American culture, Spanish-American culture, even Oriental-American culture. They don't want anything to do with being Indian because Hollywood has portrayed Indians as beggars, thieves, rapists, killers. When I was growing up, that was what I thought an Indian was, always on the warpath and stealing something. Or always drunk or something like that. That's what I thought an Indian was when I was young. Came to find out that we are the exact opposite. We are people of love and compassion. A lot of our people don't know that. That is where that depression comes from. That historic trauma. What happened to our ancestors long ago, that's what affects us today. And it's hard to get out of that hole. What we have to do is to educate our children, give them a sense of worth.

There are some reservations and Indian tribes that are thriving, or so it seems. Casinos and gambling and all that. That is what most of the people see, they don't see the poverty, the degradation that exists in a lot of areas, such as this one. Somehow, the government can help people all over the world, but fail to help its own.

We see everybody as the same people. When Christians are done praying, they say 'Amen'. When we are done, we say, "Me ta qu yea onasi"(sic), and what that means is that they are acknowledging that we are all related. It doesn't mean that just you and I are brothers, it means we are brothers to the buffalo, to the winged nation – the birds; we are brother and sisters to the fin nation—the fish; the coyote, the deer, the insects, the tree nation, the grass; because we all came from one place: Mother Earth. Everything that makes up your body, the calcium in your body, everything that makes you up is found in Mother Earth and we all carry this—the buffalo, the trees, the birds—we all have it, the exact same make-up inside of us. To us the Creator is called the "Wankantanka," the Great Mystery; that is how that translates.. We don't have a picture of him; we have never seen him. It is neither a man nor a woman. It is probably both. Nobody knows. To us, the Creator is an energy; a life force that all living things have in them. That is why everything was honored and everything was so sacred, because even that tree out there has a Creator inside it, that same life force. I have never seen a picture of the Creator before, but religion has Jesus in photographs and they say that is what he looked like, but if we go back in history, we find out that Jesus had dark skin; he looked like a black man.

Anyway, that is who the Creator is to us. He is present at all times and in all things. To us, prayer is the most powerful thing in the universe. We are a very spiritual people and it wasn't something where we went to a teepee called a church every Sunday, laid our sins down outside, went inside and got forgiveness and then came back and picked them up again. To us it was a way of life. That's how we lived our lives. Long ago, every step a woman took on this earth was done in prayer.

My tribal name translated into English is "Two Arrows," just like my grandmother. That was what my mother named me. There aren't many of us today who have an Indian name, as they call it. That is something today that is earned. I didn't earn my name until I came back from overseas.

I was a sergeant when I left the Marine Corps, having earned the rank of sergeant in five years. I loved it, I miss it every day. But I decided to get out because both my parents were older and needed my help. Some people thought they were actually my grandparents. They both became ill and needed extra care, so I decided to give up my career. I had intended to make a career of military service which is why when I came back here to the reservation I joined the Army because it was close by.

To us Dakota, the youngest son of the family is the one that takes care of the parents and that duty fell to me, as the youngest of fourteen. Thirteen brothers and sisters. So I gave up my military career, came home and moved in with my parents and took care of them until they died.

Of course, I got help from my siblings. There are four of us that live on the reservation. Two of the four are severe alcoholics and likely won't live much longer. They are young, in their forties or fifties. Everyone on the reservation has been touched by suicide or alcoholism in some way, shape or form. And the cancer rate here is unbelievable; just unbelievable.

I had an elderly uncle who passed away a couple of years ago. He was the type of person that would always bring a smile to your face, no matter what. He always had a joke or something funny. He was getting sick and they couldn't find out what was wrong with him. One morning I went and loaded him up and helped him into the clinic here, and we finally get in to see the doctor. The doctor said, "What can I do for you today?" My uncle was sitting there and said, "I want an autopsy." The doctor said, "WHAT?" My uncle said, "I want you to do an autopsy." The doctor said, "What do you mean?" And my uncle said, "That seems to be the only time that you find out what's wrong with us is when we are dead." And my uncle was sort of semi-serious about it, but he was trying to make a point. And I guess that shook the doctor up quite a bit. Probably didn't make any change.

Out there in the white world, everybody out there thinks that we are just unbelievably rich. That we get all this money from the government, that we get free medical, free housing, free education. That's not the case. Unless you have tried it, you don't have any idea what free medical care is like; you get what you pay for. And it's government-funded, which means it constantly suffers cutbacks, less services, less care. Everybody out there thinks that because we have a casino that we are wealthy. In fact the casino only barely provides employment and that's all it does; if we even break even, it's a hell of a day. All it does is provides jobs here. The electrical bill is unbelievable every month. The Corps of Engineers took this land along the river from us and they built a dam there. They seized it under Eminent Domain back in the fifties, and said, "We're going to build a dam here." According to the original agreement, we reservation Indians were supposed to get free electricity. But to this day, we pay the highest rate in the nation. The average rate per kilowatt nationally is about 7.8 cents per kilowatt and we are paying almost thirteen cents. Unbelievable. But that's why it's so hard to develop this place economically. There are constantly people coming and saying that ... When we started looking at wind energy, you wouldn't believe the companies that showed up. It's so hard to trust anybody. They wanted to grab everything for themselves.

For years, growing up here, I sat back and watched white people come in here and just bend us over ... just completely take advantage of us, and everything. It's so hard because we can't do it on our own and we have to form partnerships to get these things going, because we don't have the technology. And trying to figure out who to trust so that it will benefit the tribe is almost an impossible task because everybody here has an alternate agenda, or so it seems to us. Especially the State. We have no trust for the State at all. Although we have tried to run for statewide political office, the white voters greatly exceed the Indians. And even if one of our people won, what good would that do? They would be one Indian in an ocean of white people.

The public doesn't hear a lot of history about this place, and it's easy to see why. The governments really don't want to publicize their actions.

There are a lot of things that happen around here that the whole tribe tries to remember. For instance, on every December 10th, we leave here on horseback and ride three hundred and sixty miles all the way to Mankato, Minnesota. We spend about two and one-half to three weeks riding horse, and that's to honor those thirty-eight Indians that were hanged on the day after Christmas in 1862. I descend from one of those that were hanged there, and like a lot of us here, we descend from them – that's our people that they took away. And it's to honor them and to never forget and to teach our history to our people, our young people, that we undertake the ride. There are a bunch of us from across the Dakotas and Montana and around the world. We have riders with us from Germany, Japan. Austria. It's not just for Indians, but it's for all people. We depart on December 10th and we spend two and one-half weeks and we ride right through Forestburg. In fact, last year we were caught in a huge blizzard and had to stay around Forestburg for a while.

That's where we spend our Christmas, doing that ride, me and my family. My little kids ride, my seven, eight and nine year old. It is a ceremony and very spiritual. And all the time we are riding, we are in prayer for our people. We pray for reconciliation between us and the white people. We are trying to say that we are sorry, that those things happened. It was ugly back then. There were no heroes at that time. It happened: let's move on. Move on together into the future.

It's called the Dakota 38. Some call it the Memorial Horse Ride. We ride for healing of our nations, healing from the historic trauma, healing for all the addictions that our people suffer from. We ride for reconciliation. Once we get off the reservation, we ride through a lot of towns that when I was growing up, my mother told me to stay away from. She told me that I was not welcome there because of who I was, that I might not come back from that town.

There were a lot of our people killed off our reservation and the killings were just swept under the rug. It was not uncommon at any of the reservations here in South Dakota. No justice. But, these are communities today that we ride into and we go to the schools and talk to the kids, showing just whom we are. We try to educate them that we are not the rapists and the thieves and killers that you think we are. This is who we truly are. We love you and we want to embrace you. There is a documentary that the Hollywood people are showing up trying to buy, but it's not for sale, it's so that we can educate our people. And educate the people that we are trying to reconcile with, which is the whites of South Dakota and Minnesota and wherever else.

But this is an event that is very near and dear to our hearts. This ride is very trying, very tough and we spend all year getting ready for it, getting our horses ready for it and preparing ourselves physically and mentally and psychologically. Sometimes it's quite cold. The horses are very sacred animals. We average probably thirty-five to forty miles per day. We time it to show up at the execution time of 10:00 a.m. on December 26th, which is the anniversary of that mass hanging. We pray for Mother Earth and all the people upon it. We pray for our own nations. We get together and we eat and just celebrate life. It is beautiful; it's very powerful, very spiritual. Then we scatter in the four directions until December 10th of the next year. We do stay in contact all year and visit each other from time to time.

The people who are involved in this are some of the most beautiful anybody will ever meet in the world. There are people that are just incredible people, bend over backwards and do anything they can to help. They would literally give the shirts off their backs. The warriors were hanged just because they were trying to protect our children. It happened and we want to just leave it there and move forward. I have a lot of friends and a lot of family that are white, so I know there is really just one world, one people. And we are all—each and every one of us—part of it. We do not ask for charity, we only ask for what is ours, what we have been promised. Isn't that fair?

Lind, Dell
Seaman First Class, United States Navy
1947 –

Dale Lind, veteran of the United States Navy, native of Bismarck, North Dakota, and recipient of the Purple Heart Medal as a result of being wounded in action during his service in the Vietnam War combat zone, is heavily involved with the Prisoners of War/Missing In Action cause. Dedicated to the pursuit of the final resolution of each missing veteran from all wars and all branches of service, Lind and his fellow veterans are determined to continue their cause until each and every veteran is accounted for, and the veteran or the veteran's remains are restored to their family.

*****

Yes, my name is Dell Lind, and yeah, okay, so I'm a 'Swabbie'. At least, that is what members of all the other branches of the armed forces call us. And no, it doesn't mean someone who swabs or mops the deck. Instead it is a title of honor. Actually, according to Miriam-Webster, it refers to "someone who operates or navigates a sea-going vessel." Of course, in my case, I really didn't operate or navigate any such vessel, however, I was—and am—a proud member of the United States Navy, because once you are a serviceman, you are always a serviceman. It isn't only the Marines who can lay claim to that status.

I first became a member of the United States Navy when I was only seventeen years old. Not only did I not want to just lay around the house after high school, but I was having problems with some of the members of my family and with other people around there. After talking it over with my family and especially my dad, I made the decision to join the Navy. It really looked good and exciting to me, like 'sail the seven seas' and all that. To make this shorter, in order to join the military at the age of seventeen, it was necessary to have the permission of a parent, so Dad agreed to sign a permission slip that would allow me to enter the Navy. He agreed with me that I should do something other than just hang around. So, with his consent, I enlisted in the Navy in 1964.

Sure, I knew that it was during wartime. After all, Vietnam was running hot at the time, and I was more or less certain that I would wind up over there. Still, even if I did, so what? I figured that I wouldn't be in the jungle fighting like some of those unfortunate soldiers and Marines who were being shot and shot at every day. To tell the truth, I never even thought much about the war and wasn't concerned about the glory of being a warrior or any of that stuff. Actually, it was more of an escape for me to get out of the situation that I was in, so I signed up and just went with the flow.

As a matter of course, served for four and one-half years in the Navy, going through boot camp, which I guess some services refer to as 'basic training'. They really kept us busy, and I was learning a lot of stuff, discipline and all that. Frankly, it was all new to me, and to be honest, it was thrilling to be a part of something as large as the United States Navy. I must say that I kind of expected it, and sure enough, in 1967, I was in the Vietnam Theater, the real combat zone.

Unlike many of the young sailors that I served with, I don't believe that I was ever homesick. Naturally, I missed my parents, but my new surroundings kept me from missing anything else. And in the service, especially for an enlisted man, they don't give you all that much time to be lonely. And, it's hard to be lonely when you are surrounded by a lot of new people. So, when I'm asked, as I often am, I must admit that I really didn't miss anything much from here. It was all a new experience for me. North Dakota is a pretty isolated place, so all the new stuff was fun; fun and fresh. There was never a time when I really wanted to come back.

I still live my life at present just one day at a time, and I think it was the same way back then, too. Just one foot in front of the other. I guess that I did miss a few of my friends, a friend here and there, but otherwise, I just concentrated on what I was supposed to do day-by-day, one day at a time, just going with the flow like most young kids that are away from home for the first time. It was a pretty good time to be in the service for a young person. I was able to see a lot of the world, and meet a lot of new guys. I guess that's what I concentrated on; it was a lot of fun. You could always see the guys back home, I guess, but getting to know the new guys was a lot more fun. It was good to share a few with them. Sometimes more than a few.

When I'm asked about mentors that helped this young man fit into his new world, I can easily name two almost immediately. These two guys were from the Philippines; Oscar and Palino Galveras. They each were black-belt holders in karate and instructed me in the same art. After duty hours, of course, and we had a lot of fun together. We were stationed together. They were good Navy men, proud of what they were doing. We shared a lot of time. You make friends in service; they come and they go. You hooked up with a few, shared drinks with a few, and develop a common bond. But, that was back then. It can't be the same way in today's military; they aren't allowed to have as much fun. We had a good time over there.

I was injured on different occasions, but it was a stray bullet that caused the major wound. It caught me, and that's about all I want to say about that.

I can definitely say that at the time it happened, the wound really bother me, didn't affect my state of mind at all, it was just another one of those things. Later on, it did begin to affect me somewhat, but it really wasn't about the injury itself. It never was. It was about the other injured. It was about the other guys that didn't get to come back here. It's never been a personal thing about me really; I guess it didn't take effect on me. It was just one of those things that happened. But the real concern was to protect each other and try to get everyone home safe, but some didn't make it. That was what was on our minds constantly. Like I said, there were some minor scrapes and bruises, but the only major wound that I suffered was from that stray bullet. After I came home there were no lasting mental or physical effects, at least not from the injury. Not that part of it. On the other hand, it was the remembrance of the things that went on;

the brothers that were lost; that's the tragedy of it all. It's not about yourself, it's never about yourself; it's about your brothers when you are in a situation like that. That's how it was for me. Instead of remembering the little things along the way, you block those out and you don't remember things. But you will always remember who were there, who did what and all that. A pretty influential time in the life of a young person. You don't forget too much. But, it's about your buddies. I've got a couple here and there that I talk to, but not many. Most of them are gone now, so there's really not much contact with anyone from that time.

Later on in life, Agent Orange did come into play and affect me. But that's a tough little subject; a very emotional subject. It's something I don't talk about much because it involves deep down feelings about our government. My motorcycle is painted orange in memory of all the Agent Orange victims. That idea was just something that popped into my head one day, and I thought, "We should do this." I think about it and those guys every time that I look at it. I guess I like to react positively and not negatively, but the situations are there.

I'm definitely happy with my decision to join the military and to me, all-in-all, it was a good—possibly great—experience in my life. I made a lot of friends. I learned how to work with people better; I was never very good with that in civilian life, and thanks to the Navy—and a few Marine—buddies, I was able to change that. It was a good experience; I can't be the least negative about it. It was my choice, I wasn't drafted, I enlisted. I made the choice, and I always live with my choices. But, all-in-all, I got to see a lot of wonderful things in life and got to participate in a lot of neat things too, so it was good.

There were more good times than bad times in the military. Coming from an old drunken sailor, if I can remember ... it was good and I let those good times flood my memory. One event I especially remember was when I was stationed at Yokosuka, Japan. In a place called Kamakura there was a great Buddha statue. And they offered up food to him every day on a tray. We were there one day and looking at the Buddha and decided to sit on the steps and eat his watermelon. Didn't go over too well with the locals or the local police; they told us we couldn't eat the Buddha's food. I really remember that incident. It was one of the good ones. I wasn't sober at the time, otherwise I probably never would have done that.

I'm somewhat aware of some of the programs and organizations that are out there to help the veterans and their families. We have a military vet center that I'm hooked up with, and we are always willing to visit with other people and talk to other people. But, there's still too much negativity about the Vietnam War, and that era. I get involved with other veterans and talk about stuff and all that, but one-on-one seems to be the best approach to things. I know there are some guys that are beyond that; they need some other stuff. It's like anything in life; some people can't get over things, but you have to remember to continue on with what you are doing. Keep positive, and help others be positive. It works on some, but not others. Even so, you don't give up; you keep trying. You learn to live with talking about things you normally wouldn't or shouldn't talk about with other veterans and people who lost sons or whatever ... it's just a give and take in life. A person told me once in life that a battery has a positive post and a negative post. You can hook up to the negative post and stay negative forever, or you can hook up to the positive and get going. Personally, I choose to hook into the positive aspect of that. Life is good … life is good. You have to make what you can of it. It's too short the way it is, so the choice's yours.

When I'm asked about 'The Wall' back in Washington, D.C., I respond that I have never been there and that I never want to go there. I have seen pictures of the Wall, and that is more than enough for me. I can remember easily enough.

Of course, my recovery is an ongoing thing and I have help. I have a lot of friends so it's hard to name them all, but there is one. I have a special friend, Bill, who is my ninety-one year old airplane guy—a pilot in World War II—and his positive outlook made a big difference for me. He's fun to talk to. He's a vet from a different era and I respect and honor him for what he is. He got to win his war: we didn't, so that part of life has always been hard to accept. But that's all political, and once again, that's hard to accept.

Bill is a genuine veteran, a genuine person. Talking to him keeps you grounded, keeps you thinking about the people that we need to respect in life, and that's the ones that gave us what we have; that's the World War II veterans. And the Korean veterans. There has been a lot of mistreatment of our service people in the past, and it continues on. It's a heart-breaker. Watching the new guys come home … my happiness comes from seeing them come home, and being welcomed home the way they are. I hope they don't have to stumble through life as a bunch of bums like we do. That's really a special occasion, to see them come home. We need to make sure we welcome them home.

But those are my hardest memories, our welcome home. And it doesn't matter if you were in Vietnam or not. I am in a motorcycle club and we have veterans that were in Germany and other places, and the welcome home at that time for them was just as hard. They wore uniform too. It's like Bill told me the other night, it doesn't matter if you are in Washington, DC, typing a paper. You are still part of the chain, still part of the military. You served. That is as important as anyone in the military, as far as I am concerned.

My three-wheeler motorcycle club is much like the military; it's a brotherhood. Somebody's got your back all the time. The gathering, the fun; there's a couple of guys that keep you in stitches all the time. It's a riot, it really is. And it's not only our club, we are connected with other Vietnam Veterans Motorcycle Clubs, like the 2nd Brigade here in town. We do things together that are all veteran-oriented. It keeps you very well grounded in what you are, who you are, and what you are capable of doing for your community. That's our big issue.

The P.O.W. issue is our most important issue. The POW/MIA flag is a symbol of concern about US military personnel as 'prisoners of war' or listed as 'missing in action'. When the flag becomes tattered and torn, we let it fly until it gets down to the white part and you can't see the silhouette of the man any more. We can let it go that far; and it's to remind us of the sacrifices—the tattered flag. It's a big reminder. People don't usually replace them before then out of respect for those missing. I've never heard of one going that far, but it is allowed to. On the other hand, we have people running around and replacing the American flag as soon as there's a stain or a beat-up flag, it's replaced. So, the POW flag, we like to see people cling to until it is tattered, it sends a better message.

This is an issue we have fought hard for and will fight hard to maintain. Most people in this country know what it is. There are prisoners of war from every theater of war that never got to come home again. We are never going to see them, but we would like to know about them. So until every one of them come home and until every story is told, that's our big deal. There's a family someplace that is missing somebody.

When they do find some remains of a MIA, it's a pretty heart-rending situation even though it might be many years after. There was a Vietnam veteran's remains that just came home here recently. There were bracelets that were being passed around with names of POWs from this area, and there was a man from here in town that was wearing a bracelet with that veteran's name on it for all these years, and he finally got to take it off, because the vet was home. While it was a neat story, that was a touching moment.

There are a few things more that I want to say. If there are any young people out there, even though we are back in the war time, back in the zone and still losing people, the service and the military is a great place to be. It teaches you integrity; it teaches you everything that you need to deal in life, basically. Depending on whom you are with, or whatever, it teaches you to be positive and not take on negativity of the world that's a raw deal. And to be proud of whom you are, even if you are a sailor and not a Marine. That's a tease as there is a Marine in the room. Being a sailor was always the best, the best there was.

A quick accurate story. We were overseas and Marines walked into a bar that was full of sailors. There was never an equal complement it seemed like of Marines, there was always just a few. I always look at the TV ad, "The few, the proud," and there was always just a few. Naturally, we would always get into disagreements as to who was best and who isn't, and we would have to physically remind the Marines that they are part of the Navy. And then from there it would turn into you know what. But, if the Army should walk through the door, it would be disaster for them because the Marines and the Navy would join forces, as they always do, and the Army was in trouble. I saw that on a few occasions. It's funny now, but it wasn't at the time. When the Air Force came in? I'm not sure I want to comment on what happened when the Air Force came in. I have a couple of Air Force guys in our club and they are great people. I just call them "ticket tinkers" because seems like everywhere I went in the world, especially Guam, was all Air Force guys handing out airplane tickets. No, really, they have their places. I was hooked up in a boat pool in Yokosuka, Japan and we did some training in a place called New Moszul. It was for air rescue. They had some modified boats and we had to teach the Air Force how to run them. Those boats were going to Vietnam to search for and rescue downed pilots. The Air Force guys we worked with were great, they were going to do their duty too, so it was good. Between the services there may have been rivalry—of course no one can do it as good as you are doing it—but there was cooperation and help.

We especially liked to pick on Marines. Or "Leathernecks" as they are called, or "Jarheads." (another tease) I don't know of any other names, but it all ends up that we were and are brothers in arms. We really have to respect that in the end, and I do have quite a few Marine friends. Life goes on.

If I could add one more thing, the world is black and white. It's right or wrong. At least it is to me. It either is or it isn't. And it's the same as our POW fight. It either is or isn't. That's kind of how we go through life here. I've had a good trip and I can't complain. The World War II, the War to End All Wars was the big thing to me. Since then, things have not been the same. The Korean veteran had to go through a lot of the same things that we Vietnam vets did, maybe not as severe, but there was some. And the veterans still go through those things, unrecognized as whatever it might be. But I just tell people: be proud of the American that you are, this is still the greatest country in the world and if you are not willing to make a sacrifice, then don't complain. If you won't make the sacrifice, there is always a brave American that will. Thank God. Thank God.

Martin, John B
Staff Sergeant, United States Army Air Corps
(Prisoner of War – Germany, World War II)
1921 –

Veterans from World War II are becoming lesser and lesser numerous as more and more of these veterans of "The Greatest Generation" pass away and leave this earth.

Sergeant Martin is an excellent example of that generation, a living memorial to those valiant men and women who struggled against the mighty power of the German Empire and its Axis allies. Not even the unexpected and undetected sneak attack by the Japanese that almost destroyed the United States Navy on December 7, 1941 could extinguish the fire of patriotism that flowed through the blood of an entire generation of

American citizens who rose in anger and demonstrated to the world the power, the courage, and the true grit of "The Greatest Generation," as exhibited in one of our elderly citizens, ninety-years-old Staff Sergeant James B. Martin of the United States Army Air Corps. Long may America be blessed with such heroes.

*****

Yes, okay, I am John B Martin, from Preston, Idaho. I have lived here almost all my life except for the time I spent in service, most of which was overseas during the war. Born in 1921, I am now ninety years old. I don't normally talk much about my service time, but I don't mind a bit talking to young people, especially young people who want to learn a little more about the people that served in the military before their time. I served in the Army Air Corps before the United States Air Force was formed. I can't lay claim to being a volunteer to serve my country, actually I didn't decide to join the military; I was drafted—not that I wasn't willing—as were many people at the time. I entered the United States Army in 1943, and served a little over two years, from 1943 to 1945, almost until 1946 and fought in World War II.

I was just part of the whole draft thing, I guess at that time. I wanted to get in to be with all the others but didn't really know exactly what it was all about or how to go about it. I just believed that I should do my part and to go and serve our country, as best I can recall. I was married before I got selected so despite the fact that they tried to keep us pretty busy and despite being surrounded by a lot of other people, I pretty much missed my home life and especially my family. My oldest son was born after I got into service.

I'm proud now that I am the father of three children. Actually none of them have served in the military. They were all too young to be either in World War II or in Korea, and I guess they were too old – or possibly too smart – to get in the military during the Vietnam period.

Like I said, I missed my family and many of the good things that we enjoy here. There was more than one time that I did want to chuck it all and come home, but you couldn't let your buddies down. Even so, there were times, especially the one when I was shot down in Germany, that I felt that it would have been a good time to have been back home in the US. I know I was ready at that moment because that was the worst time, I guess.

I was in a B-17 when we were shot down…that was the plane that won the war… My job was that I was the bottom turret gunner. There weren't many of those who survived being shot down. The bottom turret was a difficult place to be, especially if a plane blew up. There was virtually no chance of survival. I know I was the lucky one. I have never suffered an injury from gunfire during wartime and had precious few injuries of any kind. Thank the Lord. I was at my position in our plane when it suffered a direct hit. The plane blew up almost immediately and there were only three of us who got out alive; three guys out of nine guys.

One problem with being a bottom turret gunner was that you were not able to wear your backpack chute while you were in the turret, there just wasn't enough space. So I was fortunate in that at the time we were hit, I was carrying my chest-pack chute. I had it snapped onto about a four foot cord so that I could just carry it under my arm while I was in the turret. Of course, when we got a direct hit, the plane blew.

Part of my job in the bottom turret was to watch the bombs coming out of the plane, making sure they all fell completely out. We were on a bombing run and I was fortunate in that the turret was pointed straight ahead. You could only get out of the turret when it was pointed either straight down or straight ahead, and it was straight ahead when the plane got hit. I opened the exit door and of course was immediately outside. I had to unhook my oxygen mask and the connections to the heated flight suit that I was wearing. As I got out of the turret, I guess that I caught a snag on something and tore a rip in my suit, but that didn't slow me down. I jumped out and once clear of the plane, put on my chest-pack chute, realizing even as I did that I had put it on upside down. However, the chute would work either way, except that instead of pulling the right hand ripcord, I had to reverse myself and pull the left hand ripcord. No problem, just a minute of fright, then I remembered. The chute opened and several minutes later I landed.

As I looked around, I found myself on the outskirts of Munich. For a couple of days, I never saw a solitary sole. I hid my chute in an old shed that was close to where I landed. I don't know if anybody ever found it. I remembered all of the instructions that we had been given regarding bailing out of a plane, I think, and that helped save me. I also remembered most of the instructions we had been taught about what to do if we were forced to land in enemy country, and getting out of my flight suit was one of those instructions. Then, we were supposed to try to make our way to a neutral country. I spent the first few days traveling in the direction from Munich toward Switzerland. Part of the escape plan was to hide during the day and travel at night.

An interesting – and now, amusing – situation is that in the rural part of Germany, many of the houses are built over a stable where farm animals are kept. So I spent several nights sleeping with the cows. And horses and goats, but mostly there were cows, and of course that part of the cow which smelled the worst. I had traveled about sixty kilometers, or about fifty miles, away from where I had landed, and then I got captured – caught as I was trying to get something to eat.

It was about a week after the plane was destroyed. I was able to get out of Munich without any difficulty and knew that I had to head toward Switzerland, where I would be safe. As I went along, I bummed food from willing people a couple of times. Of course I could not speak German or nothing, but I had to kind of go through the motions and they fed me, a little, and I got by. We did have an escape kit and there were some C-rations in the kit, but not very much. They didn't last very long and frankly were not very good, either. We had been advised not to drink local water so the kit contained pills to put in the water, and stuff like that. There was also a razor in the kit. I kinda holed up in the daytime in the forest—it was heavily wooded country, and I was able to hide during the day and walk at night. I don't know or don't remember exactly how it happened but I ran into an Italian work crew. Even though I don't speak Italian, still I traded my flight suit to one of them for some civilian suit, and a little hat with a feather in it. I got by pretty good.

I came to this little town, and it was very dark at night. There was a building or a house that had lights on and I could see through the window. I saw a lunch bucket in there and I said, "I'm going to get it, I'm going to get something to eat here." I went to get it and a guy got me. Captured in the act.

Of course, they searched me about every five minutes, and that went on for about a couple of days. Then I got shipped back to Munich. I was held in a camp near the airport close to the town of Munich. It was kind of strange because the Germans would land their planes at the airport and then as soon as they got a bomb alert warning they would fly off and try to fight our boys, but not strongly because it was getting near the end of the war, and I think they were trying to give up. They would land and almost right away then there would be a bomb alert, and then off they would go. That happened pretty much all the time. The British would bomb at night and we would bomb them during the day.

Actually, as a prisoner, the Germans didn't treat me too badly, certainly not as badly as they could have. Of course, we didn't get much to eat. After all, they could hardly feed their own people, much less the enemy. We would just get soup ... almost as much water as soup. No meat or anything like that, and very few vegetables.

There was quite a mixture of nationalities in the group where I was located. I was sent to Wesler, I believe it was. It was where they interrogated the airmen and pilots. The interrogation took place in a place just about the size of a small card table. I was at that location for about a week, and then they moved us to ... actually, they put us into boxcars. There were about a hundred prisoners in each boxcar, so there wasn't just a lot of space to be moving around in there. Anyway, we were shipped to Nuremburg. There were about, oh, ten thousand prisoners there; all mixtures. With that many prisoners, you can imagine that we didn't have anything to eat, to amount to anything. So that was kind of a bad deal. But it was better than being dead. We were in that boxcar for a week or better, no food or anything. Guys got pretty hungry.

We got strafed twice by our own planes while we were at a railroad station. Then, on another time, they had marched us out of Nuremburg to Lewisburg, a little way outside of Munich. We got strafed by our own planes again. There were six P-47's in the attack flight, I think. The first one came down and strafed us. There was an old kind of a soldier in the back of our group and he had a partial American flag. He pulled out this flag and the pilots could see it and the other five didn't fire on us. But then, every day after that a plane would come over and waggle its wings, and all. Frankly, we thought we would be quickly rescued. Didn't happen.

Altogether, I spent about a month in Nuremburg, I guess, and that's when they marched us down to Lewisburg, toward Munich a ways. There's where I was when we got liberated. When I saw the American tanks and soldiers; that was a good feeling. Yeah.

Before we were shot down, there had been other times when we took hits. On a previous flight, my co-pilot got killed on what was our tenth mission. My waist gunner got wounded, and I froze my hands. That was our shortest mission ... and our worst, except the time we were shot down. The flight was along the coast where the fighter bases were. That was the only time we got hit by fighters, and the co-pilot took a 20-mm right in his chest. He was a large guy and we had difficulty getting him out of the plane seat, but finally made it. We also got two engines shot out on that deal. Our oxygen system was shot out and we had to drop down to a lower level. We were alone and that's usually when the fighters would hit, when there was a lone plane almost defenseless. Fighters never hit our flight very often, probably because of all the guns in a flight. At the end of the flight when we landed, we had had two or three hundred holes in our plane.

Actually, we got some flack on virtually every mission, a little bit, but it wasn't too bad. But then on the 17th ... that wasn't good.

I flew spare missions after that... by that I mean that they broke up our crew. That hurt me kind of bad, after all, I had gone through school with all those guys and all.

I flew four missions as a spare and then I was assigned to this other crew. They hadn't flown any missions prior to that, and I hardly knew them. I wasn't with them at the time they got shot down while they were on their third mission. They didn't even live in the same barracks that I did. I was only slightly acquainted with any of them, but then later I met up with the engineer of the crew when we got down to the same prison camp. He told me that he thought that the crew's tail-gunner got blown out when the plane blew up. He told me that the pilot had gotten out safely, but decided that he needed to fight those Germans. The pilot took out his .45 caliber pistol and the Germans shot him.

The leaders always told us at that time not to even take our pistols with us, although most of us all carried our .45's with us almost all the time. They also ordered us to avoid contact with the enemy if at all possible, presuming that we would be able to survive longer if we didn't meet the enemy at all. Of course, those prison camps weren't too great. I only had one shower all the time that I was there, just a little more than two months. You can guess how we all smelled.

I'm just lucky to be here now; that was quite a deal and I'm glad it's over, except in my memory. That won't ever be over.

But it's little enough to give for my country.

Moszer, James P.
Lieutenant Colonel, United States Army
1963 -

Lt. Col. James P. Moszer and his sister, Lt. Col. Jan Carter, deployed to Iraq with the North Dakota National Guard Engineer Brigade, 34th Infantry Division, in April, 2007. Moszer was the officer in charge of the Baghdad Area Office responsible for more than one hundred and fifty projects valued at well over six hundred million dollars. He worked with seven brigade combat teams and fifty-three battalions improving essential services to residents throughout the capital.

Moszer is proud of his older sister. He points out she enlisted in the National Guard in 1975 and received her commission six years later. That was her second deployment to a war zone. Activated for Operation Desert Shield/Storm in 1991 as an operations officer, she earned a Bronze Star as well as a field grade promotion. She later became North Dakota's first female battalion commander.

Moszer knows construction. He worked as a brick mason, with concrete and structural steel for over a decade. He then made a career change and for a period of time worked for the North Dakota Association of Counties in their Homeland Security Training and Exercise Program. He was responsible for training emergency responders in western North Dakota including law enforcement, ambulance squads, and firefighters.

Like his sister, Lt. Col. Jan Carter, James A. Moszer was wounded in combat in Iraq and now resides with his wife and family in Bismarck, North Dakota.

*****

Moszer, James P., Bismarck, North Dakota, Lieutenant Colonel, United States Army, Soon to be retired. November 19th, 1963. Three days before President John Fitzgerald Kennedy was assassinated in Dallas, Texas, a day that no American will ever forget. Like my wife tells me, all the good-looking guys were born in November. I was actually born and raised in Bismarck and I'm most pleased to still call it home. I am also a proud member of the North Dakota National Guard and have served in that organization since 1980. I have to say up front that while I have agreed to talk about my military history, I may wiggle around a little bit as my A.D.D. takes over. While most people around here are familiar with my story, I understand that relating my experiences may be of help to veterans in other parts of the nation.

I'm not certain that I ever considered any career other than the Armed Forces as my entire family was military orientated. My brother was a full-time technician for the North Dakota National Guard for many, many years and retired as a Lieutenant Colonel after thirty-six years of service. My sister – who just recently retired and was with me in Iraq at the same time that I was there and who was injured in Iraq at the same time, she was ... she retired as a Lieutenant Colonel after thirty-five years of service. My sister's husband, who has now been deceased for about six years, was a full colonel in the North Dakota National Guard. So I think my path was destined to go there. Not only do I serve, although the three of them are retired and I'm soon to retire, I have a nephew who is an aviator mechanic crew chief in the 112th Aviation in Bismarck, here. He has been working flood duties a lot lately, and is just back from Iraq. My niece is actually the executive officer for the command staff of the North Dakota National Guard. She is out on maternity leave at the moment. She is a captain. Her husband is a captain who works full time for the National Guard over at the United States Property and Fiscal office, so it's sort of a family deal going on here in North Dakota and the National Guard and it is just part of our lives, my life, and my make-up.

People often ask me why is it that I do the National Guard and some of the other things that I do such as public service. When I was very young, my father was what they called during World War II, a '4-F', which meant that physically he wasn't able to serve in the military, but he always thought that community service was a great thing for everybody. He thought the guard was a way to give back to the community, and that's the way the whole thing started.

My sister lives in Glendive, Montana, and in fact is moving back to Bismarck. Her name is Jan Carter. She had served in the Desert Storm, and she has been in two combat zones, just as I have. Ironically, I was wounded in October, 2007 and Jan was injured in the same combat zone at some time, I believe, in January '08, roughly three months after I was hurt. She remained in theater for a while longer and then when she came out, they did the fixing up of her affairs and all that. They got her all fixed up and ready to retire.

A frequent question from people who know me is the question of how long I will continue to serve. About that, I'm not at all sure. I joined in November, 1980—November 22, 1980—and that will be thirty-one years of service in November, 2011. As to when I retire, it just depends on when the Army gets me back to full medical benefit, as they call it; then the next path for me is to retire out, because it's been a long, long haul. I've always been in the National Guard. I have spent thirty-one years in the National Guard but for the equivalent retirement pay, they will compute it at fifteen and one-half years of active duty. Even though we are supposedly "part-timers," that's how much equivalent active-duty time I've accumulated over the thirty-one years.

I was on Stabilization Forces 14 in Bosnia in 2003 to 2004, which was the NATO operation over there. And I was Operation Iraqi Freedom, starting in 2007 until my injury in October, 2007. If I needed any inspiration or motivation to continue my career in the Armed Forces after what I saw in Bosnia, that motivation to continue fighting came from my sense of loyalty to my brother soldiers. I had just returned from Bosnia—in fact, when I initially went to Bosnia was when they were first lighting up units for OIF-1 to go into Iraq—and when I returned stateside, I was on my 'dwell' time. My unit, the Engineer Brigade of the 34th Infantry Division, was put on alert for mobilization, and my best friend was the commander of the unit. The unit was heavily laden with officers and there were folks that weren't available to deploy at that time so he ... he really didn't ask me to volunteer, but I volunteered anyway to go over there because most of the guys I deployed with have been lifelong partners and peers throughout all our military careers, from enlisted through the whole ranks of the officership. My friend, by the way, ended up becoming the Director of the Joint Staff and has just recently retired. So, it was more ... I guess it was a ... a feeling of guilt, as my wife puts it, that all my friends were going to Iraq and how would I feel staying back, knowing those guys were going over there without me. That was one of the driving forces for me to say, "You know what, it's my time to suck it up again." And I had only been home for maybe eighteen months when we started training to go over there. So, that was the real impetus of me going; all my brothers were leaving and they were leaving me behind. I guess it's like if you have siblings and they are going to the Dairy Queen to get a cone and you get stuck with the stick at the end. So, that's really why I volunteered to go back into combat. There's a feeling of comradeship and the feeling of being brothers with those guys, knowing how to work with one another, and the knowledge that they have your back just as you have their back. I just had to go.

When asked what I missed most while serving overseas or even just away from home, the answer is simple: my wife. The bottom line up front is that I missed my wife immensely, and in fact, we were pretty lucky at the base we were on, we had pretty much instant communication, voice over internet, it was called Skype, and I could call her every day. That worked out in that it was categorized as a local call. There were other troops that didn't get that opportunity. In fact, on the day that I was wounded, I had called her. Sometimes I would tell her, "Hey, I'm not going to call you for a couple of days," and she knew that meant that I was outside the wire or at a different post. I called her about ten o'clock in the morning, North Dakota time, which was about five o'clock p.m. Iraqi time. That afternoon, I had just gotten back inside the wire and called her and told her that everything was good to go, and about five hours later she got the call that I was in I.C.U. in Bagdad. That was an interesting time. Yep, missed her tremendously. The other things I missed were my two girls. We have no children but Wendy and Lexus, our dogs—they are family—missed them immensely as well.

There are times when I'm asked by someone if I ever thought or if I ever felt like quitting, like just packing it in, I can't give just a simple yes or no answer, that doesn't tell the whole story. Actually, it's sort of difficult for me to explain it all. Engineers on the battlefield only do two things: we build it or we blow it up. I was in charge of the reconstruction of Baghdad for the Army Corps of Engineers, so all the projects in Baghdad came under my purview. There was about 1.4 billion dollars of construction going on at any one time. During 2007, we were one of the "surge" units, so I got a little crazy. Did I ever want to give up? I think that when anyone gets to know North Dakotans as they travel this great state will find out that we have a 'never give up' attitude.

Folks over there had been living without electricity, potable water, or running sewer system in a city that you would think of as a major metropolis for ten or fifteen years before this war started. So getting those essential services available to the citizens of Iraq was really an important mission. There were those days when you bang your head against the wall and say, "God bless America, what am I doing?" For an example, we would get a call where we were putting in a water line or a sewer line or something like that. And the trench was opened up and left open overnight. And sure enough, one of our units would be going by and some of the insurgents would have placed an IED in our trench, and you feel a little guilt as you thought, "Did I hurt one of our guys or one of the coalition troops?" So those days became very tough, but still ... We were known over there as ... Remember 'Larry the Cable Guy'? We were known throughout the Iraq as the ... "Git 'er done boys," because if there was something that needed to be done, engineering wise, they would always come to the North Dakotans. This patch that I am wearing is representative of the many units that went before us and they knew the patch. And we were just very well known.

Our unit, once we got into country, was separated into nineteen different locations throughout the whole country, in charge of engineering and reconstruction for ... not only did I have Baghdad, but I had Iraq, as well. My sister was down in Tallil; we had folks in Basra, all the way down to the south; Umm Qsar, all the way north to Tikrit, Arbil, Monsul; and we were over in the Marine sector in Fallujah and in Armadi as well as Blue Diamond. It was really cool, so we got to do all sorts of engineering but it was all rebuilding Iraq. So, when I'm asked, 'Did I want to go home'? Sure. I missed my family ... In fact, I was going to come home on leave, but the date was two weeks after my incident occurred. So, come home, yes ... but give up? No. That's not in the vernacular of the North Dakotans to do that. We just took care of it. And that's the story there.

The manner in which I was wounded is a long involved story, but the short and sweet of it is that on October 10, 2007, we were having a Change of Command ceremony between General Mike Wallace and General Jeff Dorko. That day I had been over see some of my brothers who lived in the International Zone, Col. Dale Adams, Co. Lanny Rump, Col. Mike Averly; all close friends and guys that were also well-known to my wife. The last I said was that "I love you guys and I'll see you tomorrow," because I had to go back to the I.Z. the next day for a meeting. I lived over in Camp Victory. That evening, I was headed to another meeting and all of a sudden we had sixteen .107 millimeter Katyusha rockets—Iranian made—rain in on us in a very densely populated area. The rockets wounded forty and killed two. That was in just one incident. The majority of my injuries were that I ended up with a traumatic brain injury with sheer lesions. To describe sheer lesions, it's as if you should take a straw and push it from the top of my brain all the way through to the spine, where the brain tissue actually separates. That was one of the injuries, but I also suffered trauma to my left shoulder, my hearing as well as my left eye and my left knee. The doctors and the medical personnel tended to believe that my injuries were a cumulative effect as I had been in two separate IED incidents before that. So, I had been in concussive events prior to that but this was the main one that finally took me out.

One thing that I did remember from the event was—I became friends with a girl from Texas—I didn't remember the event or anything until I had been home with my wife for some sixty to ninety days, not remembering anybody—but while I was in the hospital, I kept drawing pictures of that girl's ring finger, her wedding ring. I remembered that ring somehow. I don't know exactly why, but ... she ended up losing her leg just below the knee and I was dragging her out, trying to get her into the bunker. I didn't know I was doing it, they just call it the 'soldier's reflex' or a 'training reflex'. But

I can still sketch her wedding ring even now, probably because that was the hand by which I was dragging her. I can draw her wedding ring perfectly. I wouldn't say that I saved her life, but the soldier's instinct and the training ... I don't remember anything else because of the impact, but from what they were thinking and from some of the witness reports that I have – of course, I was injured, but there are instances when soldiers are doing things they don't why or even remember, just like Marines or soldiers or airmen. I must have instinctively known I was in trouble after I woke up from the blast, and must have just instinctively grabbed that girl's left hand and started dragging her. We have become pretty good friends since then. She doing great, got a couple of kids, and we still talk. It was just one of those automatic, instinctive events that occur. It's just another of those side war stories. To me, the interesting part is that I can still draw her ring; it's got a pattern, like a full gold ring with a marquis diamond and two little diamonds on the side. That's all I remember out of that whole event as it happened.

My shoulder injury was truly aggravated because of what they figured was the direction of the impact. When a mortar round comes in and explodes, the kill pattern goes out in a 360 degree spread. When a rocket explodes, the kill pattern is much less, around 37 to 45 degrees spread of the shrapnel. They figure that the rocket that injured me hit some five to seven meters away from me, but they weren't sure if it hit in front of me or behind me. I had no shrapnel injury, only concussion, but the girl that was running beside me was in the fan; either one of them, but we're not sure. Iranian-made rockets, dangerous, but the Man upstairs was watching out for me. They opine that when I was knocked unconscious I fell forward and that my body twisted over my shoulder. And my ACU's (Army Combat Uniform) were just a wreck. Although that's the way it happened, I remembered almost nothing. At the time.

But I do now.

It was just outside the chow hall where General Patraeus was eating. So they figure the enemy was targeting that hall, because they knew he was in there for sure. But we did get them, got all seven of the gunners through our return battery fire. Redemption.

The effects caused by brain injuries vary, of course. It depends on where in the brain the injury occurs. Mine was in the right frontal parietal lobe, I think they call it. Anyway, I could not write at all, actually had to relearn how to write, had to relearn how to speak, relearn everything because my cognizance skill and my short-term memory were pretty much all erased. So, some of my memories of Iraq, I have to look at a picture to realize what it was. I was in cognitive therapy for over two years. It takes a long time to get back. And my wife still has to help with some daily activities. For example, I had to relearn how to drive. Now some people take that as ... I had to relearn how to ride a bike, my sense of balance was all horsed up.

So that has been very frustrating because being an officer and a college grad and all of the professional development we go through, and then all of a sudden, we just sort of lose it. It's very, very tough to recover. But I think that I have done fairly well. A lot of folks don't know or even realize that I struggle. I ended up with aphasia. It's where everything can be mirror images or it flips. Most people don't know what that is, so I'll give relate an example. The easiest way I can explain it is to take the word 'did'. Under aphasia, it can be 'did', it can be 'bib', it can be that I'll take a '9' or a 'b' and turn it into a 'd', so I usually see stuff in mirror images. It can be '7' and 'L', it can be '6' and '9', so a 'd' or a 'b' can be a six or a nine, so when I read something, I have to very much concentrate on what is happening. Another example—and the brain is fairly wild—I can probably write a name or a word backwards as easily as forward. It really happens mostly when I get tired. I have a few neurological deficits that will never come back, but we work through them. You've got to have that positive attitude. I've always been that kind of person ... my wife calls me 'the eternal optimist'. I keep telling her that the bad side of the story could have been a hell of worse than we have it now. I try to give her funny examples. Cherie knows Bismarck well. When I'm supposed to take my truck to the Chevrolet place for an oil change, I may end up on the other side of Bismarck, over at the Cracker Barrel restaurant. So, I have to call my wife and ask her, 'How in the ... why am I sitting here in the Cracker Barrel, because I'm not hungry. I'm just sitting here." That is just one of the things we have learned to overcome. I always carry a g.p.s. or a Tom-Tom with me. So, she's like, "Don't you know Bismarck?" And I respond, "Not quite." But we are okay. There are just things like that. I will turn on the left blinker to turn right. With aphasia, sometimes I don't know if I'm going fifty miles per hour or five miles per hour. It's ... It's wild. But it's mostly just when I get really tired. Yep, traumatic brain injury is a huge problem to the guys over there.

Quite a few people ask me to speak at events and talk to them about brain injuries and the effects. Like right now, my left eye is twitching for some unknown reason. But, I think I go back to what probably fazed me in this whole deal of my brain injury is that I had a great ... The Army has given me A-1 medical support. I mean there are no questions asked, regarding their wounded. Yes, there some that may fall through the cracks. You hear the horror stories about the Veterans Administration or you hear about down at the Brooks Army Medical Center about guys committing suicide and stuff like that, but they are few. I am certain the thing that helped me out the most was my wife and my family.

An example was when I was stuck in Fort Carson and they sent me home on convalescence leave. My wife got home, got me settled in and I had some other serious issues as well. I was anemic and I had MRSA infections in my legs, and so my legs were cut open. Anyway, I was just a mess. She left, she had to go to work and she said, "You know what? You're going to be home by yourself for a day, so here's the four tasks I want done." I don't remember any of them too well but she said she looked up through the window in our house and I had a cup of coffee in my hand, looking out the window, probably watching her disappear. And when she came back from work nine hours later and I was still standing there in the front of the window with a cup of coffee in my hand, just standing around. It's likely that I had put the coffee cup down, but I don't know that.

I was just standing there and she came in and said, "This ain't happening. You're going to get off your dead ass and you are going to start getting better. And, we are going to work on this together. Like I said, my whole family has been a very integral part in it, but, in reality I think with brain injury is vital to get the brain stimulated again and get it awakened and get it working. Get active, physically as well. I still have problems around town when people come up and say "Hi" and I just look at them and I'm going, "God, do I know you?"

I think when it's coupled with the P.T.S.D. I have, it's an ugly deal. And I have to overcome both of them. I think it comes down to a little maturity level, but my wife just wouldn't give up on me. She kept saying, "You're getting better. I don't know how you are going to do it, but you are not sitting on your ass in this house feeling sorry for yourself."

She's been around twenty-five years, so she knows this Army gig, watching me get on a plane and then watching me come home, and she was just ... enough is enough, so she pushes me very hard. The saying is that behind every good man is a good woman ... or two. Better take that off the record ... no, I was just kidding, although I believe that I still have my sense of humor. Without her, I couldn't have made it.

I went into so much detail about my injuries and the effect not because I'm looking for sympathy, rather because I sincerely believe it may help others out there that are much in the same situation. Maybe they will think or say, "Maybe I'm not so bad off, look at what Moszer did with his life." In truth, you just gotta go. You gotta go. And your family must support you.

Continuing along the way that my injuries have affected my life here at home and in the community, there are four or five points that I could make, or I'll do a Colonel Robinson with three points. First off, the North Dakota National Guard is so small that we pretty much know each other. It is like one large family and it starts right at the top with General Sprynczynatyk. He is a ... I don't to use the words death and taxes, but I will ... he cares for his soldiers. He truly does. He wants to know what happens, when it happens; not only just when we are in combat zones, but even on flood duties and all the other things that the Guard is involved with. In the Predator mission and just ... all the way down the leadership, everybody just truly cares. The General also cares about our families, which is ingrained throughout the entire leadership. You gotta care for your families; if your families are hurting the soldiers or airmen can't heal, or they can't move on. He's a huge proponent of that. And I think the last thing is he's ... the employers. Big employers' support for the Guard and Reserve, big program, and General Sprynczynatyk is continuously out there out there pushing that along with General Dorman. So that brings that family along.

Community wise, I don't want to tell this story in the wrong way, but when you first get home and people find out that you are injured in combat, it's like ... well, my niece. Nobody would talk to her. It's like, "Well, what do we say to her?"

And then the rumors started that I had lost my eye and I had lost an arm, and all this stuff. Anyway, when you get back and you go through the demobilization process ... I'm still on active duty in the medical program ... but the soldier or the trooper—I like to use the word trooper as it covers everybody—I was literally overwhelmed with support. It got to the point that I had people calling from Minneapolis, checking from Fort Snelling because I had a brain injury. And the County Social Services people, and ... it's all great. It's really just all great. But you really don't have time for it because my wife's idea and my mind set was, "he needs to heal and you need to leave him alone, let him recover."

One great organization that helped me out was "Rivers of Recovery" out of Utah. I actually went on a fly-fishing trip with those guys and they really helped out, but North Dakotans, once again, will—someone is going to hand you a Kougan. A Kougan is a local pie, a custard pie. But people that I didn't even know would bring over meals, people that I had never met would stop by the house and they would bring dinners or gift certificates to Blockbusters, Applebee's, Ground Round, and on and on. They would just give stuff because I was injured. And of course that ruined my figure, I probably have 'abs of pudding' now. It's just that we're like a huge family.

I don't think I ever went to closure until my unit came home, because all my brothers were still overseas in the fight. It was difficult for me to adjust to home life and accept all that gratitude while they were still over there. I don't know if they call it "North Dakota Nice," but I can even go to Fargo yet, and the people there will look at me or look at my uniform and go, "Oh, you're the guy that was hurt." Yep. And they remember. Great community support; absolutely the best. North Dakota is awesome, and as patriotic as hell. We—North Dakota—have the highest rate of enlistment in the military in the entire nation per capita other than the Virgin Islands and Guam. And the lowest attrition rate in the nation, by a huge margin.

It's almost like you can walk down the street and someone will say, "My second cousin is in the Guard, do you know him?" It's likely that the cousin is in a Guard unit that I haven't seen in twenty-five years. But everybody knows everybody and they take a great amount of pride in their soldiers and airmen and troopers around here. We even have a Marine Reserve detachment in North Dakota. Actually, most of us—North Dakota, South Dakota, Minnesota and Montana—we are very tight-knit people. We are the kind of people that built the nation.

Often asked if despite all my difficulties if I am satisfied with my decision to join the military, I always vigorously respond, "ABSOLUTELY!" No second thoughts; none at all. And I've been asked several times if I would go back again. In a heartbeat. And I'm sure most other veterans feel the same. Actually, I would like to go back to Iraq just to see what the little kids think now. It was like ... I heard a story from an old guy ... don't guess I should call him old, he's a Lieutenant General now ... about Bosnia. He was with the forces that first entered Bosnia. He was on the first train. Then he had the occasion to go back some of eight or nine years later and he got to meet some of the people who had been kids when they put up bridges and put electricity into a lot of the homes. He said that experience was ever so gratifying. I've often wondered what it is going to happen ten years from the date I left Iraq. If I could go back and meet those little kids for whom we built schools and all that and see what they have grown up to be. I tell people that 99.9 percent – 99.99 percent of the Iraqi people that I dealt with just wanted the same things we have. They wanted clean water, electricity, just kids to go to school and have a safe and secure environment for their family to grow up in. They wanted to go to market and watch a little T.V. and go on vacation. That's all they wanted. Then you have the .01 percent insurgency out there that just led by fear. Still, it was great interacting with the Iraqi people and I'd go back in a heartbeat. Maybe someday I will get the opportunity. There is a program out there, I believe it is 'Return the Warrior' or something like that, ran by the Department of Defense that takes us back in to sort of put closure on our area.

We pledged to the Constitution of the United States and this grateful nation to do probably some of the biggest acts of selfless service that could be asked of a human being. As I have said, my parents were big into community service and I didn't join the Guard for the college benefits, I joined the Guard to be a part of something bigger than I. It's always about the team.

There are tons of well-meaning programs out there that are doing great things to help combat wounded veterans and their family. Rivers of Recovery out of Utah, the Purple Heart Society of America, Remember the Wounded Ride, Operation Military Embrace to name a few. I try to be active in as many things as I can. There are traumatic brain injury groups I speak to, Post Trauma Stress Distress groups I speak to, but some of those organizations, I think, don't have the most honorable intentions. So, I'm very careful of what I get involved with, trying to understand what they are doing and what their angle is. Even so, I believe most of those organizations are trying to do the right thing. A lot of people want to help and sometimes it can be overwhelming for the troop, but overall, I can't say that I've had a bad experience. Not one. I always say—and I don't mean this talking as an Army guy—but some Americans are notorious for short memories. I guess I can leave it at that. But, I'll give an example. The average guy physically could not tell that I was injured in combat. The average person physically could not tell that Lt. Col. Steve Hernon was injured in combat. Because I am not missing an arm nor did I didn't lose a leg. My face is not scarred and disfigured. But some of those folks are visibly injured ... I don't know ... I'm injured badly, but my most of injuries are internal and it's very hard for people to comprehend that, they just look at you and think, "Well, you're not missing anything, so ..."

But, the sacrifice is the same. There are many of those groups that seem to want wounded soldiers to almost feel like we owe them, to speak to their group, and it's like I told General Sprynczynatyk a long time ago, "I'm not going to be the Purple Heart Poster Child for the North Dakota National Guard." And most of the Dakotans feel the same way, we don't want to be put out into the spotlight, we just went over and did our job. Now, my job is right here; it's healing and move on to the next event.

There are organizations out there that are doing a lot of stuff with our combat-wounded veterans and they are showing only the veterans that are missing body parts; an arm or a leg. That is fluff. Those organizations are pulling on the heartstrings of the American public, and the people who see that go, "Oh. Oh. That's not good." And they put people in commercials that they really shouldn't. They are just trying to use the veterans.

I wear a bracelet—a battle bracelet, or a memorial bracelet that was given to me after my gunner was killed. The other day, I found out you can go on Facebook and you can get, I don't know, forty thousand different colors now, and it supposedly goes to support our troops. And you go on the back side of their website and you figure out that they are just a 'for profit' company. And they don't give a damn ... they haven't given a dime. How in the hell do they get off selling a battle bracelet or a remembrance bracelet – I believe they call it a 'survival bracelet – and they still don't give a damn. As for my bracelet, the only time I have taken it off is for the four surgeries on my left arm. This one came from my gunner when he got killed. That's the kind of stuff that really tees me off. We are losing the meaning of these bracelets. They are using some dude over in Iraq for their own purposes.

When people see me in uniform, they often ask me "gotcha" questions. One of them is, *"how do I feel about gays in the military?"* Well, the Department of Defense is going to tell me how I'm going proceed in this next venture with that. *"Well, how do you feel about the anti-war protesters?"* I always answer over and over again, "Well, I'm the guy that's fighting so they have the freedom to protest." Now, as long as it's not personally attacking me, and it's not sordid and sick behavior like protesting at a dead trooper's funeral—which is about as sick as a thing you can do—but he still fought and I fought and hundreds of thousands of troopers are still fighting for those individuals to have the ability to carry out such nonsense. And, that is my answer to them.

When I was in Iraq, a true example—I suppose that I really shouldn't use his name but, shit, he can sue me—Richard Ingle, NBC News. We were not allowed to talk to him. Or to Katie Couric, either. Now, as the officer in charge of the reconstruction of Baghdad, who do you think he wanted to talk to all the time? We had many requests to talk with Richard Ingle, but what really hacked me was that there were certain areas of Baghdad during the surge where you didn't go in unless you were in an Abrams tank or a Bradley. I didn't have military guys escorting me; I had Blackwater-type guys. Going into those hard combat areas, I had to ride with military guys. We came in off patrol and we pulled into the IZ or the Green Zone. And it just really irked my banana, because there was Richard Ingle standing there with his back to a big puff of black smoke, and all his battle rattle, in a secure area, doing a camera shot about a car bomb with his back to the smoke. He wasn't even out of the Green Zone. He was just standing there giving a false-ass report. And I was just like, "Dude, I'm not going to be a part of that kind of crazy crap. If you want to see that, go outside the Green Zone ..."

And he did, he began to go outside, but if you watched his continued reporting of the war, it became very, very skewed. At the time in Iraq, all we received were the three channels on AFN and we never got to see those reports. My wife would call, or I would call her and she would be like, "Jesus, Moszer, Richard Ingle sounds like the whole city of Baghdad is rubble." I'd say, "No, that's not true, dear. There are pockets of ugliness, but ..."

I don't care if he sues me, he can try; I'll take my chances in an American court. Anyway, I've read his book, and it pisses me off. I didn't do reports with him. And we avoided Katie Couric like the plague because of her taunting questions.

Looking back, I've already bragged about my wife, Leslie is her name, although it's impossible to brag too much about how she put me back together and helped my recovery. She has just been stalwart through the whole ordeal. And there was General Sprynczynatyk, who was an inspiration. He does things for his wounded guys in North Dakota that no other state does. He has flown to Sioux Falls, he has flown to Walter Reed, and he tracks all his wounded guys. There's a weekly report that goes to the General, telling him where his wounded guys are, telling him what they are doing. He flew to Sioux Falls once a quarter to see us all together. He has all the wounded service members in North Dakota get together. He wants to make sure that we are all properly taken care of and that we are not forgotten about. And he is adamant about that. If you go and ask General Sprynczynatyk right now how many wounded guys—or gals, because we had some female wounded—he could tell you immediately. He has it right on top of his bean. He certainly was instrumental. Then there was Colonel Dale Adams, Retired. My best friend and he checks on me every day. "What are you doing right now?" "Well, I'm fishing." "Oh, you can't be doing that."

There is also Mike Averly, upstairs and Mike Wallanaugh.

Wal takes great care of me. A true friend, he was over in Iraq when I got hurt, so he went through the whole thing, he's been there since day one. They take care of me. And the whole Guard family. The North Dakota National Guard is just a special breed of characters. I am very proud to say that. People say, "You must be in the Army." I am, the North Dakota National Guard. I wear the uniform very proudly.

As I come to end of this rambling recital, I would like to say that the military teaches us three unalterable pillars to success. We have to be physically, mentally, and spiritually able to handle anything that comes forth. We do and see things that most people will never experience in their lives, especially if they are lucky. I go back to my uncle, a World War II guy, 164th Infantry, saved the Marines asses on Guatemala Canal, by the way. That's an aside to a Marine friend. I've heard that there's a great book out about the 164th, first Army unit in direct combat operations in the Pacific theater. My uncle was part of that. Company A, 164th Infantry, and sixty-five years later we got to give him his awards that he earned in World War II. That was really an interesting event. I think of the veterans that have gone before me and I'm grateful because they set the path to success. And lessons learned from the past always seemingly continue to come up. Counter-insurgency operations weren't new; they were changed by General Patraeus and now we have a different way of dealing with counter-insurgency from lessons we learned in Vietnam and from lessons when we were in Korea, lessons learned from World War II. It's hats off to those who have gone before us; it's also off to those who paid the ultimate sacrifice for the freedom so that we can do the things that we do today. They were the forefathers and the people we really need to remember. My family is utmost important. Anybody can understand the military link that I have to them, and we are all damn proud to serve and to have served. And I'm appreciative to those out there for keeping us in the forefront. Once again I go back to the collective memories of this country, and sometimes they forget. And if it wasn't for the P.O.W-M.I.A. cause and things like that, man ... I started in this post-Vietnam time, in 1980. I remember the long hair and the Guard wasn't anything more than a beer-drinking bunch of bums. My short-term memory may not be shit, but I sure remember that.

What we have transformed into is this sweet, modern force that can be called upon and the unique advantage of being in the Guard and having a State and Federal mission where I can help my neighbors in Minot, or down on Fox Island, in Bismarck or in Stafford. Those folks need to be thanked and then the current list of leaders and mentors that I have in the Guard right now, because they ... I've done my watch and now they feel it's their turn to watch over me to make sure that when I transition out of this military life and hang up my boots for the last time hopefully in the near future. I've been begging to get out but the Army doesn't want to release me yet, but that's okay, Uncle Sam ain't released me yet.

Hopefully, I can still have an input into the younger generation that is coming up and tell them, *just do your job, do it right and just carry on the proud tradition of the North Dakota National Guard.* Not everybody knows it, but there's only one state that has more Medal of Honor winners than North Dakota, and that is New York. Of course, winning the Medal of Honor is not always probably the best thing in the world, because it is usually posthumous, but we have a very, very proud lineage in this state and it is my honor and privilege to serve in the North Dakota National Guard for the people of this state and this nation. It's been a hell of a great ride, and I'm still kicking that horse. I did love it. I do love it. I will continue to love it.

Nobody would ever guess what I did in my former life. I was an auctioneer. Really, it's true. And I still can do it. I even auction as I ride down the road. That's how I remember numbers. I had to work hard at it after the wounds, but hard work pays off. It's amazing what a brain can do ... with a lot of hard work.

Watching fireworks on the Fourth of July is fun for a lot of people, but for the most part, not the wounded veteran, especially a brain-damaged combat veteran with P.T.S.D. It all comes back; the nightmares and all those memories.

Finally, it's just my opinion but I think that real recovery comes a lot from maturity. From where I sit, a lot of young folks are struggling. They are struggling with money. They're struggling with ... they want to do the extreme sports. And they can't get enough. I think that a lot of the recovery from my injury was because of my maturity. I'm an older than average guy; in the military, I'm a combat engineer. I am the guy with a brain injury that went and got a Masters degree in business. And that was an absolutely torturous event: to re-learn accounting. But, I think it's maturity, at least the greatest portion. Sammy Coleburg, from Fargo was one of the first guys to get injured, lost his leg in O.I.F., a mature young man who went on to do wonderful things, and you couldn't even tell that Sam was even hurt. Some of the young guys that have been hurt, they are struggling. Money and families and divorces; I think it's maturity. Of course, it's tough. It's craziness.

I don't want to be the sad story; I'm the up-beat guy. Never in my life would I have thought I was going to run for political office. Never—not no way. I ran for County Commissioner, last time. Yeah, I got beat out by a few votes. Not many, but ... I'm going to run again. People ask me why I want to be an elected official. It's because during trying times, the leaders go to the top, and there are trying times in Burley County right now. There are trying times in Minot. There are trying times at the federal level, but guess what? One of these days, I'm going to retire and I'm going to need something to do. People know I have a brain injury and go like, "why would we have a brain-injured county commissioner." I joke about it and say, "Just look at what you are dealing with now." I don't speak ill of any elected official, but I think it would be fun. And I would certainly have time on my hands. Of course, at the live official meetings, we would have to have the seven-second delay on, because I'd be like, "What? What was that? What did you say?"

During the campaign, we had these open forums where any candidate can speak. This guy was running for re-election and he was the head of the County Commission. He was really after me. The question was asked, "Are you fiscally responsible?" He responded, "Yes, I've asked the head of each of my departments this last year to trim five percent out of their budget.

So the next turn comes to me, and being a little bit of a smart-ass as I usually am, "I would like to sorta debunk some *facts* here concerning the commissioner's track record on cutting the budget and being fiscally responsible, because the County Commission just approved the preliminary budget and there was no five percent cut; instead there was a six percent raise. And what we need to understand is that is an eleven percent swing."

Of course, he was like, "Oh, you just don't understand the way budgeting works."

So, I said, "I understand this. If I have a dollar and I take ten cents away, then I've only got ninety cents. And it doesn't matter if you have forty-six million dollars and you take five percent away, that's still 2.3 million dollars. Now you start adding that up and that is a five million dollar swing in our small little budget for our county. Sooner or later you're talking about lots of money."

"Well, ... er ... we covered workman's compensation insurance this month ... blah blah blah."

It's those kinds of things that interests me. And I think it was because of my brain injury, I just flip those kind of thing. They ask me, "Why do you think that way?" Well, it's like a damn wrench: righty tighty, lefty loosey. I think it comes from my enlisted days, because I was an enlisted man many years before I had my frontal lobotomy and became an officer. Like an old Marine, I'd rather have a bottle in front of me than have a frontal lobotomy. I was enlisted for quite a few years, so I learned a lot of that common sense stuff.

I believe I will get elected next time. I don't think that I will have to brush up on much, because I have two of the best flood fighters in the business sitting right here: General Dorman and General Sprynczynatyk. They have fought more floods than FEMA, and General Robinson is one of my mentors. I've got great mentors and down-to-earth folks who teach a couple of things: **'Never lie, cheat or steal or tolerate anyone who does'**, which is the officer's creed and around here you won't find North Dakotans lying to you. As far as cheating, General Robinson worked flood ops with FEMA, and all his office wanted was that in the event that he was going to do a 90/10 share with FEMA, then, *"fine, give us our ninety percent, we're not going to ask for a dime more, and you folks just go away, we'll take care of business right here. We know how to budget. We know how to run those things."* But some politicians, as I have said, five percent here, six percent there, that's all political. That's the way we roll around here, as they say.

I love public service. I'm doing "Cops and Kids" soon. It's my passion. I love to fish. "Cops and Kids" is when the local law enforcement share with the underprivileged kids and we take them fishing for a day. So, I get to take my boat and my dogs and ... it's going to be wild. Four kids and two dogs in a boat ... But I will survive, after all I survived Iraq. Anyway, a brain-injured guy needs a little mental gymnastics: taking apart lines, untying hooks, and more. I do stuff like that all the time. I love it. And, what is an old, retired man going to do anyway? Can't just sit around and loll in the mire, because my wife ain't going to let me. A five-foot, two-inch stick of dynamite named Leslie. We've been married for twenty-three years. She's just ornery, a real kick in the pants: my pants. "Get out the door. Get out the door."

Olzweski, Robert
Chief Warrant Officer-4, United States Army
1948 –

The Army warrant officer is a technical expert, combat leader, trainer, and advisor in a variety of basic Military Occupational Specialties. They serve in all branches of the service, spanning the Active services, the Army National Guard, and the U.S. Army Reserves. Warrant officers command the Army's vessels and most bands and aircraft. In addition, they may be found in command of various small units and detached teams.

Chief Warrant Officers 4 (CW-4) are senior-level experts in their chosen field, primarily supporting battalion, brigade, division, corps, and echelons above corps operations. They typically have special mentorship responsibilities for other WOs and provide essential advice to commanders on WO issues.

It takes a special breed of person to be elevated to the rank of Chief Warrant Officer, a man such as Robert Olzweski, CW-4, United States Army.

*****

Okay, troops. I'm Robert Olzweski, currently from Bismarck, North Dakota, but born and raised in Sanger, North Dakota. Population zero right now. Everyone has either moved out or died. It was a small little town back in those days just after World War II. I grew up working on the one hundred and sixty acre family farm with my dad who came from Poland. Sanger is north of Mandan, North Dakota, maybe ten miles or so. It is along the Missouri River and, of course, it's flooding right now as I speak.

Anyway, I was born in 1948 on that farm, and learned what hard work is really like. I entered the Army in 1967, just after I was nineteen. I began as a Private E-1 and finished up in the reserves as a CW-4. Roughly a total of thirty-eight and one-half years; I started out in 1967 and had a short break and finished up in 2008, nearly forty years. I didn't volunteer to join the military; actually I was drafted. I came from a real small town with large family, and I decided wanted to do something else and get away from the farm. I was always interested in military and wasn't a bit reluctant to report once I received the draft notice.

I went to recruiting office and talked to them, hoping that I would get to go to Germany. I wasn't really thinking about Vietnam at the time; it just didn't come to mind. That's basically what happened. I went to basic training and off to Germany I went. I loved ... once I got to Germany I was supposed to be assigned as a mechanic. I didn't want that kind of work as I had done a lot of that on the farm. So they said, "Okay, here, you can join an Army unit." I thought, "Whoa. I get to drive the tanks and things like that." I thought that was hilarious. I did really well on the tank ranges and everything with the tanks and three personnel carriers and the other vehicles. All of a sudden, they said, "We need you over in Vietnam," so ...

The one thing I did see when I was in the service. When people have really good experience and the experiences are brought up for consideration, I think the powers that be have a tendency to look more at those people for leadership qualities a little bit more in considering promotions, and the skills I had developed on our farm in repairing equipment was really helpful to me as I was going through my military career.

I served on active duty for two years and nine months, from 1967 until approximately 1970 and then again in 2003 and 2004. I served in the Vietnam War in 1968 and 1969 and I served in "Enduring Freedom" mission in 2003. During Enduring Freedom, we were actually stationed at Uzbekistan, which was close to the Afghanistan border, so we were housed in Uzbekistan, but our functions required that we had to go down into Afghanistan to support the different units that were down there. We supported Marines, Air Force, the base camp, and also Special Forces units that had small compounds outside Uzbekistan; we had to support it all. That was some pretty rough duty right there.

Although the times were hard and the duty difficult, I never felt like giving up or quitting. I don't believe that I needed any special inspiration or motivation to serve during this period. I wanted to challenge myself to do a little bit more. I wanted to see the different types of the world. There was so much more out there to see, to feel.

I've always felt that every person should serve in the military. To me, I'm giving something back and I want to make sure the United States stay free, so that was one of my goals; to go into the military.

When I got orders to active duty in Afghanistan, it wasn't all that difficult for me, because what helped me out was my experience in Vietnam and I knew that eventually the United States would probably have to go, especially after 9-11. And what helped me get my unit ready was my leadership and experience from 'Nam, because we had a lot of people ... a lot of soldiers that were in the reserves that didn't even dream that this was going to happen. Pretty much, they were going into the reserves, they were going to get their school paid for and stuff, and all of a sudden the balloon went up and they said, "What, we're going to fight the war?" And I said, "Yes we are, we're going to have to go do our part." And they were just really pleased that I had been in Vietnam and had the experience to help them get through this dangerous year of 2003.

One tremendous thing; we were able to bring back every one of our men. Men and women. We also had women in our support role. I was the second in command. We had... I've got to back up a little bit. Desert Storm hit. That's when it started bringing up the reserves. Desert Storm and Desert Shield. My unit was at about eighty percent strength. Throughout my reserve career, I've been the commander about eight to ten times. We can't keep second lieutenants and captains, they have to get promoted. In the reserve structure in Bismarck, the highest rank you could achieve when we had our headquarters here, you could make, like, light bird (Lieutenant Colonel...Ed) and so, it was hard to find a commander. So when it first started, our unit was supposed to go over to Iraq. But we didn't have a commander. So, what happened was, a general from Salt Lake came up and said, "Chief, are you ready to go?" I said, "Yes, Sir, we are." He said, "Are you sure?" I said, "Yes, Sir." He said, "No you are not, you don't have a commander." I said, "Yes we do, I'm the commander." And he was like, "No, no, you need an officer as commander." I said, "No, we don't need one, we're ready to go." But he insisted and then, lo and behold, we found one. And we were just about ready to go, and be deployed, and then they called it all off.

We were real close to going to that one, but we didn't go. So, that commander went up through the ranks and he left, and then we got the call to go on Enduring Freedom. I was the commander again. And it was the same thing. "Nope, you've got to have a commander to go with you." And I said again, "No, I'm ready to go. We are good to go." And lo and behold anew, they found a commander and we did take him along with us. And I'm going to leave it right there.

As to what I missed the most while serving overseas, it was my family; my wife and my grandkids. I have ... we have two grandkids. The littlest one, my granddaughter, didn't really understand why I had to go. And it took almost a full year later when I got back home before she got fully involved with me again. She was scared that I was going to leave again. It took a great deal of time. She would get involved a little around the edges, but not that touchy-feely, she didn't want to be unhappy if I should leave again. Young ones just don't understand. And there's no counseling for those left behind, not for the families, the spouses, not for the children. And it's pretty much when you come back here in North Dakota, and I'm sure it's like that in a lot of other states too, that the veteran can go and maybe get some counseling. But I don't see too many families taking the whole family going to the Veterans Administration and trying to get some help. A lot of the families are tired of it, they don't want it now, they don't want that, but there must be something there for them.

I'd like to read something. *"My Hero by Aryan. My hero is my grandpa. It's because he was in the Vietnam War and saved my country. I want to be like him because he keeps my country. Your grandpa sounds like a great person.* That's from my granddaughter, not my daughter. She was quite young. And she is seventeen years old, now. She really supports me on this one.

A question that is always asked of veterans is about deciding to walk away from it all. There was never a time when I ever just felt like throwing up my hands, quitting and coming home and saying to heck with it all. That's because I knew what I was fighting for and especially the last group of soldiers that I went with, I felt it was better for me to stay with them and make sure that everyone came home. That is the most important mission; that was the biggest thing. It's just the way that the soldiers were in the day and age before the 9-11 hit, they weren't really geared up. It was pretty much that, yes, they were serving their weekends and then they went to school or back to their day jobs. And then reality did hit and they … we made a resolve that now it's time to roll up our sleeves and step up to the plate, and I wanted to make sure they had good leadership and that I would bring them all back home.

I did suffer an injury in Vietnam. But, a little background. When I left home, I told my mom and my dad that I would not tell them if I got injured. So, I got a couple of scrapes first, got patched up and told the doctors to send nothing back home. It wasn't enough even to earn a Purple Heart. But somehow they got word back home that I was wounded. When they found out, that was more heartbreaking than actually what happened over there. I just didn't want them to know what was going on so that they wouldn't worry.

When I did get seriously wounded, I received shrapnel all the way from my hip to my legs and actually got grazed by a bullet from the side. I compared it to being back in good old North Dakota and getting a bee sting. I wasn't worried about it, my adrenalin was high and I wanted to make sure that everybody on the tank was okay, but we did lose a soldier. And the chopper came in and the medic came over to me and he said, "Specialist, you've got to get on there because you have blood all over." So, I looked down and I said, "No, I'm still able to fight yet." So, I said, "You make sure everybody gets on the chopper." When the fighting was over and my people were safe, I kinda went down on one side and another chopper came in and I was carried aboard that chopper and evacuated.

As it turned out, what had really happened was that the night before or rather in the early morning, we started taking hostile rounds in; artillery rounds started coming into our base camp. So, we got the call to go out and seek and find where they coming from. Our company took off and we went up to the DMZ border and we got into a firefight with the North Vietnam Army, and that's when it all happened.

After I was injured, I believed that I may be transported to Germany. That didn't happen. I was on a hospital ship. Now, I don't know if this is true or not, but someone told me it was on the Bob Hope Show. Anyway, it was a big ship; it was nice there.

I just went there for a little bit and then I went to a base camp all the way the rear, to a MASH unit. It was safer there. They still got some incoming artillery, but not much. Even so, I just could not stay there because there were too many soldiers there that were seriously hurt or wounded. And most of them were wounded so badly to the point where they couldn't go back to the battlefield or didn't want to go back. I had to get out of there. So I told them, "Just give me a pair of crutches, I want to go back to the fighting." So, lo and behold, they found me two crutches, and I got on a chopper and went back to my unit. I couldn't take it back there. They were trying every way not to go back to the firing line and there were some of them that should have been sent back to the front. They didn't want to go back to Hell. I couldn't bear myself being there and hearing all the lame excuses as why they couldn't go back and be with their unit.

I was missing my comrades, so as soon as they got me a pair of crutches, I was out of there. Back with my comrades. Because I'm from good old Sanger, North Dakota.

There was no one from North Dakota in my Vietnam unit. They came from all over the country, but not a one from my home state. One thing that I wished for but I never got was my 'tanker' jacket. It was left on the tank when I was evacuated and I've never seen it since. That was one thing that I wanted but I never did get. I flew our North Dakota flag and our United States flag on our personnel carrier, gave me a little extra adrenalin.

The wounds that I suffered had only a little effect on me, either mentally or physically, during the year that I was in Vietnam. But when I came back stateside, it was different. Things got pretty hectic. When I first came home from Vietnam, we actually landed in Fort Lewis, Washington. And that was the worse scene I have ever seen. That was a time when the protestors were talking about killing babies and, they were actually throwing eggs and things at the plane. And once we started getting off, people were yelling, "Why didn't our sons come home? Why are you guys coming home?"

There were only about ten or fifteen of them but we just wanted to turn around, get back in the plane and go back over there. I had never seen people acting like that. I didn't even think that Americans could act like that. And it set in pretty hard on all of us; very difficult to accept.

After that, it took quite a while; probably took me about six solid years to get back to a more normal life. Because the pain went too deep with the depression and everything. There wasn't really too much help that we could get at that time when we came home, and the only way where ... I actually helped myself. I went on a running program. I just ran and ran and ran, at first for exercise and then all of a sudden, something just hit me. And I came back to normal again. We could have gotten divorced and the whole ball of wax, but my wife stuck with me. Don't know how or why. We will be married forty years in August.

When I came back into the reserves, I was a sergeant. The first thing that the commander we had said, "The first thing you do when you get down here, is that you don't talk about Vietnam, you don't talk about war." And I said, "What am I getting into?" It was just sad. He didn't even want us to talk about it or mention it to any of the young soldiers. "You don't talk about none of that stuff out here." And I'm like, "Oh no, what am I getting into?" I just let it pass and then in a few years, things changed a little.

There are things available to veterans today that were not available to us at that time. I work a lot with the local veteran facilities around here. I'm thankful that I was able to find a way to overcome a lot of what I went through. Reaching out to others is a vital part. There are a good many counselors out there now and a huge part of the problem is getting the people to come to the counseling. It's difficult to get anyone to admit to a problem, but they must admit it before they can be helped. I would never have admitted to anyone that I needed help; too much of a weakling, or so I thought. So, I had to find a different way to do it, and I'm lucky I did. I could have gone off the deep end. It would be good to have an organization like they have for people with a drinking problem. They have the AA. It could help the veterans. Or if we could persuade them to go to a vet center, there's normally someone there to talk to. Not a counselor, but just someone to talk to. Eventually, they may be able to open up a little. Sometimes it takes a lot.

The wounds that I suffered haven't really bothered me much in regular life. My hearing is affected, of course; not drastically, but some. My wife says it's only selective hearing. But actually, it's the lower voice. I just can't pick it up. And the higher tones. I went to the V.A. to get a hearing aid, but I can't use them. Because when I put them in, the ringing is so loud. And it seems almost like I'm sitting in a tunnel. When you drive through a tunnel and you can hear that echoing and ringing; that's what happens when I put the two hearing aids in my ears, it drives me crazy. So I have to just say, yes it's there and bear with it. The doctors say that there is nothing they can do. They say they may have something pretty soon. They say with surgery, maybe they can correct it, but the odds are ninety percent against it. And when I lay down it gets worse.

When I was in Vietnam, I would get about two hours of sleep per night, because I was always worried about my troops and what was going down. I had seen too many people get killed to sleep deeply. Since I came home, and to this day—and people have a hard time believing it—my best sleeping time is between 10:00 p.m. and midnight. I cannot go to sleep; I just toss and turn from 12:00 o'clock on. And I've done that since day one. And I understand that a lot of other veterans are pretty much in the same boat.

The other thing is that 4 P F condition right now. I haven't got Agent Orange yet, but it's right on the border. I know some people from North Dakota that were over in Vietnam and they've taken insulin and everything else, and still some of them are dying from that. There was a lot of stuff over there and I was over there under it. It's not going to *hurt* you, they said, but it *killed* all the foliage.

Despite my injuries, pain and sacrifices, I'm completely happy that I joined the military. I love the good old United States of America. I've gained a lot of experience from the military, and one thing I still love to do—and I am retired from the military and from the Department of Transportation of forty years also—I still like to help the veterans. The experience that I gained from the military I keep on line, and I keep up with the benefits and programs, and I like to share that with the veterans. That's what I like to do. I consider them my brothers.

I haven't really kept up with or studied the various organizations that are trying to help the veterans. One major one that I am familiar with is the AMVETS. The AMVETS in North Dakota are active, and when I was commander of the local AMVETS, veterans would go to the County Service Office, and if the veteran was not a combat-wounded veteran or had not served in combat, they would call me at the AMVETS to see if we could provide them some food or shelter. Nine times out of ten, we didn't have any kind of funds to allot, so often when I would get a call for food, I would go to my own pantry and get food out for needy families when they had to have it. I would try to help them until they could get back on their feet. And when we would have our 'stand down' at the end of the year—I worked with the local Reserve center out here and I have a storage bin with all the clothing that is left over. A lot of times the veterans would need extra clothing or cold weather gear to get back on their feet, and we would do that through the AMVETS. We would try to support them that way. And the AMVETs are big, big supporter. I think the Legion and the VFW are too, but we have a pretty good club to help us and a few funds now, so we can help the veterans a little bit more. To us, they are all one, whether they are combat or not, they are a veteran. To me, a veteran is a veteran. There are about twenty-nine million people that have served in the military. And they have all done their part, whether in a combat theater or not. Every one of these veterans deserve our support.

And the organizations all need to join together. There's just not enough support out there in the community for the VFW and the Legion and the AMVETS, and Operation Military Embrace, Remember the Wounded Ride, and on and on. Perhaps if it were to be one massive nationwide organization, it would draw the public's attention. We need them to combine most of them into one organization that can help every needy veteran. And their families. Especially their families.

One thing I can't emphasize enough is that I owe my very survival to my wife Pat. Without her, I probably would not be here today. She has lived by my side. Especially during the last war. She was a mentor, not only for me but for our troops. When we were to deploy, we were twenty-two soldiers short. We had to go out to eight different states to get those twenty-two soldiers to go with us over to Enduring Freedom. Pat was Family Support Coordinator for my unit. She had to take care of all those twenty-two soldiers' families when things came down the pike. All over the country, from those eight different states. And she's not even in the military.

That is how the military takes care of its own. Not surprisingly, they will call her any time of the day.

When I was overseas, it was hard for her to call me or a member of our unit.. Now you can call into a combat zone almost any time but in 2003, it was tough. When I'd get back from a mission, it was like. "Oh, oh, there was a phone call waiting. What's wrong with that so-and-so's family now? They are calling from the States."

I think that part of today's technology is great. I believe it's fantastic that the soldier can communicate back and forth with his home and family now. There's some of the stuff that we could leave out. I'm going to leave it at that. I know that people want to know back home, but it's hard to fight a war when you've got someone sitting there with a camera. And it's not safe for either party.

Finally, I want to say thank you to all of the volunteer organizations that are trying to help our veterans and their families. It's a great, great thing they're doing for all the veterans in the United States. Thanks to you, the American citizen; you fantastic volunteers. It takes people like you to support the veterans. The veterans are grateful for you. You're special. You are extra-ordinary people doing extra-ordinary things.

God bless.

Reynolds, William E.
Seaman 2nd Class, United States Navy
Aviation Cadet
Second Lieutenant, United States
Marine Corps Reserve
1920 –

Veterans of the Second World War, members of what the American people know as "The Greatest Generation," are becoming ever scarcer as more and more of these great veterans leave us. Honored we are indeed to meet William Edger Reynolds, former Seaman, former aviator and always a Marine. At the ripe age of ninety-one, not only does Reynolds' mind retain its sharpness, he has embarked on another career in the Arts field, both as a designer/artist and a author. He is a shining example for the younger tuned-out generation of what is right about America, and a living guidepost to the meaning of being an American citizen with the privilege of serving his country.

*****

To start with, I'm William Edgar Reynolds. Born in Helena, Montana, I now reside in Bismarck, North Dakota. It's actually the second time I've lived in Bismarck, first from 1976 to 1991, after which I moved up river to Washburn from 1991 to 2008, and then back to Bismarck from 2008 to the present day. I was born on June 17, 1920 and I am still alive and kicking. I've agreed to tell my story, that is, if you can stand the rambling of an old man. Actually, I'm not old at all, ninety-one years young and just getting started. I'm not really sure why anyone would be interested in hearing about my life, but I have been told that it may help other young people to understand what has made America so great for so many years. They call us the "Greatest Generation," but I think there are great people in every generation.

My military career started when I enlisted in the United States Navy; Seaman 2nd Class. I suppose that I kinda knew what was coming ahead of time. What happened was, at Winston Churchill's insistence, Franklin Roosevelt back in 1940 got an act put through for a civilian pilot program because Churchill said, "You're going to be in the war sooner or later, and you are going to need a lot of aviators, so get a head start." I also felt that we would get into the war and there was this selective service that had been established in order to draft people into the Army. I didn't really want to be in the Army so I chose the Navy.

I got in on that civilian pilot training program so that when we actually went to war I was automatically, you might say, a member of the flying services and when I was taken into the military, I went straight into the Naval Aviation Cadet program. When I was first inducted, I had a choice between Army and Navy and I took Navy. My older brother had gone into Naval Aviation and I always kind of followed his footprints. I couldn't consider the Army with my brother in the Navy. My brother had more hazardous duty than just fighting; that was flying patrol in the Aleutians where the weather was such a querulous factor. He did two tours of duty, flying patrol boats out of the Attu Islands, Alaska.

After I enlisted, I was chosen to be a Naval Aviation Cadet. I then became a 2nd lieutenant in the United States Marine Corps Reserve. I've always said that I wasn't such a great Marine because I didn't carry a rifle.

I went on active duty about the first of June 1942 until December 1945, just that short time. All of my active service was during World War II. There's a reason I didn't go to Korea, but that had to do with my physical condition; otherwise I would have been in Korea as well. When I'm asked what gave me the inspiration or courage to join the military, I respond that it really didn't require a lot of courage. I can remember plainly though, while I was still in college and the first guys that had to leave college and get drafted, there were a lot of mixed feelings about it then. There is something about it. Once you get into a draft contingent, in most cases, or once you get in the group that you are going to be going with, all of a sudden, it's just like being a member of a football team. You've got a lot of instant buddies around you and you're saying, "Let's go!" You are all hyped up. That was the way it was for me and I think it was the same for most of them.

I certainly remember when I first deployed overseas. It was kind of a long process. I was training in Mojave, California. "We are going to ship out." *"Well, thank God, we've been here long enough."* Then we got on a ship and got off in Hawaii. We did some more flight training there. "Are we going to sit here until the end of the war?" Then all of a sudden, our squadron, "You are going forward." That was quite a thrill; a very strong feeling ... it was quite a relief in a way. Really exciting. We were going forward. We didn't know just where, but we found out shortly, after we were in route, we would be stationed on a particular aircraft carrier, the Essex. And now the fun starts.

As far as really missing anything back home, I don't believe that I did. Actually, life aboard a carrier was unique. I still dream about it and think about it all the time. The noises, the smell, everything that was related to it; it all comes back. I always thought I was very lucky to be able to see that part of the action and that type of duty. I think there is a terrible, terrible dull and dreary duty that most guys had to go through, living in the mud and fighting the elements, but we didn't have all that. Carrier duty was, yes, very dangerous, but nevertheless when you are working in danger, you are having a wonderful time.

There are frequently odors and smells that bring those memories back. After you get out of service, for the first twenty or thirty years after I got out, I didn't think about it all that much, but now the older you get the more you think back on it. I'm older now and I think about it all the time.

Although military duty kept me extremely busy at first, I did miss my family while I was serving. I wasn't married, but I had always been close to my mother and my dad, especially my mother, I guess; I wrote to them as often as I could. And there was my brother; we were very, very close. I managed to keep tabs on him. We only managed to get together one time before I went overseas. He had just returned from a tour of duty in the Aleutians. I also kept track of a lot of my college friends all the way through. I did an awful lot of letter writing to people. I doubt if they kept a lot of those letters.

There really was never a moment when I felt like I wanted to quit, to just walk away from it all and come home. I bet I was like virtually every other veteran. Well, of course, when the war was over, and I could see that all of a sudden ... I was just back from my second tour to go for an invasion of Japan, but Japan capitulated before we shipped out. So, I was just sitting in Hawaii, deciding whether I wanted to stay in the Marine era or go home. During the war, things were pretty relaxed and not so much disciplinary, and I'm not cut out to be a military man in the first place. And then all of a sudden things started getting what I call G.I., everything. All of a sudden you had to be in a sharp uniform all the time, you had to salute everybody above you, everything started get real tight and I'm like, "This is not the life for me." Then, I was released from active duty. I was never discharged, just released from active duty.

I found that I liked the fighting and action, but not the garrison stuff. And it had become different. An airplane squadron is a small unit, like a band of brothers. It's not like a real military unit at all. I used to wear a horsehair belt instead of the regulation belt and things like that. Anything that I could do that was a little bit out of uniform made me happy. Bucked the system you might say.

The different types of planes that I flew started when I began flight training with the N-2S, a biplane; the 'yellow perils', they called them. I flew them at

Minneapolis. Then on to a BT-12, which was a single-winged monoplane. And then on to the AT-6 which was a very nice North American advanced trainer with five hundred and fifty horsepower. Then, I wound up with a seventeen hundred and fifty horsepower Brewster Buccaneer dive-bomber. They had quit manufacturing them, but the Navy was still using them for training planes. Then I did a little time in the Douglas SBD. I was trained as a dive-bomber pilot and by comparison, the Douglas SBD was a wonderful plane but was awfully slow. Pilots flying the SBD used to say that you could light up a cigarette in the cockpit of an SBD with the cowl open and the match wouldn't even be blown out because the slipstream was so weak. In truth, it was a slow airplane. Then the Navy needed pilots for the Corsair up in Mojave. My name was the second from the top on the volunteer sign-up sheet to transfer out of the SBD squadron and get into the fast airplanes. Toward the end of the war when the Navy said—after we had gone out and proved the Corsair as the fleet fighter for the Marines—the Navy said, "Okay, we want all of the Corsairs for ourselves."

When I got back to Mojave, we got the cast-off Navy planes, the F-6F Hellcat, which was an awfully good airplane but not in the class of a Corsair for speed. So, I finished up flying the – if the war had not ended, I would have ended up on a small carrier, flying an F6F, Grumman F6F during an attack on the Japanese main land, but as it turned out, the war ended, so that was it. It also turned out that the last planes that I flew were those Grumman F6Fs.

I believe that I flew some forty missions in all; we really weren't out there for any long time. The worse flights were when the fleet was on the edge of a typhoon and the decks were just heaving and swaying. They would gave you take-off and you would slam the throttles all the way to the firewall and you look down at the deck and you don't see anything but a dead wall of grey water ahead of you. But they time it right; by the time you get to the end of the ship, the ship is pointing up into the air. Then you just better put your nose down with your stick forward before you stall out. And then you're flying up through the terrible, terrible squalls and stuff in the typhoon, getting blown around so badly, and then finally, you find the right ship again, and go home. That is scary. Sometimes you go into the soup (fog) at six hundred feet and it keeps getting thicker and thicker. And the guy that's flying beside you, it's so thick that that you can barely make out his wings' tips. Then you have to burrow your way up through that stuff to eighteen thousand feet. It takes quite a while to do that. I would often get vertigo in a situation like that, lose control and orientation. And then, they're gone. Those flights were not pleasant. The actual strikes against the enemy where you could fire your guns and see everything around you, those were the good flights. Just as some of the take-offs were hairy, so were some of the landings.

Before I went aboard ship, I underwent the same training that every Naval Aviation Cadet goes through. It goes back to the earliest training that any of us received. As a cadet, Navy aviators were always taught "small field procedure." If you were to watch a Naval Aviation Cadet landing a training plane and compare that to an Army Aviation Cadet, the Army pilot starts his let-down way out there for miles to make a long, gradual approach to the runway and then lands the plane whereas the Naval pilot has a very short distance, even steep let-down and a fairly steep approach to a short, quick landing, always training for a short-field landing. Next comes field carrier landing procedure. In which case you have a landing signal officer on the runway and you simply fly at slow speed on your approach and follow his signals. After you've done fifty or sixty of those field carrier practice landings, you learn that whatever you are doing relies on the man there. He can tell the speed, if you are going a little too slow, or too fast; he can signal you to move a little this way or that way, or up or down; to land or to go around again. Follow that man because he knows, he's done it thousands of times. You just read every move he makes. The very first carrier landing I made, I was going downwind and the carrier was ahead. It looked about the size of a postage stamp. It was a small carrier, a jeep carrier. The landing deck was only four hundred and eighty feet long as opposed to the nine hundred feet deck on the larger carriers. So, here I go; I just came around and I'm coming up to the ship, and as soon as I see that guy with the paddles, I forget all about the ship. I forget about everything except him; if he wants a little more throttle, I give him a little more throttle. Or a little more this. Or I move up or down or side to side as he directs. Then when he gives ne the sign, I chop the engine, and then I look ahead and see the end of the ship, but I'm sitting there safe and secure. All in all, I believe that the landings are perhaps safer than the take-offs.

In effect, you are entrusting your life into that man with the paddles, the one waiting down there for you as you are coming in. And of course, you take care of that man.

I had one very, very exciting experience. I had taken a few hits and my hydraulic system was kaput on my airplane. I reported in and at end of the flight I took the last place position so that they would know what the score was. I thought they would—as had been done before—tell me to go out and fly over the picket destroyers at the edge of the fleet and either bail out or ditch. They gave you the choice.

In this case, they said, "Baker five zero, hold your position." Then they said, "Baker five zero, can you get your landing gear down?" I reached down and there was a CO2 bottle down there. I twisted the handle and surprisingly the landing gear came down. 'Course everything else that was running hydraulic didn't work, the flaps didn't work, the cowl flaps didn't work, none of that worked. But the landing hook itself was mechanical; the hook released and dropped down. They said that they were going to bring me aboard. I looked down at the ships and I could see the wakes getting longer and whiter. There wasn't much wind that day, so they were trying to give me as much wind across the decks as they could. I thought to myself, "For this lieutenant in the Marine Corps and for one Corsair, they're going to spend tens of thousands of dollars in extra fuel to see if I could land without any flaps." I'm like, "Okay," so I came around and had to bring it in a little faster than normal and I'm approaching the deck, and then **"Wave-Off."** So, I go around again and I make the same kind of approach and, **"Cut."** And I landed. They had dragged out a lot of extra wire because of my speed. Later the approach officer said, "On the first try you made a perfect approach, but I gave you wave-off so that you would go around again and I would be able to get a good look at your undercarriage." So when he had given me the wave-off it was so he could closely examine the undercarriage, the positions of the wheels and the landing hook. Never before was a Corsair without flaps actually landed on a carrier. And I suppose it was because the Admiral wanted to see if it actually could be done. I can't quite say that was exactly a wonderful experience. However, it was *an* experience. It actually was a little hairy because without flaps, the stall speed of a Corsair increases quite a bit. I was just hanging onto the props, ready to spin in at any minute, but I didn't. I made it.

I'm asked about the quality of the Japanese pilots. In truth, most of their better fighter pilots had been eliminated before my group got out there. I flew with people who had flown against the Japs in the South Pacific. Their opinion was that the Japanese pilots that they had to face during the time when I served with them almost didn't know what they were doing. At one time Japan had some marvelous fighter pilots but the superior number of American pilots as well as attrition took care of most of them. Actually, I didn't have much air-to-air combat action, only on four occasions during the short time that I was out there. The rest of the time I was banging away at ground targets or dropping bombs. Or dive-bombing. The Navy gave up on flying dive-bombers. After all, if you could hang bombs on a fighter plane, why would you have these slow dive-bombers flying around the place? Put the bombs on a fast fighter plane and then after they get rid of their bombs they could do a lot more things. At the end of the war, the dive-bomber was gone. Just like Germany eventually eliminated the Stuka dive-bombers. Didn't take them long to get rid of those. Especially after our Air Force shot down so many of them. Kinda hurt their pool of pilots, for sure.

There was a good bit of time between missions to rest. Sometimes, we would fly a mission one day, and the next day fly a Conrad air patrol, which was nothing but a take-off and circle around for a while, keeping a look out, and then land again. I just dreaded those flights, because they were so boring. That is, most of the time it was boring. The times it was less boring was when you had to tunnel your way up through fifteen thousand feet of dense clouds and come out with beautiful pillow of clouds around you and the hot sun. Fly around in a circle for three hours, and then go back down into that stuff again.

Those kinds of hops were no fun at all, but they had to be done, so that was part of it.

Escorting bombers became a part of my routine. By that time, the Navy had already eliminated the dive-bomber, but they had many squadrons of TBFs (Grumman Torpedo Bombers) and the torpedo bomber could also be armed with ordinary bombs, which is mostly what they carried mostly anyway. So we would escort the TBFs, fly high cover over them, watching them peel off, go on toward their target and see all this smoke and destruction going on. We would follow them down and escort them and protect them. That wasn't too often, perhaps a half-dozen or so times. During these missions, my plane took enemy fire only once that I knew of. And that was the time that I had to land the Corsair without flaps. It wasn't until I got out of the plane and looked it over that I found out that the damage had indeed been caused by enemy fire and we could determine exactly where the damage was located.

I'm often asked if I am content with my decision to join the military when I did. My answer is always a resounding yes, of course. Actually, during war time, you had no choice, to tell it like was. But the people you are with, the guys you're going to college with, your good friends at home are all, "Yeah, we're going." It was almost like a team spirit kind of thing. "Yeah." To have not gone would have been very difficult, put it that way. There were some guys who didn't go or couldn't go, and I know that it was very hard on them that they couldn't enlist. They wanted to go so badly. Medics turned some of them down them down. That was the irony that they wanted to go fight for their country, to be with their buddies. There is a spirit ... It's like ... When war was declared by the Japs, it was like a personal affront to every single American, like a slap in the face. "We're going to go get those s.o.b.'s, yeah." That became the national reaction.

An awful lot of Americans already had that reaction before we were attacked, because the smart guys like Billy Mitchell and some of the others knew what was going to happen. There a lot of people who quit what they were doing and went to Canada or England; they wanted to get into the fight, they were so determined that the Axis powers were wrong and that democracy must win. They felt that strongly about it; they just had to get in ahead of time, and a lot of them did. I wasn't one of those. But one day I will never forget is hearing that Pearl Harbor was bombed. I was in college, a little college in Minnesota. I waited tables to earn money when I was in college. I was head-waiter during my senior year and was walking across campus with some of the waiters. We had just finished our job for the day over at the girl's dormitory. This girl came racing out of the post office building and said, "Pearl Harbor has been bombed."

I said, "My God, what is this all about?" So we ran into our rooms because most of us had radios, and listened to the radio and heard all the news. Word was sent out that the faculty was having a special meeting. A bunch of different professors and the whole student body gathered into this one hall and heard these people giving their opinions on what was going to happen and so forth, because all of a sudden ... some of the smarter students were not all surprised because they because they knew we would be in the war sooner or later, but to the average person, it was just a complete shock to them. All they were trying to do was to get a passing grade in psychology or biology or stuff like that, but world affairs were something else that didn't affect them. All of a sudden, it came home to them. It shocked people, a real genuine shock.

There is naturally some similarity between 9-11 and Pearl Harbor. The thing about 9-11 is that it is so unforgettable. It was so visible. America got to watch it. And you couldn't believe what you were looking at; the fire, the buildings coming down. It was horrible, just horrible. Pearl Harbor was different. It was all on radio, but there was no visual stuff at the time, which made it a little more remote. Of course, months later, they released some films showing Japanese blowing up our battleships in Pearl Harbor. That part was different, but psychologically, it was the same type of reaction by the majority of the people. Perhaps more so with 9-11 because of the fact that people didn't have to just believe it, they could actually see it. They knew it for the truth. It was happening right there in front of them. One of the most unforgettable of my life was 9-11, probably much more so than December 7th, 1941.

I receive the veterans' publications from the Legion and the VFW, so I'm somewhat familiar with some of the programs that are available for veterans; but I never got involved with anything like that. My involvement with the veterans' organizations didn't really begin until I moved to Washburn, North Dakota and then I got pretty well involved with their programs, and so forth; but mostly just their local programs.

I must admit that I do have a hobby, but I'll have to explain. Although artwork has become an important part of my life, if I had lived somewhere else I may not have become so involved or as successful. I know that I'm quite lucky. I'm not much of a pictorial artist, but I can get by. I've had a bit of a flair for design work and it has been fairly easy for me. Perhaps I should have been an architect, but as it turned out, the way the cards were dealt, I did more of the graphic design work.

After I was married, I went into the advertising business, a family business that my wife's family owned. That involves a lot of design work and as it turned out later on, engineering as well. Putting up a structure, large advertising structures such as billboards and so forth, I was sort of a self-taught engineer in that sort of thing. Eventually, I decided to go out on my own and moved to Bismarck. I did a lot of work for a couple companies down here, a sign company and an outdoor advertising company – Newman Outdoor Advertising Company. That kept the income coming in and then, on the side once in a while, I would pick up requests for design work for buildings. Well, I'm not an architect, but put it this way. If a developer had an idea for a piece of land and he wants to develop and build a certain type of building or structure, I would work that out for him including the parking area, the access and all that for a commercial enterprise. But the main thing is that I would draw a picture of it so that you are looking down at it as if from a helicopter, so you could see the surrounding neighborhood and all that. Then the developer could take the rendering out and use it to raise money to back the thing up. If it went ahead and achieved success, as it did many times, then he could go to the architect. Spending a thousand dollars with me rather than spending ten thousand dollars with an architect right off the bat on something that wouldn't fly, so that's kind of way that it worked. Of course, the architect would always change what my idea was. Guess he had to earn his ten thousand dollars.

So, when I got going on more design work, the better I liked it. Eventually, I quit doing any work for sign companies and just relied on doing design work of all types until I retired, and of course, I never did retire, because every time I would try, there would be a request. When I moved up to Washburn, some of my customers just followed me up river with their requests. Not many, but enough to make quite a little extra money. So, I've been very fortunate because my eyes have kept up. Oh, my brain hasn't quit working entirely, but it's slowed down quite a lot. When I'm asked how slow I am, I respond, "Well, I'm like the Queen Mary with an EverRude motor." The speed is gone, but at the age of ninety-one, I'm a most fortunate person, and can see as well without glasses as I can with glasses.

Of all the memorials that I have designed, the Medal of Honor Memorial gave me the most passion, means most to me. Of course, there was a lot more put into it. We were not restricted except for a few do's and don'ts by the owner of the property where it was going to go, the Minot Park District. They said 'No', to my first original design. So I came up with a circular design that didn't take up so much land. They liked that. I'm very happy with it. I've designed a lot of stuff before and after and always wished I had done a little more of this or a little less of that. But, I can't think of anything I would have done differently on this Medal of Honor Memorial. It was the most ambitious design that I have ever done and turns out that it is my favorite. The Concrete Association gave it first place in a certain division. It was written up in the Minot newspaper but I don't think it was in the Bismarck paper. It could have been highly publicized had we arranged for it, but I didn't want to be the one to do it and when it was finished, the chairman of the thing said that he had other things to do, and then he went on, kinda forgot about it.

One of the Medal of Honor winners attended the dedication, a Mr. Fitzmorris. He was the shyest, most unassuming man I have every met in my life. But his bravery and what he did after he was wounded was a real story in itself.

The last Medal of Honor recipient from North Dakota was Woodrow Wilson Keeble. He was a full-blooded Sioux Indian. He had already won many battle ribbons, several Purple Hearts, and other special awards for his service in World War II. He would not have had to go back to war then with all the Purple Hearts that he had won, but he said, "Somebody has to teach all these kids how to fight." So he went back and won the Medal of Honor. He had already been awarded three Purple Hearts and had been decorated for bravery, but his comment was only that someone had to show those kids how to fight. He was quite a man. Of course, he was awarded the Medal after he was killed.

I owe much of my happiness in my lifetime to my wife. She's kept me from going off on bad tangents. She's always been a good backer; staying the course when I'm doing things right and a damn good foreman when I started doing things wrong. There have also been good people around me who have been influential on my life. One is a man named Rusty Kruger. I've done a lot of work for him, but it went far beyond that, because of his values and his honesty are on a level above most people, and that relationship has meant a lot for me. And it was through Rusty that I got to meet another person for who I have a great deal of respect and admiration for, and he's sitting right over there, Dell Lind.

I've had two special birthdays recently. On my 91st birthday, Rusty and I had a party at the three-wheelers club room over in Mandan with a beautiful big cake and ice cream, and oh, boy! But the one the year before was more exciting.

For my 90th birthday, we went up to Washburn where we used to live, for my birthday party. Rusty and Dale came up to Washburn for the party and there were about eighty-eight other people that showed up. That was some week. I got a lot of nice presents and wonderful cards; some of them had a lot of money in them, which was nice; that's such a friendly way to say congratulations—just hand over a little money. That was such a good party and a few days after that these barnstormers came through with all their old biplanes. I just had to go down and look at those planes. I ran into Dell and he said, "I'll see you in a few minutes, I think you're going to be going on plane ride." He came back in half an hour while I was still looking at the biplanes. He said, "Well, tomorrow morning at 9:00 o'clock, you are going up in a biplane. Rusty and I are sending you up." The next morning at 9:00 o'clock, I was there and ready. I hopped into the biplane and had my half-hour ride. She let me let me fly the plane quite a bit at the time. It was the same style plane that I flew when I first trained in when I joined the Naval Aviation. Steerman. They called it N2S, but anyway that's the same plane I flew when I first went in the Navy. So it was a lot of fun. Couldn't do anything crazy, though; we were not wearing parachutes, so automatically they said, "No inverted flights." Oh my God, I would have loved to ... I always miss the biplane because there is so much you can do with one so easily; the slow rolls, the inverted loops and just everything. You couldn't to all that with most of the other planes.

We were doing what we call the 'Lazy S'. You dive and then make a climbing 's" turn. I started getting steeper and steeper with the maneuver, and then she said, "I'll take it now." Really hated to give it up, but it was her plane. It was a thrill to be up there. A natural-born pilot is in heaven up there in a plane, just to be up there, just sitting there flat and level. It was most enjoyable for me, perhaps not to the degree of the natural-born pilot; I'm not one of those but I still like to do a lot of stuff with a plane. It was quite a bit of fun. I probably don't have the right stuff to be a test pilot; that takes a certain kind of guy to be a test pilot. I never thought that I had the right stuff for that, but I knew there were certain things I could do that was above and beyond what the average pilot could or would do, at least in a biplane. I was just itching to do that, but of course, I couldn't do anything then; not without parachutes. She wouldn't have permitted it, the gal who owned the airplane. She said, "I'll take us home now."

Their airplanes were stacked up in groups, four here, another four there, in a box formation, sixteen planes come in and fly over. Poetry in motion they were, as they would put sixteen planes on the ground in less than a minute. Just plunk, plunk, plunk. And that's the kind of flying I miss.

I don't care for the flight's landing today; just lowering the plane landing gear and flying what seemed forever in a straight, extended line right up to the runway. The Navy guys had it figured it out right, you can see the runway much better when you're curling into a landing and being at the edge of the runway at the end of the curl. Uses much less time and less distance.

After I got out of the military, I pretty much ended my flying career. I was going to school, and I didn't have any money anyway. I could have gone; one guy tried to talk me into continuing flying for a company, saying that they were looking for single-engine pilots to retrain. He said that they didn't want Army pilots that were already fully trained and who had too many set patterns; they would take single-engine pilots and train them to fly twin-engine planes, but fly them in the manner that the company wanted. I thought very seriously about it, but in the end, I wanted to get back to school. I was going to school on the G.I. bill. It was a design school and I wanted to specialize in design work. I was very anxious to get at least one more year at that school. I thought I had better return to school. So, I did.

I don't have any one single major regret about anything that I did or didn't do that comes to my mind; probably a lot of little mistakes that I made along the way. Perhaps someone that I slighted and didn't intend to slight him. Little things like that. My life has been full of little faux pas. Things I should or could have done. But there isn't any one thing that I would change in my life that would change my life; it's been a full life. I can't complain.

By no means am I a linguist, anything but; however I did write my memoirs of the times that I went into service until we went into combat. I kept a diary during that time and I wrote it up. When it came to the actual combat, that was when I quit writing, because hundreds and hundreds of accounts about combat have been written and I wasn't just going to be another one of those. My little history from the time I went in until I went into combat had some kind of amusing stuff going on, and I thought it might be worth going to print. I wouldn't even have thought about it except that I was illustrating a book for another author, a gal I know, and she told me how inexpensive it was to publish a book. She said that I ought to publish a book. I couldn't believe that I could get a book published for that small amount of money because five years prior to that time, you were looking at fifteen to twenty thousand dollars to get a book published. But I could get it published for seven hundred and fifty dollars, *Hah!* This computer technology is something. I write—I print rather well, actually, and this gal for whom I was doing illustration did the typing and she sent it all to the publisher, got it back for a proof read and so forth. I sent the publisher five hundred dollars and then for another one hundred and fifty dollars, I got fifty books. They sold right away, so I just kept ordering fifty at a time for a while, and finally ... It's not a great book or anything like that in high demand and not everyone in the country is going to want a copy, but it's just kind of a fun kind of diary, and it's title is "Diary of a Lucky Leatherneck Throttle Jock." I have a few illustrations in it. And that's how I became an author. I don't even have a copy with me, I sold my last copy. On the other hand my wife does have her own personal copy. Autographed by the author, of course.

Digressing a little, an amusing thing happened to me when I was on my way home from the war zone. I was coming back from overseas and our transport home was an Essex-class carrier coming home for repairs. I stored my gear in a little cubby-hole and then I went up on deck, which was covered with bunk beds. I heard this voice say, "Hey, Bill!" I looked around and it was my buddy from my home town, Jack Mayhan, another Marine pilot. He's on his way home, too. He was in dive-bombers and I had been flying Corsairs. So we were chatting and I said, "Hey, Jack, when we were transported over here, I saw a ship way down at the end of the pier with really different camouflage colors on it." I said, "I want to go and investigate that –" It was a small carrier. I said, "It might be British."

Right away, Jack said, "Well, if it happens to be British, we can probably go aboard and have a drink.'

So off we go down there and pretty soon, glory be, there's the British flag flying from the yardarm. *Alright!* We approach the gangway and there's a great big Royal Marine standing there and he gives us a great big salute, an actual rifle salute. Just for us? Just then a quiet voice behinds says, "Would you gentlemen care to go aboard?" I think, *Oh God, would we.*

"Yes, Sir. Thanks."

He says, "Follow me and we'll go the wardroom." A nice-looking little guy. We went down to the wardroom and up to the bar and he said, "What would you gentlemen care to drink? We don't have much to offer, except Scotch."

"Well, Scotch would be fine."

There's a kid behind the bar who looks like he is maybe thirteen years old. A good-looking little devil, but anyway he fixes up a couple of Scotch and waters, and I started to say "Now how do we pay?" The man said, "It'll go on my tab." I said, "Well, you don't ..." He said, "You see, I don't drink. We have a two pound allowance ($7.00 US dollars) per month here in the wardroom. So you can have as many drinks as you want on me." I said, "Two pounds?" He said, "Well, each drink you have is about the equivalent of three cents American."

He took us around and introduced several other people. Everybody we talked with had a bandage or an arm in a sling, one guy was on crutches. I said, "Everybody here is sort of battle-damaged." He said, "Well, I wouldn't call it battle-damaged. You see, we've done nothing but transport; doing this for the past eight months and that can be very boring duty indeed. So to relieve the boredom, we have formed a field hockey league. The games are played on the flight deck. And sometimes in the heat of the contest, one of the laddies can't resist having a bash on an officer." Britannia rules the waves.

Later on, we're going back to our ship, and I say drunkenly to my buddy Jack, "Just think. There are a thousand guys on our Essex-class carrier sitting around with nothing to do. And two of them found the best place on the island of Hawaii to spend a few hours."

Of course, now I still stay in touch with Jack, but he's on kidney dialysis and feeling rotten. Way back in 1952, he was the Commandant of the VFW Post in Helena, and for the clubrooms he ordered four paintings from me. I lived in Butte, Montana at the time. I painted these pictures; one for Army, one for Navy, one for Marine Corps and one for Air Corps. Each painting was about 2x2.5 feet, painted on masonite panels. They were

… I framed them and they went to Helena and hung in the VFW clubrooms until they sold their club and the paintings were put into storage. But when Jack Mayhan, my buddy, was given a post, Richard Nixon actually was President at the time; Jack was the Chairman of the Un-American Activities Committee in Washington, D.C. He brought the paintings to Washington, D.C. and they hung in Washington, D.C. for twelve to fifteen years. Later on, when Jack returned to Helena to private law practice, he had them shipped back to Helena and put into storage. When the National Guard built a big metal building out there at Fort Harrison in Helena, they decided to have these paintings cleaned up and hung, and have a big dedication.

So, two years ago, we drove out there; it just happened to be Jack's birthday. We drove to Helena and met with Jack. The next day we went out to the Fort and they had the big doings about the dedication about those four paintings that I had painted way back in 1952. The paintings are all oil paintings, of course. The painting for the Marine Corps shows that famous scene at Iwo Jima. Of course, at the time I painted it, that was before it became so famous. I found that picture. In the Naval picture, I show the battle of the Coral Sea. For the Air Force I show the contrails from the heavy bombers going into Germany up high, medium bombers below and the P-47 doing the ground attack work. Then for the Army, I show the landings at Hollandia. As it turns out, the Army unit was a Montana unit that made the landing at Hollandia, and that blended in very well. Goes without saying, if I painted them today, they likely would be a lot better.

I must admit that my nickname is "Whisky Bill." It began in when I was at Mojave, California. At the Marine base, every now and then, the word would get out that you could buy whisky. There was a shortage of whisky in the entire country during the war. We could sometimes buy whisky at the officer's club. However, you could only buy one fifth of whisky per customer. So, I would buy my fifth, and then ask the next guy, "Are you going to get your fifth? Can I have yours?" And the next guy, "Can I have yours? And so on. At the base where we were located, we were only twenty-six miles from an Army base by the name of Muroc. There were a few guys I knew who were stationed at Muroc and they couldn't get any whisky at all, so I would get it for them. Not just for me, but also for them. Muroc was later renamed Edwards Air Force Base. So this guy in our squadron who had invented nicknames for several guys in our squadron, so he started calling me, "Whisky Bill," and it stuck. It wasn't because I drank whisky, although I drank plenty of it, but there were guys in the squadron who drank a lot more than I did and could have easily been called "Whisky" but I got the name and it stuck. I've had a lot of nicknames in my life, but that's the one that stuck the longest. I kinda like it.

Usually, I wind up a long, boring talk with a joke or something to reward a patient audience, so I'll let you in on the story I told the other night at my birthday party. One hundred and fifty years ago when Britain still owned India, there was a retired Colonel who had did all his service time in India and he was being interviewed by a writer for one of the London periodicals. The reason the writer was interviewing the Colonel who had no distinguished career at all except one thing: this Colonel had this uncanny ability to single out and destroy man-eating tigers. So, that was the subject of the interview. The writer said, "I say, Colonel, this is smashing information and our readers are just going to be riveted to it. Now, tell me, Colonel, one other thing. What was your narrowest escape? Your closest call?"

The Colonel said, "Well, that probably would have been south of Jodhpur. There was a man-eater running loose. He'd done away with twenty-five or thirty of the poor devils in that neighborhood, so naturally they called on me. So we went there and while my C boys were setting up camp, I went out into the elephant grass to look for signs or spoors. Mind you, it's not too wise to go out into that tall grass, which is as tall as a man's head, excellent cover for those clever tigers. Nevertheless, I was out there alone and I noticed over there movement in the grass and it moved over this way and kept moving and ... Aha! A tiger, and a clever devil, getting downwind of me. Then it stopped. I got my rifle ready. Then it moved closer and closer. Suddenly, the tiger sprang, and 'ARRAHHH'."

"My goodness, Colonel, what did you do?"

"I messed my britches."

"Well, I don't wonder. You must have been terribly frightened."

"Frightened? Frightened, my boy? I have never been truly frightened of anything in my life."

"But, Colonel, I distinctly heard you say that you messed your britches."

"Huh? Oh. Oh, yes. Quite right, so you did. Mind you, that was not when the tiger sprang at me. That was only a moment ago right here when I went ARRAHHH."

There is an old, but true saying: Once a Marine, always a Marine ... America, Semper Fedelis.

Sable, Marty S.
Sergeant, United States Army
1959 –

Yakima Elks Lodge 318, serving Yakima and Selah in the state of Washington, is only one of the many Elks Lodges that provide services to the veterans of the United States Military. Their motto from 1917 has been: *As Long as there is a veteran, the Benevolent and Protective Order of the Elks will never forget them,* is evident in the variety of services available for the veteran. Among these services are the *Leather for Veterans, Playing Cards for Veterans, Veterans Remembrance, Freedom Grants, Adopt-a-Veteran, Army of Hope, Re-Creation USA,* and last, but certainly not least, *Operation Military Embrace.*

Indeed many of the members of the BPOE have given their lives in the service of their country and countless thousands of others have suffered painful wounds in defense of this great nation. Still others have served during times of war, watching as comrade after comrade dropped from enemy fire or suffered from the blast of enemy bombs. Helping a wounded fellow soldier became a way of life for many of the servicemen as war swirled around them, causing them to become leaders in a way they never expected. These veterans were heroes, not just to their grateful nation, but to each other.

One such veteran is *Marty Sable* of Yakima Lodge 318. Like other veterans of his ilk, Marty is proud of his service, albeit reluctant to accept accolades for his service, stating that he was *only doing his duty*.

Acknowledging that by telling his story he could help other veterans who have served in the fight against the enemies of the United States, Marty did consent to let America know more about him.

As an introduction, Marty Sable, Esquire and former In-Guard, is currently the Veteran's Chairman of his Lodge, and his story is only one example of a veteran's service to his country.

*****

To introduce myself, I am Marty Sable, formerly Sergeant in the United States Army, and currently member of Yakima Elk Lodge 318, Esquire and Former In-Guard; current Veteran's Chairman. Honored to be both a veteran and an Elk.

I got out of Monroe High School in 1975, about the time that the war in Vietnam was ending. Deciding that I wanted—and needed—an income of my own, I immediately found employment in a lumber company, building roof and floor trusses for my stepfather. At the time I was earning six dollars an hour, which wasn't bad for a recent high-school graduate, but it wasn't something that I wanted to do for the rest of my life. I had been working there for some six months when a bunch of my high-school buddies said, "Hey, we're gonna join the military. Want to come along?"

At the time, I wasn't really interested in being a soldier or a sailor. Or any other kind of military enlistee. Even so, a little later, I talked about it with a really close friend, Chuck Whitfield. Chuck had decided to join the Army and explained the reasons to me. He said that the real reason he was going to enlist was to get away from Monroe and try to see and learn more about the big wide world that was out there, just waiting. Chuck and I had each been an exchange student. He had been an exchange student in Sweden and I was in Japan, so we both had an understanding that there was a far bigger world out there than just our little hometown. It was Chuck's opinion that joining the military would be beneficial because it has a presence all over the world. The Army was a great place to go see it all. He told me that he was going to go to Europe and become a parts clerk. Not exactly sure what that was, I asked him what that meant and he said, "When things or units need parts, I will secure those parts for them and that would be what I will do. The military identifies the type of work that you will be doing by a Military Occupation Specialties code number, or MOS. Being a parts clerk will be my job and the army is going to train me to do that. I'll undergo three months of basic training and then three months at this other school—a 'tech' school. After that, they will ship me off to Europe and I'll be over there for two years."

I started thinking about my situation and realized that if I just stayed there in the truss plant eventually I'd be working for the lumber yard. And I'd be exactly like my step-dad, who was close enough to me to be my father. That would be as far as I would be able to advance; I'd either be a truck driver or a fork lift operator and that just didn't sound too intriguing to me.

I started thinking about my situation and I talked it over with my step-dad—my father—asking him what he thought about me joining the military. His advice: "It ... Go for it. It's the best thing for you at your age. You will get more education in your first six months than you will likely ever attain in your entire life or at any school you will ever attend."

So I was, like, OK.

I went down to the Military Entrance Processing Station (MEPS) and found that the same MOS that my buddy Chuck had chosen was still available and I could opt to do that. So, I was like, *Okay, why not? I will just do that.* I didn't have the slightest idea what a parts clerk or what the job entailed, but I was damn sure willing to learn. And these guys were going to teach me all I needed to know, so how could I fail? That's really why I joined: I joined to be with my buddies.

There was another guy ... There were actually two of my classmates that went to Germany and there was kind of a strange and funny story about how we all managed to get together at the very beginning. Chuck ended up in a place called Neuweller, near Stuttgart and I was in Bad Kosching in Bavaria, the northern part of Bavaria. Not just the northern part, but the very northernmost area. If you drove ten miles north, you would actually be out of Bavaria. This other friend of mine, Jeff Jensen, ended up Fulda, which was only about fifty miles away to the north of where I was based. This was something that I didn't know at that time.

I had agreed with Chuck during the time that we went through basic training together that when I was stationed over there, I would notify him as to my location in Germany. Not having any way of contacting Chuck directly, I mailed my address back home to my mom and asked her to take it to Chuck's folks. That way they could send it to Chuck. The weekend after the letter had reached him, Chuck was going to come up and visit me. He would have to take a train to try and find me, but he went a little too far. There was a station where he was supposed to get off the train but he missed the stop and ended up going all the way to Fulda. When he got off the train, Jeff was standing on the platform waiting for his girlfriend.

Chuck didn't see Jeff and started to get on a train going back the other way when suddenly he heard someone yell in English, "Hey, Chuck!" To Chuck's astonishment, running across the platform toward him was Jeff. So, happily, and much to our surprise, we all ended up being together. That's really the major reason that I had joined the military ... to be with my buddies.

I served in the United States Army, joining on the 2nd day of January, 1976. After thirty-four years, my last day of service was the 31st day of August, 2010. There basically is really no difference between the between the Reserve components and the active Army. We do the same commissions as do the active Army, except we don't get some of the sexy missions that they do. You can say that you are in the Army National Guard or that you are in the Army Reserves, but the reserve components are fully integrated with the active units. You are in the military.

Like many other American military personnel, I served in Operation Iraqi Freedom II. Perhaps President Bush's proclamation in May, 2003 that the war was over may have been a little premature. Although the major battles were over and the main fight had been won, there was still danger at later dates. My unit went into Iraq in 2004. The war had started in March of 2003 and we were there in February of 2004. We were the second phase of the military to go in there. I also served in Operation Iraqi Freedom 2008 & 2009.

Very proud to have served, when people ask for the truth, I have to say no, that there was never, not ever, a point at which I wanted to quit and come home. I am certain that ever troop will say this: "There is never a point when you want to give up your buddies." It is as if you become family with your fellow soldiers or sailors. Emotions between military people, male and female, run deep. I mean, there is nothing in this world that is so traumatic as the feeling of comradely that exists between soldiers who had been to war together. In truth, if my father or mother had passed away, I would have never ... I may have come home and taken an emergency leave and taken care of business, but I would have gone back over there because those guys needed you ... you're part of a family and the family you are with, you had been through the shit together and you wanted to continue to go together through the shit as long as you were going to have to be in the shit. And in fact, the last time that I was deployed, my step-mother of 51 years passed away while I was over there. I would have had to come home on emergency leave. I found that I had to go talk to the colonel and a couple other people. I had to go talk to the chaplain before I could make a decision. I was torn. I felt the need to go home and be with my family, but I didn't want to leave my guys. I believed that they really needed me.

The chaplain said, "Go home. You need to; just go home and take care of business and then come back." And that's what I did.

It was very traumatic for me to go through that situation—being torn in two different directions by people you love. That's how strong you have feelings for your fellow troops.

The number one thing that gave me the courage and inspiration to serve during difficult and trying times was the fact that I looked around at the guy next to me and discovered that he was struggling with it just as hard as I was and he's making it. If you're gonna be the first one who gives up, what's gonna stop him from giving up as well? If you look ... if you're in a group of fifteen people and one decides to quit ... I guess negativity is contagious, kind of like a disease. Once the disease takes begins to root, everybody will be infected and then they eventually will have a bad attitude. Bad attitudes are just something you just can't have in a war zone. And Iraq was a war zone.

I saw action during out first excursion into Iraq. We were taking vehicles out of Iraq and were coming through Bagdad at 9:00 o'clock in the morning which is, like, prime time for IED's. Two vehicles ahead of us, a truck was struck by an IED or Improvised Explosive Device, which is really a dangerous roadside bomb. Well, the truck kept going for another two miles ... the driver somehow actually kept the truck on the road for another couple of miles. He did an excellent job as the IED had blown the front tire completely off of the vehicle and a hole in the side of the engine and the transmission. Finally, the truck just completely gave out.

We got out of our vehicles. We found ourselves on top of a bridge and kind of exposed to everything because we were silhouetted against the skyline. I walked up to the driver of the damaged vehicle which was still second in line ahead of me. The driver had actually been injured when he had first gotten to Iraq earlier that year, in April, and had returned to Iraq because he had healed enough, and like I have already explained, he wanted to be back where his buddies were. That is what we do. So he had gone home and healed, at least in his opinion, but he in truth he wasn't quite healed. His name was Brad

Barnes, an excellent guy who has since that time taken a discharge because of that injury.

I said, "Brad, I know your knee still hurts and I know it must be quite painful for you to go fast, but we don't have any time left. You need to run. Everything needs to be at a running pace." And he said, "Yes, Sir." And enough said. He ran. It was impressive. He just sucked it up and started moving and that's the kind of thing you just never forget.

I'm one of the fortunate. I've never been injured myself; at least, not physically. The only injuries that were sustained by my unit during the first go-round were to one of the vehicles that were in the convoy ... they had taken a prisoner from our base in Balad down to another prison in Baghdad. The soldiers in the convoy had delivered the prisoner to the prison there and were on their way back. Just as they pulled out of the gate, they were hit by a car bomb. A suicide bomber drove a vehicle into them and detonated it. The car bomb did its job and one of our soldiers was killed. The one guy who was killed, Sergeant Tran, had been standing in the gunner's hatch and his body was half way up out of the hatch. When the blast went off, the sergeant was maimed to the point where he lost all his blood. Part of the blast had come up through the heat duct and almost severed his lower torso. It took him out. He had no chance at all.

And the one officer that was in the vehicle, Dave Ammon, was also injured. Although they were in an armored Humvee, the bullet-proof glass window wasn't completely closed; it had been cracked open a little, as some of the occupants were smokers. When the blast went off, a bolt from the car flew through the small opening and struck Dave in his helmet, just above his left eye. The bolt embedded itself into Dave's helmet and blew the helmet completely off his head. A little lower and it would have blown Dave's head off. The third soldier in the Humvee was not injured at all.

That soldier was our only fatal casualty. There were wounded people ... Dave may have a wound on his face from the shrapnel that came out of that explosion, but I don't think that's where the whole wound was located. Part of the wound was the turmoil inside Dave and I don't know if he's ever going to conquer that demon.

It's surprising what they say; the old saying is that bad news doesn't get better with age. It's true. We knew something had happened, something that wasn't good. We knew that somebody had died. We knew that a bad event had happened, but it happened so far away that a lot of us didn't know the true story about what had taken place. Initially, we had heard that one guy had died and one guy had been taken to the hospital. Well, I called up to the unit, to the Battalion Commander's office and spoke to an S-2 up there. I said, "Hey, what happened?"

He goes, "Well, Sergeant Tran was killed and Dave Ammon was taken to the hospital."

I said, "How's Dave doing?"

"Ah ... oh, I think he passed away." Not knowing ... He didn't know it, he just said it.

Initially, I was just, "Oh my God!." I dropped ... I hung up the phone, got in my Humvee and drove around the post ... his company was all the way around on the other side of the post. So, I drove all the way over there and I talked to a man, a Mr. Doslin, Doug, another warrant officer who worked with Dave. So, I talked to Doug and I said, "Doug, is it true what I've heard?"

He goes, "What did you hear?"

I go, "I heard that Dave passed away."

And he goes, "No ... Dave didn't pass away."

I go, "Are you sure?"

He replies, "Yes, I'm sure.'

I ask, "Just how sure are you?"

He answers, "I just got off the phone with him. He's alive."

That relived all my fears because Dave was a good friend of mine; always was and always will be.

You are aware, I'm sure, that bad news like that just sucks the life right out of you. You just think, like, "That can't happen." It was very traumatic for everybody, not just me but for the entire unit as well. Everybody felt that way. Maybe they weren't as close to Dave ... I didn't really know Sergeant Tran as well as Dave knew him, but I knew that Dave had told me that Tran was a good troop, and to me that was golden. I really can't say anything bad about the man. I did go on one convoy with him and don't remember anything spectacular about the convoy, but Tran knew what he was doing and did it well.

I received the Bronze Star for the support that we did and the things that we did while we were there. *(Editor's comment: The Bronze Star is the fourth highest award for bravery, heroism or meritorious service that can be awarded to a member of the military)* Our initial mission ... well, I went into theater as advance party and ended up spending about a month and a half in Kuwait before our brigade even showed up. I set up all the logistical side of what we needed to do as far as us moving us from Kuwait into Iraq and then, before the brigade left Kuwait, I flew up to Iraq and set up the infrastructure that they needed to have when they got there; the housing, the buildings and all the other stuff for the people coming from Kuwait. After that, I helped set up the motor pool as well as the maintenance section for that battalion that was going to be there. Additionally, I set up the areas from which the battalion was going to conduct its missions. While I was there that time, I went on six convoys. I went twice to Baghdad and back and forth to Kuwait twice. I never got to go north. There were convoys that did go north, but I never did. But I wish I had. It was fun.

Of the people and things left behind while I was overseas, I missed my family the most. There are no soldiers over there that don't miss their families no matter what their status may be between themselves and their family. Everyone misses family. The other things you miss are the freedoms, and the ... If you were to take away everything that you have in the world and go down to where you have just a water bottle and a place to sleep, that's where you really find yourself. That is the core – the basic beginning. That's where you're going to start. Whatever you can do from there – whatever you can do to make happen and make it better for your troops, that what you try to do. You are packed, ready to go, and you are living out of a bunch of sacks. All your worldly possessions are in those sacks and they go with you everywhere you go. The most uncomfortable thing you go through when you leave the States is that period of time when you are living out of those sacks. 'Cause, that's it. You don't have a refrigerator to go to, you're drinking warm water, you're drinking a warm this ... or a warm that. If you have cool drinks, that's great, but it's not going to be where you are, because there are no coolers. There wouldn't be enough coolers to do it. So pretty much the creature comforts that we have in the United States that we take for granted every day are the things you miss the most. The military tries to do a good job to get it to them for you, but a lot of times it's just not available in the places that the troops are stationed.

A question that I'm often asked is whether or not I would do it again. And my answer is always, yes. Yes, I would. I would do it all again in a heartbeat. And I know that to a man ... There were some people that I knew that were disgruntled, but I know that there are people from the first go-round that I still talk to, people who have gone off to their own civilian life, people who have gotten out of the military entirely, and there is still a kinship there, a kinship that was created there and at that time. A kinship that you just can't get anywhere else. You can't just go into a ... Even in an Elk's Lodge. There is a lot of kinship there, but it's not to the extent that your fellow troops have been through. If you have been through a war zone with the troops, it makes a whole big difference.

Most of the kids we were with—and here I'm a ... the first time I went over there I was forty-eight and the next time I went, I was fifty-two—and I'm looking at these kids were half my age or less that are going over there and being thrust into this environment where they can't be a kid anymore, they had to be an adult. The ones who could handle it became an adult—and remained an adult when they came back to the States. And the ones who couldn't ... that you knew couldn't handle it because they never had—or couldn't develop—the maturity needed, they either got demoted or ... they pretty much screwed themselves while they were there because they just couldn't cope with situations that required them to be an adult.

Those who were professional and knew why we were there and realized the situation became mature adults. And we're talking about twenty-two and twenty-three year old kids who matured and were thinking like thirty –five year old mature adults. A war zone just, at the snap of a finger, instantly ages them.

As an older man, a lot of the young soldiers came to me for advice. I wasn't reluctant to pass along my thoughts, however, to each person I emphasized the need for the soldier to consult with his or her family and not rely strictly on my advice, as my version of the world was solely from my own perspective. I reminded them that it was likely that their father or mother or other relatives may see things from a different slant, and they should consider that. I didn't want anyone to rely solely on my opinion or on my suggestions without considering alternatives, especially young people who were just entering their early adulthood and subject to a variety of emotions and tumult.

We had both male and females working with us, and the females were good-looking girls, but they were twenty-one and twenty-two years old. In fact, this one girl turned twenty-one while we were there. She was a very smart young woman by the name of Christine Cooper. We all called her by a nickname, "Coop." Christine had a boyfriend when she arrived at our base and her boyfriend decided to break up with her. In a war zone, emotions are at an extremely high peak, and Christine became despondent, a sulky person that was difficult to handle. After a period of time, the other Warrant Officer that I worked with, Mike Davidson, and I called Christine into our office and told her, "You're either going to suck it up and be an adult and quit acting like a teenager, or we're going to have to bring someone else in on the team and move you out."

Like I said, "Coop" was very smart and instantly realized that she had been in a snit. Again, at the snap of a finger, she became a totally different person, and became the real Christine that we needed. Mike and I knew how smart Christine was and that was the reason behind the "pep talk," and Christine reacted exactly as we expected. Like I said, instant maturity in difficult situations. All Christine needed was someone to point out, in a nice way, that she was acting immaturely and she became a valuable member of the team once more.

One thing that made my transition from civilian into the military and kept me going during tough times was that both my step-mom and my dad supported me one hundred percent. Additionally, my brother was behind me as well. My brother, Ray Hallett, he ... if there was anything that I needed, all I had to do was write him an email and whatever it was would be instantly sent.

Because of his position as a business man, Ray could do things for his family that no one else could do. He had the means and the financial wherewithal to be able to just jump on a plane and fly to Washington DC. There, he would hit on those Congress people and Senators and say, "What is wrong with you? Why aren't you asking the military about this? Why aren't you holding someone's feet to the fire?"

The first thing he got on his contacts about was night-vision goggles. Ray had a nephew, Joe, who was stationed in Bagdad, just south of where I was stationed. Joe was in a transportation outfit. They constantly had to go on the road in the darkness and didn't have enough night-vision goggles for everyone. Ray got on a plane, went to DC, and told Patty Murray to go into the Armed Forces Committee and asked someone why the Army didn't have enough of the goggles, and to get the Army the money they needed to provide the goggles. Initially, nothing happened for the first month or so, but before Joe left the theatre, the entire convoy had a sufficient supply of night-vision goggles for everyone.

People like Ray deserve our thanks and the appreciation of all of our soldiers who receive the best equipment of any armed forces in the world. And while I'm on a gratitude kick, let me express my appreciation to Penny, here at home, without whose support I would have had much more difficulty during Operation Freedom 2008 and 2009. As a matter of fact, I may as well go all the way and thank many of my comrades. I'll try to remember all and can only hope that I leave no one out. If so, I'm certain that I will hear about it and I apologize in advance. Furthermore, I hope that I've spelled everyone's name correctly. Let's see, there were Sergeants Horme, Ward, Wolfe, and Baker; Specialists Cooper, Edwards, Scott Baker and Comacho. Finally, there was Sergeant Pease. Master Sergeant Pease.

Sergeant Pease was a special case. At the time he deployed with us on our first excursion, he was approaching sixty years of age. He was a couple of years away from receiving his retirement letter and saying "Hit the road." Pease fooled us all. Everyone thought that he would be the one that bailed on us but it turned out that he was the hardest-working guy that we had. He ran that shop. We gave him that authority, Mike and I did. We said, "OK, this is the way that it's going to fall out." Mike was the lead guy, the overall manager of all of the maintenance activities that we had on the post. He said, "Marty, you run the shop."

Well, I looked at Pease and said, "You're my foreman. You run those people. You just tell me what jobs you're working on and what problems you're having and I'll solve your problems. You solve the problems out there and I'll solve the problems in here." And, he was just a hell of a guy.

And this last deployment, I had a kid named Guardo Saenz. Unusual spelling, but it was a Hispanic name. Sgt. Saenz was an ex-Marine, and just a little hardheaded, young and full of p ... er ...'vim and vigor.' I also had an old crusty veteran First Sergeant that worked with me, Dane Case. First Sergeant Case had been my First Sergeant during my first deployment so we had years and years of experience of being around each other and working together. It was a pleasure to work with those guys. Still, Saenz would do something stupid, just because he thought he could do it. He would never ask permission, that's the kind of person he was. He was, like, "I'll lean forward ... I'll go 'balls to the wall', but I'm not going to ask permission to do anything."

This attitude led to a funny situation with Saenz. It ticked him off, but I ticked him off for a reason that made life better for all of us. We had this little 'gator'— or buggy—that we ran around with on post. That was the only method we had of getting around, to go to all of the little places where we had to go in order to coordinate all of the stuff that had to be taken down to a pump house on the Tigris River. One day, I was trying to get the coordination done. I would always set up my missions two or three days apart. I would talk to the people involved in moving us to the pump house so that all we had to do was jump in the vehicles with the equipment we needed and they would ferry us down to the pump house. We would do our jobs there and then be ferried back to the post.

I had given a spreadsheet to Captain Raines that covered a entire week's missions and in order to make sure that we could comply with the schedule, it was necessary to brief all of the people involved. Without that coordination, it wouldn't be possible to stay on schedule. I would tell the captain, "OK, this is what we are going to do, and when." The coordination had to be done in the short period between missions. Because we working between military and civilian personnel, it was necessary to travel to multiple locations to brief all groups, as the telephone communications between military and civilian were not fully integrated, so my physical presence was vital.

Saenz was off-duty that particular day, which was a scheduled day off for all of us. Saenz had taken the buggy and driven it over to his housing area. Although it was a day off, it was necessary that I still do the coordination so as to prepare for the next mission, and of course I didn't have the buggy. Because I really needed it, I had to walk from my office to Sanez's housing area, more than a mile and a half, in ninety-plus degree weather. Thankfully, the really hot weather hadn't arrived yet. When I got there, I knocked on his hut and he came out. I asked him, "Sgt. Saenz, have you got the buggy?" He said. "Yes," and came out to the buggy with me, then started to take off.

I said, "Whoa, Whoa, wait a minute." I said, "Who do you work for, Sergeant Saenz?"

He goes, "I work for you."

I go, "No ... no. You work for First Sergeant Case. So, who does First Sergeant Case work for?"

"He works for the Colonel."

"No ... no, he works for me, Sergeant Saenz. And, who do I work for?"

"You work for the Colonel."

"No ... I work for ... " (Darn, why am I forgetting his name. I can see his face, but I just can't recall his name) "I work for the Major. Okay, who does the Major work for?"

"He works for the Colonel, right?"

"Okay. Of all of those people, all of the way down, who did you tell that you were going to have this vehicle over here?"

He goes, "Nobody."

I said, "Okay, this vehicle belongs to me. And you have to go through at least First Sergeant Case in order to have this vehicle down here."

He goes, "Oh."

And from that period on, we never had a problem with Sergeant Saenz.

Before I finish my story, I do want to say a few things about organizations such as Operation Military Embrace and other organizations of the same ilk. There are several operations that are out there helping, and I don't think that we ever can have enough of them. Even if they are small and only helping four or five veterans—or even if it's just one veteran—those organizations should be recognized and appreciated for the help they are giving. The nation owes a gigantic debt to the veterans of the military, every branch of every military, and veterans of every war.

The United States government is not ... they do have the Veteran's Administration, and the Veteran's Administration is doing the best that it can with this huge bureaucracy that pays a bunch of people a lot of money that never ever filters down to the actual ... where the rubber meets the road. Well, it's up here where the body of the car is. These organizations are at where the rubber ... they are the rubber that meets the road.

I don't know why the Veteran's Administration ... I do know why ... it's because of the laws that have been written. They have been poorly written ... they are well intentioned but they are very mis-worded and very misguided. Those laws are the reason that the V.A. is such a headache. Organizations such as Operation Military Embrace just bypass all that crap. They are there for one purpose and one purpose only: they are there to help the troops.

Once the government wakes up and realizes that's what they should be doing ... which we may never see it ... These organizations have to exist at this time ... they have to be here, because there's nobody else out there that is helping that much. Without them ...

Finally, I am relating my story to a fellow veteran. I'm no hero, only a veteran. And like so many other veterans, I am proud of my service. But, I must admit that I am changed from the person I was before I went overseas. All veterans change, especially those that experienced a war zone. Many are physically wounded with wounds and scars that are visibly evident. Others are wounded in ways that are not as readily evident. But all are changed. They too are proud of their service, and proud of their nation. A nation that owes a great debt to her veterans. Valiant veterans, both men and women who gave their all for their fellow Americans. Many made the ultimate sacrifice and gave their lives. Others suffered painful wounds or mental scars that will never heal. And a large part of the American public is unaware of the magnitude of the debt owed to the veterans, a debt that will never be repaid. Yes, the public is unaware, and that is because there is a dearth of information about their service and the reality of their situation.

The media does a pretty darn good job in covering the war. They are on top of the news whether it concerns an earthquake in Japan or on the East Coast. They rapidly and thoroughly expound on the destruction of a tsunami as it ravages the land and kills thousands, causing millions of dollars of damage. But when it comes to the veteran, the soldier or the sailor, the airman, the coastguardsman or the marine, the female soldier or the young boy who played soldier as a kid and now has died in the service of his country, the media does a very good job of diverting the public's focus onto something less meaningful. The surviving veteran or the family of a dead veteran is often left in dire need, ignored by the very public that he or she served, forgotten or overlooked as the media moves on to stories that generate more excitement than a wounded veteran finding that his job has been filled while he was sacrificing for his country, or finding that his wounds have caused him to be unable to perform the same tasks as before, so his employer hires a younger, more able person to do the work while the veteran loses his home, his car, his family. After all, what is newsworthy about another destitute veteran?

That forgotten veteran is your neighbor who made the sacrifice so that you could enjoy your life as a free American; you owe your freedom to a veteran. And you owe more, the fact that you can continue to have the blessings that only a free nation can bestow on its citizens, blessings that had to be earned by the blood, the sweat, the toil and the tears of a veteran of the United States Armed Forces.

Scow, Orval H.
Sergeant, United States Army Airborne
1922 –

Shortly before eight o'clock in the morning of December 7, 1941, the Japanese aircraft began their surprise attack on the fleet of the United States Navy at Pearl Harbor and the military installations on Oahu. The attack was a wake-up call to the United States citizenry.

War had been ongoing for more than two years on the European continent, and although many American citizens joined foreign armed forces to fight against Germany and Italy, most of the United States population had only a faint idea of the viciousness of the war in which they would soon become embroiled.

Following the Japanese unexpected attack, the American citizenry flooded the Selective Services offices to volunteer their blood and their services in defense of their beloved nation. Many served, some survived, few are still alive. One such volunteer and veteran of the "War to End All Wars," is Orval H. Scow, a native of Montana and a former NCO in the United States Army Airborne.

*****

Orval, here. Orval H. Scow, or just Orval, if you want. I'm being asked by a young feller to tell all of you about my story. First of all, I don't like to talk and second, I damn sure don't want to talk about the war, makes me too mad. But, this young 'un tells me that he's putting together a bunch of our stories, the stories of veterans, into a book and that it will help a lot of the other veterans, especially those that were wounded in the service of their country. So, okay, I'll tell you all that I can, but it's really not much. And now that I'm eighty-nine, it is a little more difficult.

Yes, I was born in here in Helena in 1922 and have lived most of my life around here and Manhattan – that's in Montana as you know. Mostly, I've lived around Helena. As a young man of twenty, going on twenty-one, I enlisted in the United States Army. There was a war going on, the war that supposedly was never to happen, World War II. Deciding that sooner or later the draft would get to me, I chose to enlist and get it over with. Historians have called us the Greatest Generation, and while that may be a little much, I do have to say that we did a hell of a job. While most people appreciate the sacrifices that we made, unfortunately there are still a few who still don't understand.

There were several Airborne Divisions in the 1940's Army: the 82nd, 11th, 13, 17th, 101st. and XVIII. Well, I wasn't going to just sit around forever and wait for the draft to call me and not know whether I was going to have a job or not from one day to the next, so I just decided to enroll. They day after Christmas in '42, I went down to the draft board and said to them— asked them when the next bunch was going. Of course, I signed up right then.

I served in the U.S. Army just a little less than three years, from January 1943 until October, 1945. I saw action in the war zone of the Second World War, mostly in the Asian theater, in the Philippines.

I had decided that was the place to fight because, well, those Japs got to me. They pulled a damn sneak attack on us, especially when U.S. was shipping them all our scrap iron and they were shooting it back at us. And at the same time, they had all their – their envoys or whatever they had, were in Washington D.C. all the time, trying to smooth things over, and while they're doing that to us, they attacked Pearl Harbor. That wasn't right and there was no way that we could let them get away with that.

One of the things that you miss when you are stationed overseas and especially in a war zone is your freedom. You can't just pick up and go any time you feel like it. First of all, it leaves your buddies in a crack. And then, you are likely to get yourself killed. So, you pretty much stay put and remain with your unit, it's safer that way. And you have a lot of time to miss other things, especially your family. You certainly will miss that a lot. Fortunately, I wasn't married, deciding that there was just no way that I was going to get married and then be drafted. I chose to put it off until after the war and my service was over, so I just went and signed up. Did it. Did my duty.

Some of the guys were lonesome for home and would like to have just chucked it in; quit and go home. Not me. No, no. Hell, no. Not as long as I didn't—not as long as we hadn't whipped them Japs yet. Oh, hell. It's just a rule to go by; a rule to live. We were on the Leyte Island in the Philippines and fighting was heavy. It was on Leyte that I was wounded. But not by the rifle of one of those damn Japs. I told them they wouldn't—they couldn't see towards—straight enough to hit me, so they had to get me with artillery or something. That's the only way they could get me. Well, 'cause I was a scout, and a good one. I wound up in the S2 Section as a scout for intelligence. I was right up there at the front and able to see it all. But that wasn't the day I got hit.

They're going commando for two prisoners—they were going to do a commando raid to capture a couple of prisoners, the company that I was with, 'cause I got called into the briefing that morning on a mission. Our mission was to do no fighting. If we run into—should run into the enemy, fight as little as possible, pull back and go another way 'cause our mission was just to cut off their supply line. When he—the minute the point man got caught in ambush and the machine gun opened up, why, hell, the Captain says, "Dig in; dig in." I said "Dig in, hell, Chuck. You know better. Move back."

We had an extra machine gun section and an extra mortar section and our radio section. We were a reinforced unit, but we only had a small company. Our company was only about a hundred men.

The day that I was wounded, we didn't suffer a lot of casualties; only one man afterwards. But, we got caught in a cross-fire with some other outfit from somewhere. My unit was coming up, saw some movement and started to fire. They saw some wounded so they shooting. So we were in the crossfire. My wound was caused by a mortar shell exploding close to me, resulting in me being wounded and some shrapnel that I carry still in there today. It was right in-between two ribs, right next to the spine. And it's gone out of there now. It's inside the cavity now. There is no way that I'm going to let them go in and get it out. Not now. No. Hell, no. They wanted to do that seventy years ago, and I said no. They said, "We should send you down to Walla Walla and operate." And the doctor says, "We might do more harm than good." And I says, "That's good enough for me to leave it right alone."

That wound really pissed me off. I wanted to get back into the fight, and I would have if they would have let me. That's when the commander came to tell me as they were going on a mission, he says, "Scow, I want your rifle." Of course he wanted it, 'cause I had it zeroed in. Oh hell, I would easily put seven out eight in rapid fire center into the bull's eye. I told that officer, "Well, soon as I get out of here and get this taken care of, I'll be back." Shit, there was only six months left before I got back, partly because of the wound and partially from the other diseases that I got: malaria and hepatitis and jungle rot and dinghy fever. I had it all.

Anyway, at the time I was wounded, we lost just one man to enemy fire. The point man, he's still living, as far as I know. I talked to him a few years ago. There were five of us in my section, but I haven't been able to locate all of them. Still, I found one in Chicago when I was going through there and made a stop. I went through the phone books to find their names, so I started calling and I finally found his name but he couldn't come down to see me at the airport. A year or two year later, I happened to be going to Chicago on business for a couple of weeks, so I got a hold of him first thing when I got there. He was a kid in my section. That was a great reunion. Man, I wound up driving around Chicago half-drunk; he wouldn't drive. Yeah, he just didn't want to drive in the dark at night. Oh, Christ. That was old McKinsey; he was telling me which way to go, but that's all. I never took the time to ask him what happened to the rest of the crew, so I assumed that ... I know some of them didn't make it. Two days after I got hit by some heavy artillery, I heard the section all trekked up ahead and on. The company commander that wanted my rifle, he was gone; he got it. And that one, and I think my section leader in the battalion, which I am currently, he got wounded. And he got it —it must have hit him right in the middle, so they wound a bunch of them.

Even so, in a book I that got one time, it said our kill ratio was forty-five to one; 45 Japs to every one guy we lost. That was good for us. I believe it was because of those fanatical banzai attacks. The Japanese fighters were tenacious fighters, but they were stupid. They'd run right into you. Sort of straight on, point blank. They would just keep coming. Stupid, just plain stupid. That was their government—their leader. They had to do it for their honor. There's no honor to that.

Something that few people knew about was that I found it necessary to take over the command of the company for a period of time. I haven't talked to anyone about it, I'm no hero. Nobody around here knows about it except my wife and my son. I really don't like to talk about the war. Well, when I finally get the outfit going and back to the CP, my section leader Lieutenant come up to me and he says, "Good job, Scow." Well, that made me feel pretty good. Sort of took me off the hook, if you know what I mean.

I don't have a lot to complain about throughout my tour, though I get a little soured on the Army doctors on the front. I remember when we were—we got stuck on the hills for three weeks after I got hit because we found it necessary to stop on one afternoon, getting ready for camp—set up our night parameter. We're sitting up on the hillside just about sunset, and we looked back out and over to the west, heaven help me, we saw a bunch of planes coming in. I go, *"Oh, those are a bunch of bombers coming back from a raid."* Well, a couple of days later, we found out it had been the Japs and they dropped 'chute troops back on our land that was right back there, and they shot up all our supply planes. So we had no supplies. There were no roads 'cause our area was remote and mountainous. So we didn't have any supplies for a full week, but of course, we were still short even then.

But the aid station there—or the field hospital as that what it actually was—that's where the docs operated on me there to try and get to the junk out of me, but they couldn't find it all 'cause they didn't have an x-ray or anything. So I was there about bout a week, unable to be transported and we didn't have much in the way of supplies as well. So everybody was pooling their sources of what they had left out of a K-ration or a C-ration or whatever. One guy said, "Oh, I'll buy a chicken from this "phlip shack" (Philippian house)." They had a "philip shack" just across the way from our tent about, oh, 50, 75 feet maybe at the most. And they had some chickens, so the guy said, "Look, look, look, a chicken. I'm going to make some chicken stew." I had some powder for making broth. Chicken broth and stuff. And so I put in what I had and have some, and they had something else or what they had. The soldier took his helmet and built a fire under that helmet; hung it there; put some water in it, just broth and stuff. He got —

bought the chicken, even butchered it and cut it up and put it in our stew. That's all that we ate for a while.

Better than the C-rations. Yeah, yeah.

I remember one day we went down the trail and we stopped just about ready to camp for the night, and we finally decided to spend the night there. And so one guy was —he was from Georgia or Tennessee or someplace down there, and he's kind of skunking around 'til he found some sweet potatoes growing. So hell, there was bunch - he dug a bunch of them. We all got together and we had a ... we had received a box of 10-in-1 rations one time on a draw about a week before that. We had been hanging onto the can of bacon that came with the rations. So one guy says, "Well, I got these potatoes, but we don't want to boil them." I said, "We'll fry them." I said, "Well, look; jut fry the bacon and then cook them in the bacon grease; the sweet potatoes." Well, that was a meal. Yeah. Beats the hell out of a K-ration.

The docs out here in Fort Harrison, they're as good as or better than many of the doctors they have in the civilian hospitals here. But I got soured on those military doctors when I was trying to get out of Leyte on Christmas Day. We had just gotten back down on the coast. It was like, the 24th, and the next day was Christmas. We were there a couple of days 'til they could get us out. They took us down quite a long ways to another landing strip where they could get out and put us on a hospital ship. And goddamn, the first night out here, it had become dark as night but on top of the ship there were glaring, bright lights out there. I was up above deck 'cause the ship was full, and so they had dumped us up on the top upper deck. I hollered, "Douse them lights. And then another guy started hollering at me I repeat, "Douse them lights." He says… he says, "Oh, this is a hospital ship. I said, "I don't give a damn. They don't care who we are."

No, they didn't. They didn't give a damn. In fact, the only reason I was in that base station up in the mountains there ... about a couple days after we had cooked that chicken up, I ... one morning I had the GI's, and the slit trench is about as far as a football field away from the tent. And after sundown, nobody moved. Nobody walked around the place because you might get shot. So I—well, I just had to go. So I crawled off the litter I was on and bellied out under the tent and moved to the slit trench and squatted and took care of business, and pulled my pants up, turning to go back being careful to crawl back. When I was just crawling under the tent flap, a machine gun opened up from that damn "philip shack," from the doorway. The "philips" had let—had disarmed our set traps and stuff and let the Japs in here, and they had set up a goddamn machine gun, and then they just turned right on the tent just about thigh high. Just like those machines—just like a sewing machine going across the tent. And it didn't hit a man. The Lord was watching over on us that night. And Captain Brady, he was on a cot, almost that high and he had his mosquito bar around him. How he didn't get hit, I'll never know.

We were—we didn't have any weapons. One of the guys from the tent went out there and grabbed a rifle away from one of the guys and was trying to turn around and run back. The other guy says, *"Where the hell are you going? I want that rifle."* And the guy with the rifle sat down by the trench and started trying to pick off on snipers near the trench and stuff. He didn't hit anybody. I mean, he should have shot all the Japs and all the 'philips' there, too, 'cause they were treacherous. Well, they're Communist, the Philippinos. They're Communist, and still, that is our country. Our territory.

I like to say it like it is. Everybody knows that it makes no sense beating around the bush. Well, I think the government should ... Oh, never mind. Islam's all over this country 'cause they're trying to take this country over from the inside. That's my feelings. And I'll bet you in time, it will prove true. And our government should just let the Islamists over there kill themselves off if they want to. We're losing, and for nothing. As for that damn traitor, Pakistan, I wouldn't trust Pakistan as far as I could throw a bull 'cause it's already proven that they'd hid that Osama bin Laden for six years. As far as I'm concerned, that's too much. And we've been pouring money into Pakistan, money which should be going to our guys.

I admit that's a hell of a way to feel, as we like to help people, but when they're after you—when they're trying to beat you and kill you, take over your country—it's time to cut them off.

I didn't have any problems after returning from the war. The wound that I suffered didn't bother me at all. Not physically, not mentally. I understood what I had done and that I had done just what I had to do. When I came back, I didn't have any trouble getting jobs. I've got nothing wrong with me. Hell, I janitored in bowling alleys in Helena. An auto dealership wanted me to go janitor for them. And I thought, *"No, no. I'm not going spend my life janitoring."* Unlike a lot of young people today, I took any work available 'til I could get squared away. I actually retired from the local telephone company. I was a building engineer.

After my service, I went to school for a couple years. Went to business college. I figured if I ever owned a business, I'd want to know something about that—what happens if I owned a business? I started reading books and so forth and all that financial part of it, so I did study, and it got me a job at my college with on-the-job training at Carroll College up here. I spent a couple years there, and hell, I... It was tough getting by on the allotment I was getting from the government, so I was correcting papers for math teachers and stuff on the. That was to make a few extra bucks, which come in handy with a family.

Then I finally took the civil service exam and I passed it with the highest grade they'd ever had for their accounting test. That got me a job out at the Fort and a couple guys out there were accountants. They come after me one day, wanting me to go take the CPA exam with them. And I said, *"Hell. Oh, no. I don't know enough about that, and I don't have the money for it to start with."* It cost twenty-five bucks just to take it. And that was a lot of money back then. Half the money of what I was getting from the government.

Finally they quit asking and they finally quit the Fort and went to into business for themselves. I eventually started a firm, my own accounting business. Those guys took the test and I guess they passed it, as they started their own business.

Nearing the end of my story and my military service, I have to say that I wasn't going to be a slacker. What the hell? If the rest of them could go, I could go. I will hold up my end, I would anyway.

My last words will be about the DAV (Disabled American Veterans) which is the only organization that I belong to now. Just what little time I give them is all that I have. I belong to that organization for a long time. I never attend the meetings—not any more—but I support them. I pay my dues. In fact, I paid for a life membership one year. But something went askew. I never got a receipt and they don't have it on record. I got a lifetime membership card from them at one time, and when I start getting my dues, and I says, *"Hell, I'm life member." They* don't have it on record. Somehow, I've lost the card, but I don't care. I still support them because they are doing good, they are helping the veterans and the veteran's family, and God knows, their help is needed. Very badly needed.

That's it, young 'un. Send me a copy of the book when you finish.

Sparks, Richard D.
Sergeant, United States Army
1945 –

The Purple Heart is a United States military decoration awarded in the name of the President to those who have been wounded or killed while serving on or after April 5, 1917 with the U.S. military ... *In the theater of the Republic of Vietnam for wounds received in connection with military operations against a hostile force ... 1966 – Sparks, Richard D.*

Recipient of the Purple Heart during his tour in the Vietnam combat zone, Richard Sparks exemplifies the heart of the United States Armed Forces. Called to serve his country from his home state of Wyoming,

Sparks performed his difficult duty in an unpopular war in an honorable manner that brings credit to his sacrifice.

*****

Yes, Sir. Richard Dennis Sparks, native of Lovell, Wyoming with my date of birth November 18, 1945. A proud veteran of the United States Army. But, no hero.

I have rarely if ever talked about the experiences I had while in the Army or afterwards. Bluntly, it is quite traumatic, but I'm told that by letting other people—especially the wounded or traumatized veterans—have a peek inside my life that it might just help someone. And if that is the case, I don't see that I have a choice. So, sorry if it's boring, but it is my life and this is my story.

No, I was not a volunteer. I wasn't all that eager to join the armed forces. Actually, I was drafted by the United States Army in 1966. That was during the Vietnam War era when a lot of good men had volunteered or were drafted. After basic training, I was assigned to Fort Hood, Texas, where I underwent AIT (Advanced Individual Training) and assimilated into an armored division.

After training, we were shipped to Germany where only a few days or weeks later, I volunteered to be sent to Vietnam. At the time, in 1966, I felt that the Vietnam War was a war that our country should be engaged in, and I also felt that I wanted to do something for my country. That gave me the motivation and the initiative to agree to serve in a combat zone.

When we went into Vietnam, the war wasn't anywhere near as unpopular as politicians and misguided

Americans later made it. And just for the record, I want to state that I still do not regret my efforts in Vietnam, not one single solitary bit. It was the right thing to do at the time. Although I only served two years in the Army, from 1966 through 1968, and although I was drafted rather than choosing to enlist, I do not regret one moment of the time that I served in our military.

Like every soldier in every war everywhere, the things that I missed the most while serving overseas was my family. You always miss your family, and you want to get home to them safely. But, you still have your duty.

Actually, my family stayed in contact with me on a regular basis. I constantly got all kinds of care packages from them and that really makes you feel good when you're out there. One of the neatest one that I ever got was my niece's nephew ... my sister lived in Big Piney, Wyoming, and they all went out trick and treating on Halloween and they boxed all of the trick or treat candy and everything they got and sent it to me over in Vietnam. When I got this box, it was nothing but all kinds of candy and everything. I opened it up and I mean that everybody was going crazy over it. It was unreal. Everybody was going, "I haven't seen this ... I haven't had one of these for ten years," and things like that. But, it was fun. I really enjoyed that. Couldn't eat it all myself, so I shared it with my buddies.

Despite the war and the shooting, in spite of the wounded and dead, I never had a point that I wanted to quit and come home. I wanted to stay there and serve my country and my buddies. They had become my family and I wanted to protect them. They had my back and I had theirs.

Even so, I was injured on the 27th of May. We had taken some 'LURPS' into Cambodia, right up on the border of Cambodia and Vietnam. We were to drop them off. "LURPS" stood for long-range reconnaissance patrols. I was in the Armored division, so we had tanks. We took a platoon of tanks and a platoon of infantry with us. The infantry and the LURPS rode on the outside of the tanks, so we took these LURPS up to the Cambodia border and dropped them off. They were going to go further into the country and observe and do whatever reconnaissance that was needed.

We came back to our base, which was in Jackson's Hole at that time, and we hadn't been back, I couldn't even say how many hours, when the LURPS radioed back and said that they were surrounded and needed help getting out of there. So, we went back in to get them out. Again, we had a platoon of infantry and a platoon of tanks – a platoon consists of five tanks. So, we went back in to try and rescue the LURPS, but we were ambushed three times as we were going back in to get them out. When we arrived at the location, there was a huge clearing; probably twice the size of a football field is my guess, as well as I can remember. The LURPS were on the far side of that clearing across from us, so as when we went in, we naturally deployed our tanks around that clearing so as to protect it because the enemy were just on the other side of the opening.

Our tank—I was on the platoon sergeant's tank—started across the clearing and the Vietnamese had mined the center of that clearing. We hit a mine out in the middle of the clearing and it blew the tract off of our tank. So, we were pretty much sitting ducks in the middle of this clearing. The enemy had the entire clearing surrounded, and that is when … we had to try to mobilize our tank, to get it fixed and moving, so we were outside the tank. They were firing and dropping mortar shells in and things like that. I got hit while trying to repair the tank. A mortar shell exploded close to me. Another sergeant had come over to help and asked what I wanted him to do. I stood up and faced him and the mortar round went off just behind him. He was launched over me and I got shrapnel in my arms and my legs, but the sergeant's torso had pretty much protected my vital parts because he was standing between me and the explosion. That sergeant was thrown clear over the top of me. Then everything from there, it was ... it was four or five hours before we got to dust off and got out of there. My comrade-in-arms saved my life, and surprisingly enough, he was fine, he lived through it as well. We did lose quite a few individuals and soldiers in that fight.

As far as my situation, I couldn't move. There was a sergeant on that platoon leader's tank and he and I had been close friends. He saw us lying out there – the other sergeant and me – and he came over to get us, 'cause we were stunned from the blast, plus the wounds. He came over and started dragging us underneath the tank to protect us because of the mortars that were coming in. The medic had gotten killed, so the sergeant was giving us morphine shots and taking care of us. After he got us to safe cover, he went back to his tank to continue fighting.

Even with all the damage, we got the LURPS out. We accomplished our mission. The LURPS told us that the North Vietnamese could have killed them anytime they wanted to, but the enemy didn't want just the small party, they were trying to suck in some more people. And that is exactly what they did. But, we got them out. Otherwise, they would just have been killed. Even though I was wounded, I rated the mission a success as we accomplished our goal of rescuing the LURPS, our fellow soldiers. It was worth the trip.

Actually, at least at the time, the injuries that I suffered didn't bother my mind at all. Sort of invincible, if anybody knows what I mean. Still, I was in the hospital for three months, in reality, just a little over three months in Japan, and then I went back. That was probably the worst part of the whole thing. I went back to Vietnam after three months in the hospital and that was perhaps the most difficult, because you know if it can happen to you once, it can happen to you again. No longer was I invincible. That was difficult, indeed.

Even with the pain of the injury and the worry about additional wounds, the thing that bothered me the most throughout the entire affair was that when we returned home, we were not welcomed home. Actually, it was like, don't wear your uniform home, you are hated. Things like that. You weren't really accepted at home; in your own nation. Truthfully, we never received a good welcome home. That has bothered me for several years. It seems that perhaps it's getting a little better now, as some of the Vietnam veterans are being recognized for their service, it's no longer the stigma that it was. The lack of respect did hurt badly, very badly; especially as I was drafted into the military. I well may have volunteered, but wasn't given the choice.

I wouldn't trade my two years in the military for anything, not for anything at all. I think that I probably did more growing up in the two years I served than the rest of my life. I still to this day do not regret a minute of my service in Vietnam. The only thing I regret was the way that all veterans were treated when we came home.

I don't try to attend any reunions of my unit, but I have been in constant contact with the sergeant—the person—who dragged me under the tank. I've been in contact with him every since we left the military. He was still in after I left, but … as a matter of fact, he's coming out this year for "Frontier Days." I call him on Veteran's Day and he calls me on Memorial Day every year, and we've been doing that for … since 1968 or 1969. A true lifelong friendship. I have been out there to see him and he has been here to see us. I've met his family and he has met our family. We are very close and very tight.

To be perfectly honest, one additional reason that I am telling my story to everyone now—I have the reputation of never talking about the war—is that I am undergoing counseling for P.T.S.D. and one of the things the counselor said that I really need to do is talk about my experiences, so, I guess I made the decision right then to start, and I'm glad this is the occasion. I have never even talked about my experiences to my children, or anything, so I thought, well ... No matter that it's difficult to talk about it, I'm sure that opening up will be of help.

I went over to Vietnam on a plane with a soldier by the name of Dwight Johnson. We both went to the same area. We were both assigned to Armored and we were at the same place. When we went over there, we were replacing individuals. We weren't going over as a platoon or a battalion or anything like that.

Dwight went to one platoon and I went to another, but still we got to be pretty good friends while we were stationed close-by. Dwight ended up winning the Congressional Medal of Honor. I was in the 69th Armored Division and Dwight was also in the 69th. We were both in the 'B' Company, I believe. I think he may transferred over to 'C' Company, or he could still have been in 'B' Company when he won the Congressional Medal of Honor, which was just before we both came back stateside. Dwight's tank became demobilized and was under heavy hostile fire and Dwight grabbed a machine gun off the tank and went out and single-handedly killed a bunch of the enemy. Saved all of his comrades, so earned the Medal. Quite a true hero.

The sad story there is that he had some problems when he came home. He got killed holding up a liquor store, or so they say. Dwight was only in his '20s when he was killed. I'm sure that part of his problem was that

P.T.S.D. and things like that that combat-affected military people suffer. Couldn't cope. But they admitted they weren't sure if he was actually holding up the store or if he had come in while a hold-up was taking place or what. Stories like that are sad, but Post Trauma Stress Disorder is real and if there are people out there that think it isn't, they need to do a little research.

The way the conflicts are going now, it is only going to get worse and there are going to be more people affected.

One of the nice things that's happening now is that the veterans that are coming home are welcomed home, and they can talk about it and not have to hide their service, so that helps them too. I welcome every one of them home that I see. I say, "Thank you. Thank you."

Being somewhat of a recluse, I'm not really familiar with the organizations that have been formed to help the veterans as they seek the help they need. I haven't really sought out any help, other than the counseling for P.T.S.D. that I'm taking now. But I know there are several out there and there should be more groups to help, they are everyone needed. Those organizations weren't there to help the Vietnam veterans. On second thought, there shouldn't be a need for such organizations; the United States Government should handle it all in repayment for the sacrifices the veterans made for the nation. The government isn't going to do it, not in the manner it is needed, and help for the veteran and his family has been a long time coming.

I'll have to declare that the one person that I know has helped me the most with my situation is my wife. She has stuck by me for forty-three years. I don't know how she managed to do that, it's incredible that she was able to last through it all. I also owe a debt of gratitude to my friend, Doc; my friend from Pennsylvania who came and dragged me under the tank. I really want to thank him for that. Truth is, other than a few friends like that and our families; we didn't have a lot of support from anybody else. Few of the Vietnam era veterans did.

As final thoughts, I just want to repeat that I do not in any way regret my time served and the only disappointment I have is the way we veterans were treated when we came home. I love seeing our soldiers come home now and the way they are treated. It makes some of us envious in a way, but they deserve it, and I still love it. I wouldn't deny them that kind treatment and respect in no way, and I hope it continues like that. That is the true America that I served.

I won't forget Dwight. I can't imagine going through what he went through, not after something like that. He was decorated with the Congressional Medal of Honor, our nation's highest award. He had everything going for him, and then ... But, like I said, they weren't sure that he was robbing the place or just got caught in the middle. I believe in Dwight; he died a hero.

Like many of the Vietnam veterans, we are aware that America is just now beginning to realize that we served honorably, we did our job admirably, we executed our mission in the proper manner and for the proper cause. The sad part of it is that we have lost so many that will never realize that America is finally discovering the truth. Too many have gone to their grave unacknowledged, unwelcome, and unappreciated. And that's too bad. It's so tragic that when the job they were doing so well was to serve their country, to go where they were ordered and to perform their mission to the best of their ability. I hope and pray every day that never happens to another generation. My story is no different from many. I served my country. I was a soldier for the United States of America.

Wadsworth, Shawn
Sergeant, United States Army
1978 –

Shawn Wadsworth is a native of West Virginia who currently resides in Helena, Montana, and is a member of the Army National Guard.

Although never being decorated with the Purple Heart Medal that is ordinarily awarded to a casualty of war, Wadsworth is a victim of Traumatic Brain Injury caused by numerous close-by explosions and he suffers as well from Post Traumatic Stress Disorder, incurred during multiple tours of duty in Iraq while serving as a member of the United States Army. Despite his injuries and his difficulties, Wadsworth strives to live a life as normal as possible while waiting for a nation that should be grateful for such services of valor that she would be eager to bestow upon a veteran who made such sacrifices the assistance, the benefits and the respect that the veteran deserves and has earned.

*****

Serving in the armed forces on behalf of our country has always been a kind of a tradition for my family. I'm Shawn Wadsworth, and although I wasn't necessarily overly motivated to join, there was a time when I reached a point in high school where I really didn't think I had much else to do, so I decided to join the military. I suppose that it was actually part patriotism and partially because I realized it was an excellent avenue for me to get to college, perhaps the only avenue that I had. At the time, there was not a war in progress, nor was one anticipated. It was 1997, four years before 9-11 and before the Afghanistan and Iraq situation erupted. Not that I was overly concerned, but it seemed like a good time to join the military, serve for a few years on active duty and qualify for college. As it turned out, I served on the active duty for a total of twelve years and have been in the National Guard here in Montana now for two and one-half to three years.

While I was still on my first hitch in the Army, several things happened that flipped the world—and my world—upside down. There was the attack of September 11, 2001, followed shortly by the Iraq war.

After the terrible events on 9-11, all my thinking was drastically changed. As it turns out, I was in the right place to do the right thing to protect my country and to protect my family. That became my mentality and has been ever since. That's what I do, I'm a means to defend us, to defend the American way and I take a lot of pride in that.

My war was the war in Iraq. I was part of the initial invasion in 2003 and stayed there through 2004. I was back in Iraq for a second tour in 2006, and left in 2008. Although I only served two tours, they were long tours, so I served a total of thirty-six months in the Iraq theater. It seemed like a whole lot longer, although I didn't really mind being there. I believed I was doing my duty.

Like every soldier serving in a war zone, or even just serving in foreign countries; or possibly just being remote from our home, the thing I missed most was my family; my wife and my daughter. Of course, there also were some of small things, the comforts, the freedoms, but it's always mostly just being with my family. At the time that I was overseas, we only had the one child. She was born before the Iraq War started, and we didn't know – rather, we didn't think it would be a great idea to have additional children as I was being deployed back and forth outside the United States a lot. Our second daughter was born just as I was getting off active duty, so I was fortunate enough to be with my wife at the time our youngest daughter was born. Actually, I believe that my wife became pregnant within the first four or five days after I came home from my second – and last – deployment, and our baby was born a couple of months after I ended my active duty. Is it okay to say that?

When I'm asked about my term on active duty and serving in the war in Iraq, I have to admit that my first tour was very tough. It was without a doubt one of the hardest things—perhaps the hardest thing—I've ever been through in my life, and probably always will be. The initial invasion was a whole different war than it is today where you've got the IEDs (Improved Explosion Devices, or roadside bombs) and stuff like that. In that first invasion you were actually fighting a face, they didn't do the little guerilla tactics like they do today. An enemy that actually came at you and actually fought you, so it was mostly small arms, guns, RPGs (Rifle Propelled Grenades) and that kind of stuff. It was tough. And there were a lot of times when you were under fire and hoping for an end. I remember that when we first went over there, they said we were going to be there for probably six months. Maybe. They said, *"You take that Iraqi Army and you defeat them, and you take Saadam Hussein out of power, and do the other things that are going to end the war effectively, and then everybody goes home. Mission accomplished."*

Well, six months turns to eight months, and eight months turns to ten months, and ten months turns to twelve months, and twelve months turns to fifteen months and then you're just … I think at twelve months when I found out it was going to be fifteen months, I really honestly didn't think I was ever going to leave that place. Either I was going to die there or I was just going to be there like forever … I kept thinking back to World War II; I had a grandpa in the war and my grandfather had told me quite a bit about that war. *Four years in a combat zone*; I was thinking that's what's going to happen to me. So, yes, it was tough, very tough.

There were many difficult times when a lot of things happened that could easily have made me down on myself, but you never want to fail the person next to you. You've got friends to your left and to your right and you don't ever want to fail them so you can't ever let that low feeling show. You just fight through it and carry on. You push through it no matter what happens because those people depend on you to make it home to their family. And when you fight beside people, you learn a lot about them. You learn what their feelings are, what their dreams are, what their goals are, who their families are: all that stuff. So, it's really personal. And that's what you really fight for; you fight for them. They become your brothers and a very tight-knit family. And most of those people you'll keep in contact with forever. I still talk to them, all the guys that were in my unit.

My primary military occupational specialty was in chemicals, an NBC (Nuclear, Biological, Chemical) soldier. Once the threat for NBC went down, which happened within about four months after our arrival, NBC soldiers found themselves without a job, so I didn't have anything in my field. That wasn't really good as it only meant that I was available for anything the leaders wanted or needed me to do, such as light infantry leader, SKT Scout sniper, that kind of stuff. But sometimes not, there were times when I served as training room NCO and other such tasks.

Although I never suffered a wound that penetrated my body, and thus never ended up getting a Purple Heart, I became a victim of TBI, or Traumatic Brain Injury. A lot of different things contributed to my injury, as I was blown up a lot of times from the concussions of standing on the ground next to tanks as they would go off, and loud guns and other explosions. There was one incident that stands out in my mind and the doctors feel is likely the major cause of the TBI. I was lead man on a fire-team as we were advancing, and an RPG impacted and exploded directly in front of me, just a short distance ahead, maybe ten or fifteen meters away. I was knocked out and the force tossed me through the air onto my team. They pulled me back and saw that I was covered with blood and stuff. My team at first thought that I was dead. With everything that was going on, it was somewhat crazy. As I was coming back to consciousness, I could hear them saying this; and I was like, *"Am I dead?"* But then I came to complete consciousness all the way, and I got up. The guys were like, "Are you okay? Okay?"

I said, "I think so." Actually, I wasn't entirely sure, really groggy. It was like everything was kind of blurry and hazy, and far away, echoing and my ears couldn't hear much. I was dizzy, sort of like instant vertigo. It was an interesting sensation, trying to move forward like that.

At the time I didn't think anything about my situation, not realizing that the trauma that I had suffered had indeed caused damage. There were some residual effects but I was sure that the symptoms would pass, and in fact they did lessen somewhat. I had no idea that I had suffered a brain injury and actually didn't realize it until later back in the States that I went to the Veteran's Administration. It turns out that the people there knew quite a bit about the problem. Actually, symptoms manifested by TBI is a lot different from Post Traumatic Stress Disorder, which is another problem that I developed as a result of my two deployments in Iraq. The counselors' explanations helped me understand why I can't remember things. I used to be quite good in English, in fact went to Advanced English in high school. Now I have to read things two or three times just to be able to understand what I read. There were small memory things that a victim can do, like someone gives you a list of things to do. Maybe it's three things. Then they talk to you about something else for a while. Maybe five minutes later, they ask you what those three things were and perhaps you can only remember maybe one of them. Sometimes none.

It's tough to go through life that way, either through your work life or your personal life. Especially if your wife tells you to do this before you go to work or something, and you can't remember things like that. If they are not part of your routine, or you don't write them down, they are gone. That's the result of Traumatic Brain Injury.

Unlike TBI, Post Traumatic Stress Disorder has much of the same symptoms, but can abate. My PTSD has gone down a lot. My last psych appointment wasn't exactly easy, but it wasn't hard either. Mostly it was about the IEDs. For me, there wasn't a lot of that. Because the first six months that I was in Iraq, although I had already suffered PTSD, I would roll out on patrol two or three times a day and roll for miles and miles and miles even in the most dangerous areas, and the convoys that I was with was only hit with an IED once. It wasn't until I was pulled out of the security detachment that roadside bombs and IEDs became bad, so I didn't have a lot of involvement.

As a result of the permanent effect of the TBI, one thing I'm pretty sure of is that I can't be in a civilian employment environment. I know that for sure. That's one reason that I still wear the uniform and work with the Guard. I work with soldiers and people who have been deployed; the sort of people who understand that kind of stuff. People that are civilians are for the most part are only worried about the little things that are going on in their little world; they don't know what's going on in the rest of the world except what they see on television. It's tough for me to be around those kinds of people and generally I try to avoid talking with them, so I don't think in a civilian setting that I wouldn't do too well, to be honest. Trying to counteract that, I've had some counseling with the V.A. and I even had some counseling before I got out of the service. Perhaps sometimes it might get better, but it isn't likely.

The V.A. counselors have suggested various things that I could do, like talk to people—at least those I could tell things to—and write things down, especially those things I don't want to talk to anybody about, just write it down and put it away somewhere. All kinds of things that they give the veteran to try to comfort and try to heal. But the one thing I took away them the most was that the combat-affected really needs to talk about it. He or she need to get it out; it can't just be kept inside, hidden away because it would just be something that the veteran would think about it all the time. It's always going to be there, but if you accept it as being part of your life ... You did the right thing. You did everything you could; so it gets easier.

I haven't told most of this stuff to my daughter. She knows a little because I told her a few things, but I didn't think it appropriate or wise to tell her everything; she wouldn't understand most of it. On the other hand, my wife does know quite a lot. She and a couple of our friends really have been my main go-to people. My wife never went into combat, but she deployed on life humanitarian missions and those kinds of things when she was in the military. She saw ethnic cleansing, its aftermath and stuff like that; so she has a pretty good idea of what it's like.

Some people wonder, considering my injury and all, if I'm happy with my decision to join the military and I can only respond, yes, absolutely. I've learned a lot of things and grown a lot as a person. I really feel that I've seen things and done things that are far beyond what most people are ever able to do in their lives. I believe it's something I can reflect back on when I'm on my deathbed and I'll actually be able to have something to say, *"I gave something to this earth before I left it. I didn't just ride through my life and go to my nine-to-five job and then retire and go fishing or whatever; that I actually did something with myself. I actually gave something to the world."*

I am aware that there are several programs out there to help veterans who are going through the transition phase when they get taken out of the military and they are injured and they can't work. I've done the V.A. thing, and all the paperwork is just massive and takes time. I'm glad there are organizations and programs in place that tries to help veterans maintain and keep their families together. Those organizations are important, especially to the wounded and disabled and those with little or no income. As a wounded veteran, you give up everything. Even if they didn't give up their lives, many veterans give up the ability to do those things they love the most. For example, if they were a baseball player and lost their right arm, they would be unable to play anymore. Whatever the case is, these veterans give a lot. It's great that the people who have built the Remember the Wounded Ride type of program to kind of give back a little bit.

Before ending my story, I must say that the reason that I'm close to being a normal functioning individual is because of my wife, Nadine Wadsworth. She absolutely is the person that helped me the most, through everything. The thing of it is with my family; my wife probably has what some people would consider PTSD. And even my daughter has it. To this day she has night terrors where she wakes up in the middle of the night and doesn't know where she is, and she's scared and crying. My wife went through a lot, worrying and suffering, because she didn't know what was going to happen to me. On my first deployment to Iraq, she didn't hear from me at all for the first five months. The only thing she could get was what was reported in the news. That's all she knew. It was quite difficult for her with no news. She had it kinda rough at home, too. She's a wonderful lady, and I am glad that Nadine is strong enough to endure it all.

In the last duty assignment where I was located, across the street from us lived a veteran from the Vietnam War. He had the same combat patch that I had, so we talked a lot. I asked him one time, I said, "Do the memories ever fade? Do they ever get any easier?" And he said, "No. It's the same as it was when I came home from the war. You just have to cope."

Finally, I would like to add that I love and support all the people that are in the military. Maybe my story will help one of them heal. If so ... I support them and do everything I can to give them everything I can – me – and I appreciate everything that they do for me and for my family. And they know who they are. God Bless.

Warrick, Devon E.
Sergeant, United States Army
1919 –

At the age of ninety-two, Devon Warrick of Preston, Idaho is one of the rapidly diminishing numbers of veterans of the "War to End all Wars" or World War II. Warrick served in the 7th Infantry Division where he was decorated with numerous medals including the third highest decoration for valor in battle, the Silver Star. He also was awarded the fourth highest decoration for meritorious service above and beyond the call of duty, the Bronze Star. Wounded in action, Warrick was also decorated with the Purple Heart, signifying a wound in the service of his country in an action engaging an enemy of the United States of America. As is easily noticed on his awards memorial, Warrick also won numerous other decorations, almost too many to list, for his valiant services on behalf of a grateful nation in time of great danger and peril. Like others of "The Greatest Generation," Devon W. Warrick is due all the honor and respect that a free nation, kept that way by actions of heroes such as Warrick, can bestow on a valiant and honorable warrior.

*****

Sergeant Warrick, Devon W.; Preston, Idaho, United States Infantry, 7th Division, 184th Regiment, K Company, reporting for duty as ordered.

Born 1919, I was; ninety-two years old, going on ninety-three. I guess that makes me the oldest soldier to be included in this first volume of heretofore untold stories about veterans such as I. Being the oldest, it is only fitting that I come last because I have been around the longest. After all, I'm in no rush. Got plenty of time.

Like I said, I'm from Preston, Idaho, and I did serve in the military. Although I did earn a few medals, I'm certainly no hero. In fact, I didn't join up, they drafted me. Got me when I was twenty-five, just a year or so before the end of the 'Great War'. Put me into the infantry, they did, and I served them proudly.

At the time that I was drafted, I was married with two children; one girl three years old and another baby only one year old. It's a fact, I didn't ask; they drafted me. Not that I objected. I didn't protest going to serve or even of being drafted. It was my duty. I just took a leave of absence from my job and went into service like they asked. They shipped me off to Texas; Camp Fannin, Texas. I took seventeen weeks down there and then I came back here home. They let me stay home for a week; I was living in Burly, Idaho, 541 North Elbe in Burley. After that week, I went on to Fort Ord in California. I was only there one week and then they shipped me to Seattle, Washington. From there, a lot of us were put on a troop ship and we went to the Aleutians Islands and then to the Kyushu islands, Japanese islands and then to the main island of Okinawa. There we were all unloaded from the ship and transported to the battle area and then spent the next two months, day and night, fighting to capture and control Okinawa.

I was wounded roughly two months after we first arrived, in what they call the battle of Okinawa. I got hit by a mortar shell that landed close to me and blew up and took my tail bone off, broke my hand and broke my head. My helmet was a sight to be seen.. A metal helmet that something had put a great big crease right through it. And I survived that. It was hour upon hour upon hours of duty when we were in battle on Okinawa. I never in my life ever put in such strenuous hours as I did there; virtually no rest at all.

And we didn't have near enough men and it was very slow going because' the Japanese were dug in very well. All of those rock ledges and cliffs, fox holes; they used all that coral rock for protection for themselves and we would have to burn them out, really, with flame throwers off of the tanks. We used those big tanks, to spray that liquid on them—like napalm—red hot. Just burn them right out.

I was only in the hospital—or rather a field tent was what it was—back from the front lines about a mile. I was only there for about a week and then I was able to get up and move around a little bit and then I was back in the front lines again.

I'm not sure that I can tell you how I won my Silver Star. Or even want to. It's almost too sensitive, too touching for me to even talk about it. It's awfully hard to even think about. Let's see. There was a sniper that shot a young fellow ... He wasn't old enough to ... he didn't look like he was even sixteen years old, to me. The sniper jad shot that kid in the stomach. I was the closest one to him and I crawled over there to him; he was crying and calling for his mother. At the time, we had on our jacket lapel a morphine kit – all of the soldiers on the front line have such a kit. All the time that I was there, I was staying as low as I could, keeping my head down, and this Jap sniper was trying to shoot me. I was just trying to keep that kid from dying on me. Staying as low as I could, I took the morphine kit off his jacket and gave him a shot of morphine right through his clothes, not being able to lift up enough to get to a bare arm or leg. The morphine eased the pain he had from being shot through his stomach. After I gave him that morphine shot, he calmed right down. I don't know whether he lived or died, I never did hear anything about it. They picked him up; the medics did and took him back to back to the medical facility. I want to believe and I'm really sure that he made it. I certainly hope so; he was such a young kid. Yeah, I guess they could say that I may have saved his life, but that's what soldiers do. They help their brother.

Physically and psychologically, my injury didn't bother me too much, I knew that I had a job to do and I did it as best I could, with my mind as clear as I could possibly have. I had to be alert, making the choice and decisions. I tried to make clear-headed decisions and probably saved my own life due to some of wiser decisions that I made. I was a light machine-gunner in K Company and I had artillery shoot at me, field guns, those big ones, those 88 millimeters just trying to get rid of me. Me and my machine gun. Guess I had made them mad – or scared.

After the medics picked up that young boy that was shot in the stomach, and I went back to my position, I was ... I didn't pass out or anything from my prior wounds, but you might say that I was rum-dumb from what went on. The medics came back and took me to the field tent because I had been wounded again and still pack a severe scar across the top of my head. In fact, it is easy for anyone to see the indentation in my head even today. The broken hand that I had suffered earlier was still bothersome, and I find that I have to favor it even now. I also still have shrapnel in my leg right next to the big bone in my thigh. The doctors said that it would be better just to leave it alone; eventually it would form a gristle around it and pretty much stabilize it. So they didn't try to remove the shrapnel from my leg. I'm still carrying souvenirs of the war and in fact have a little trouble getting on a plane from time to time as the scanners pick up the metal in my body. And when I tell them where it's at, they all want to see it and I have to show it to them. Then they let me go on through.

Back in the States, my injuries did have some effect on my ability to work, at least, to a certain point. Mentally, there were no repercussions; however, physically I did have some little difficulty because my tailbone had been crushed. I drove for a bus for Greyhound for thirty-two years, put in more than three million miles. That's a lot of miles. The constant sitting on my injured and crushed tailbone for long periods of time would really get to me at times. I had a special cushion that I could use on my seat in the bus that would help keep me from getting so tired and keep my back from hurting so bad. Even so, even with the pain and the difficulty, I enjoyed every minute of it; every single minute.

I've met a lot of good people while driving a bus, mighty good people. And at times there were a lot of people riding busses. There have been occasions when there were as many as four extra busses besides mine, all running on the same route that I was taking; just five of us in a line, there were so many people riding the bus. I was hauling a run on the Salt Lake to Burly, Idaho at that time. And, thankfully, all *safe* miles.

I'm completely at peace with my service in the military, proud to have served, and, yes, I would do it again, if I had to. The only that I regretted was leaving my family to go serve. I would say that was the one thing that hurt even more than anything, more even than the wounds. That was the worst thing for me to do. I wouldn't have minded going to serve as much if I didn't have a family. And the communications with those back home were not the best. We did receive letters from time to time, but often not for a month or so, and then we would get a box full of them at a time; from family, relatives and friends. Take a day or so to read all of them. I didn't get to respond to very many of them. When you are in a combat situation, you don't have much in the way of facilities to write letters. So, about the only person that I really wrote to was my wife. We would still be married, but she died in 1996. She suffered a broken appendix. I had taken care of her for about ten years. They wanted me to put her in a nursing home or a rest home, but I wasn't going to do that. I wanted her to have the best care that she could possibly get and I saw to it that she got it.

One of the really good things about being a soldier in combat was the close friends and comrades that was in battle with you and that you had all around you. Instant buddies, but staunch allies. They were there to help you, to watch your back. And you, theirs. Unfortunately lacking among those things that I missed out on was meeting those pretty combat nurses like you see on T.V. Our nurses were ugly soldiers; good, friendly, careful and caring, but ugly.

Yes, I would do it all over again if I had to. Every bit of it. Because we've got a great country here. The United States is the best; the nation's free and I would give all I had to keep it that way. On Okinawa alone, I was fighting for eighty-two days and nights and that's exactly what I mean – day and night. Some nights I might get an hour's sleep and some nights I wouldn't get any at all. Those Japs, one thing I can say about them, they were damn good fighters. They would take their shoes off at night so that we couldn't hear them coming and they would try to cross the lines through your position or do anything to hurt us. I'm sorry that I had to kill a lot of their young boys, but what else could I do? They tell us to kill them or they're going to kill us. And that was the truth. Yeah, it was hard. But I killed a lot of Japs. I don't know how many really, but I know I killed a lot of them. Perhaps I saved a lot of our lives in the process, defending and fighting for my comrades and my friends. I really don't have any regrets; I did the best I could to defend our country. That is what we do.

One last thing; this young fellow that this sniper had shot through the stomach—the sniper was shooting at me all the time that I was lying down and doctoring him and taking care of him; when I got him taken care of, I crawled back away from the kid and away from the line of fire that I was receiving from him cause he was shooting at me and coming awful close. I crawled away and worked my way back to my foxhole that I had dug in at the edge of the hill. There was a big ravine that ran below me and back up the other side and it was covered with cedar trees. That was where the sniper was, in those cedar trees. His bullets would hit the mound of dirt that I had placed outside the foxhole and I could easily see the bullets hitting the dirt. I had a full belt full of ammunition in my machine gun, so I cocked the breech back and let it go and I ran that whole belt through that machine gun. I never quit and I just kept sprayed those bushes over there and I just kept shooting until I was out of ammunition. I saw him just as I run out and I saw that I had killed him, that sniper. The next day we went over on patrol and found him, and he was dead. I think I saved a lot of lives. If I hadn't killed him, he would have kept picking us off. Most of the time, you don't know if you are the one, but I know for sure that I was the one that killed that sniper. I know that I got him.

I do not regret what I did, not at all. The biggest sacrifice that I can think of is that of having to leave your family. They shouldn't do that. It's just too hard on everybody. If you have a family, they should leave you alone; leave you at home. But I didn't protest or anything, I just went when I was told and did what was asked of me.

The company that I was working for at the time when I was drafted was Greyhound Lines of Dallas, Texas. And when I came home, they were there to greet me. They put me right back to work. All my seniority and everything else while I was gone were reinstated. I loved that job. I like to meet people and you meet a lot of them from all walks of life. There are a great number of good people out there, many more good than bad. Our there in the greatest country in the world: the United States of America. God Bless America.

*****

The story of our elder hero Devon Warrick brings America's Heroes, Volume I to a close and brings a termination to the first initial segment of the Remember the Wounded Ride operation. But it is only the end of Phase I of the mission. Phase II will continue with more stories from the venerable heroes that have protected the United States from enemies at home or abroad.

Post Ops Debriefing

At 15:25 on Tuesday, 25 October 2011, Step One, Phase One, Remember the Wounded Ride Mission came to a conclusion in Washington, D.C. as Scot King, Corporal in the United States Marine Corps and current member of the Benevolent and Protective Order of the Elks Lodge number 142, Portland, Oregon rode his bicycle into the streets of the nation's capital. Achieving the successful conclusion of Step One, Phase One required that Corporal King ride a bicycle for six thousand and twenty-three miles (6023) through weather fair and foul, scorching and frigid, desert and mountain.

King's ride passed through the capital cities of thirty-one states and took nearly six months. As a result of the ride, King was able to record more than sixty interviews with combat-affected veterans and their families; veterans from the era of World War II, the Korean War, Bosnia, Vietnam, Afghanistan, Desert Storm, Desert Shield and Operation Iraqi Freedom.

The tactical plans for Step Two, Phase One which will cover the capital cities of the remaining seventeen states of the contiguous forty-eight states are currently being drawn. (By the way, you great people in Alaska and Hawaii; I haven't forgotten you. I will get there!) The route and the timetable will be posted on www.rememberthewoundedride.com January, 2012.

After Action Report

Throughout the first segment of what has become my lifetime mission of providing long-missing succor to the combat-affected veteran and his or her family, there has been a magnanimous outpouring of aid and encouragement from people of all walks of life; the rich-and-famous and the down-and-out. At a time when our nation is struggling to keep her rightful place in the world, not one person was negative about my effort and not one person rejected me in any way. Yes, America is still great and American people are still caring. And so are many, even most of the companies and organizations of the United States. Many of these people are the very root support of my entire effort. Without these openhearted people and munificent organizations, I could never even have begun my quest and without their continued support, I never would have endured and my mission would have failed. They didn't, and it didn't, and it won't.

The facts about the mission and the success of the first phase have been reported and now I would like to take a little space to say thank you. I really would like to say much more, but the only words I have to express my humbled feelings are: thank you, thank you, thank you. And thank you.

A tremendous amount of gratitude is owed to the Benevolent and Protective Order of the Elks, especially my fellow members and home Lodge # 142 in Portland, Oregon, who provided the first boost as I began what I consider my greatest challenge in life. Without their love and care, it is likely that my mission would have failed before it started. Bu they were there: *"Elks Care; Elks share."* But, it wasn't only BPOE Lodge # 142 and its members; there were many, many other Lodges and members that helped and others that stood ready to aid me on either this trek or the next leg. With no intent to omit anybody and at the risk of leaving some out, I will identify the following: Lodge # 10, the Mother Lodge of New England, West Roxbury, MA; Lodge # 12, Harrisburg, PA; Lodge # 13, Indianapolis, IN; Lodge # 17, Denver, CO; Lodge # 19, Hartford, CT; Lodge # 37, Columbus/Grove City, OH; Lodge # 49, Albany, NY; Lodge # 53, Toledo, OH; Lodge # 80, Lincoln, NE; Lodge # 81, Queensbury, NY; Lodge # 83, Upper Sandusky, OH; Lodge # 105, Trenton/Ewing Township, NJ; Lodge # 107, Gallipolis, OH; Lodge # 120, Danbury, CT; Lodge # 125, Sedalia, MO; Lodge # 155, Fort Wayne, IN; Lodge # 158, Springfield, IL; Lodge # 186, East Olympia, WA; Lodge # 188, Portland, ME; Lodge # 193, Helena, MT; Lodge # 195, Marion, IN; Lodge 270, New Albany, IN; Lodge # 291, Vincennes, IN; Lodge # 310, Boise, ID; Lodge # 318, Selah, WA; Lodge # 319, Stroudsburg, PA; Lodge 410, Madison, WI; Lodge # 450, Harrisonburg, VA; Lodge # 466, Jackson, OH; Lodge # 524, Madison, IN; Lodge # 530, Frankfort, KY; Lodge # 566, Boulder, CO; Lodge # 606, Biloxi, MS; Lodge # 607, Idaho Springs, CO; Lodge # 622, Edgewater, MD; Lodge # 660, Cheyenne, WY; Lodge # 674. Pocatello, ID; Lodge # 684. Frederick, MD; Lodge # 714, Bridgeport, PA; Lodge # 719, Golden Spike; UT; Lodge # 734, Park City, UT; Lodge # 787, Hudson, NY; Lodge # 808, Salida, CO; Lodge # 809, Greeley, CO; Lodge # 823, Vancouver, WA; Lodge # 841, Staten Island, NY; Lodge # 878, Elmhurst, NY; Lodge # 924, Montpelier, VT; Lodge # 984, Kearney, NE; Lodge # 1016, Effingham, IL; Lodge # 1037, Junction City, KS; Lodge # 1067, Pulaski, VA; Lodge # 1087, Idaho Falls, ID; Lodge # 1187, Rapid City, SD; Lodge # 1195, Columbus, NE; Lodge # 1199, Bismarck, ND; Lodge # 1210, Epsom, NH; Lodge # 1261, Pana,

IL; Lodge # 1271, Pekin, IL; Lodge # 1389, Nampa, ID; Lodge # 1393, Rochester, NH; Lodge # 1416, Blackfoot, ID; Lodge # 1448, Caldwell, ID; Lodge # 1482, Kelso, WA; Lodge # 1554, Dillon, MT; Lodge # 1670, Preston, ID; Lodge # 1683, Weiser, ID; Lodge # 1720, Greenfield, IN; Lodge # 1751, Hot Springs, SD; Lodge # 1778, Riverdale, MD; Lodge # 1797, Lusk, WY; Lodge # 1903, Dover, MD; Lodge # 1953, Pierre, SD; Lodge # 2088, Grandview, MO; Lodge # 2257, Camp Hill, PA; Lodge # 2270, Waynesboro, VA; Lodge # 2281, New Castle, DE; Lodge # 2337, Providence, RI; Lodge # 2375, Vernal, UT; Lodge # 2382, Front Royal, VA; and Lodge # 2442, Bountiful, UT.

Thank you to the motorcycle clubs who provided me with inspiration and assistance on multiple occasions, giving the lie to the misconception that the average public has of motorcycle clubs and the character of their members. Most of these motorcycle clubs have chapters in many different states and every chapter was most willing to assist me when I was in need. Several clubs in specific must be acknowledged and they are: *Freewheelers MC*, (especially the North Dakota chapter) *Vietnam Vets Legacy Vets MC* in multiple states; *Second Brigade MC*, again in multiple states; *Patriot Guard Riders*, also in many states; and *Elks Riders East Providence 2337*. Guys, you rock. I love you all. Keep up your great works.

Thank you to some very special people; people without whom this ride would have had no meaning, people without whom my life would have no meaning, wonderful people who understood and who understand.
- First among these cherished individuals is my son, Kalib King. My only son without whom this bicycle trek would have been much more diffi-

cult, without whom there may well have been no motivation and no ride. Kalib, I loved hearing your voice on the telephone, it kept me going and it kept me strong. I love you, Kalib. Dad.

- Jeanean and Kayla Bourn: for your unwavering support when things became difficult, The more difficult, the more meaning you had in my life and in my mission. I love you both.
- Lori King. Mother of our son, Kalib. Your support of my mission and your sacrifice to care for Kalib means a great deal to me. Just a mere 'thank you' is too little to express my debt to you.
- Jim, Jennifer, Adam and Katy Adishian: for all you do and for your understanding. Jennifer, you are the best sister that a brother could ever want. I could continue because you were there to take care of our mother; I know she was in the best of hands with you. I love you all. God Bless.
- Pat Paltridge: always there for me just when I needed succor. I owe you big time. I love you.
- Wyatt Bellus: my eleven year old friend that I made in Utah. Wyatt emailed me every week, encouraged me to keep riding. Thank you, Wyatt. You will always be my friend. By the way, your family rocks as well!
- Ralph Hartmann: friend and confidant; thanks for finding me the Elks Lodges and host families that supported me on my ride. Ralph, you are an excellent vice-president for Remember the Wounded Ride, Inc. non-profit foundation. I could have not performed this mission without you. Even more, I am looking forward to many, many good years of you and I working together on behalf of the Remember the Wounded Ride, Inc.

- John Keating: what can I say? You are my best friend and you have always been there for me. Without your wise counseling about the mission, I would likely still be backpacking and not riding. Thank you for talking to me about the mission and the ride, as well as keeping me motivated and excited about the mission. I love you, John.
- Jeff Nelson: always there for me and the Remember the Wounded Ride, Inc. My appreciation for your efforts working with me in those booths at the Veterans Memorial Coliseum. I was always glad to work beside you and with your help, this mission became a reality. I love you, man.
- Don and Jan Dupuis: your concern and help was most beneficial on my trek and I can only say 'thank you.' Must say though, Don, my truck is running great. Thanks again.
- Nadene and Charles Jones: my second family. You and your family took me in like I was one of your own. I feel like a part of your family. I appreciate your help and your concern; both were a lot of help. The Outer Rim Bicycle Shop rocks!
- Mom—Boni—You have always been the rock that I could count on being there for me.
- Dad—my stepfather—Peter—I miss you. I was on my ride when you passed. You will never be forgotten. You instilled good work ethics in me and you were always there for me when I needed you. Rest in peace. Our inside joke was that the United States Marine Corps (me) were the Boy Scouts for the British Army. My stepfather served in the British Army.

- Jerry Johs: Jerry has been a very good friend to me and my family over the years and has done wonderful work for our combat wounded veterans and the Marine Corps. Jerry is a huge inspiration to me and as he is a combat-wounded Vietnam Veteran, I have the utmost respect for what he has accomplished. My friend Jerry lost both of his legs in Vietnam but that does not slow him down and it is he who helps motivate me to be a better person and proof that you should never give up when the road you travel gets rough, as all roads do. Jerry, thank you for being my friend and invigorating me with your calls to me on a regular basis while I was on my trek.
- Jerry Reed: Jerry is the founder and president of Operation Military Embrace as well as a combat Vietnam veteran and my friend. Jerry Johs introduced us and we have been friends ever since. Jerry was instrumental in helping us become a 501c3 nonprofit. I would like to personally let Jerry know how much I appreciate his complete dedication to our combat wounded veterans and their families; it is unwavering, solid as a rock. I look forward to many good years of working together and continuing our good works.
- Donna Houge: Donna, thank you for doing what you do for our veterans and for the "Throws of Love." What you do for our veterans is AWESOME and you make many warm nights for those Veterans who have received one of your wonderful hand-crafted throws. Donna is a Gold Star wife and lost her husband in Vietnam; she has committed her life to help others through "Throws of Love." Donna has given me as many throws as I need at NO charge to give to those

heroes who have sacrificed so much for this great country. Donna has also been recognized by President George Bush for her wonderful work with a trip to the White House. Love you, Donna.
- Lane Ostrow: I want to personally thank Lane for the support he has given to me and Remember The Wounded Ride. Lane, you and Products for Goods have graciously given us wonderful shadow boxes to give to many of our combat wounded veterans through RTWR. Your show of support and ongoing friendship as well as your patients has been inspiring. I look forward to having you ride with me while in N.C.

A final, personal note: to Jeaneane in addition to all the other gratitude I have for you, there is appreciation from two sources: me and Quita for your loving care for taking care of her during my ride. Quita is my dog, and the true Marine Corps mascot: she is a pit bull. She is also the best dog I have ever owned; I missed her and I love her very much. Knowing she was in loving hands set my mind at rest throughout the ride.

I must express grateful appreciation to the sponsors and groups that made the mission possible, so I will acknowledge them now:
- Outer Rim Bicycle Shop
- Fuji Bikes
- Freeze Dry Guy
- Castelli;
- 2 X U
- Products For Good
- AAA of Oregon/Idaho
- American Airlines;

- MWC Enterprises,
- Kidspace Child Enrichment Center
- Marine Corps Rings and Jewelry
- Rock Bottom Supplements
- Nite Rider
- Ortlieb Waterproof
- Fly Style
- Rose City Nazarene Church
- Johnson RV
- Nova Tattoo Studio
- Northwest Tours
- Wooden Chicken Bar and Grill
- Migration Brewing Co.
- US Support Novelties
- Truth Be Told Band
- Violetta Burgers
- Integrative Chiropractic
- Ohana Hawaiian Cafe
- Branded and the song, "Heroes"
- Portland Winter Hawks
- Crow Creek Sioux tribe

Thank you to all the host families, both fellow Elks and non-elk that put me up in their homes, made me feel welcome, allowed be to wash my clothes and take showers, fed me bounteous amounts of good food and made me beneficiary of their prayers. These people were especially wonderful. I love you all. God Bless.

Thank you to the media, the newspapers and television stations. all of you who gave so generously of your time, your talent and your expertise. A special thank you to the radio talk show host, Mark Levin, who allowed me to talk about my mission on his show one evening. Thank you, Mark. You gave me the first opportunity to reach out to a national audience. To you and to your colleagues: Keep up the good faith.

Thank you to J.D. Tynan, award-winning author from Vancouver, Washington, without who this book would not exist and these veteran's stories would remain u ntold. Joanne, you are a true friend and your work on behalf of the Remember the Wounded Ride people will always be treasured.

Finally, my deep appreciation to the professional truck drivers who didn't run me over with their big rigs. Guys, I love you all. Keep it between the white lines. God Bless.

Forward Recon

D-Day for Phase II of the Remember the Wounded Ride mission is projected for May, 2012. The battle plan is that Scot King will begin the second phase of his mission in Washington, D.C. and will travel by bicycle to the capital cities of the remaining seventeen on the southern segment of the Remember the Wounded Ride mission. Timetable and route for the foray will be recorded on the nonprofit foundation's website,
www.rememberthewoundedride.com.

The Goal

Elevate public awareness as to the sad plight of combat-affected veterans and their families and to raise sufficient funds to see that every veteran and every veteran's family that needs help get the help that they need and deserve.

The Pledge

As long as one veteran or one veteran's family is in dire need, the Remember the Wounded Ride mission will never end. As long as one veteran's trauma can be relieved by sharing his or her experiences with other veterans and with the American public, the mission will continue. Someday, with the generous help of a grateful nation and a caring citizenry, every veteran will be respected and provided with all necessary care that he or she has earned. Until that day, the Remember the Wounded Ride mission will not be completed.

Semper Fi

Through the bad times
Scot King
Come Ride With Me

And through the good

Semper Fi

Made in the USA
Charleston, SC
25 June 2012